D0468446

Nineteenth Century FURNITURE
Innovation, Revival and Reform

Nineteenth Century FURNITURE
Innovation, Revival and Reform

Introduction by Mary Jean Madigan
Edited by Art & Antiques

An Art & Antiques Book

Produced by Roundtable Press, Inc.

Editorial: Marsha Melnick, Susan E. Meyer
Art Direction: Jerry Demoney
Art Production: Tom Ruis

First published in 1982 in the United States by Art & Antiques,
a division of Billboard Publications, Inc.
1515 Broadway · New York, New York 10036

Art & Antiques: A Magazine for Connoisseurs and Collectors
is a trademark of Billboard Publications, Inc.

Library of Congress Cataloging in Publication Data
Main entry under title:

Nineteenth century furniture.

    Includes index.
    1. Furniture—History—19th century—Ad-
dresses, essays, lectures. 2. Furniture—
United States—History—19th century—Ad-
dresses, essays, lectures. I. Art & antiques.
NK2385.N56   749.2'048   81-21625
ISBN 0-8230-8004-8   AACR2

Manufactured in U.S.A.

First Printing, 1982

Contents

Introduction

Only within the last decade have the decorative arts of the 19th century begun to get consistent attention from collectors and scholars. The auction market, which is perhaps the best gauge of collecting interest in any specific field, has seen a marked upswing in the prices paid for the best examples of high-quality 19th century furniture, especially pieces by known makers. So strong has been this trend that several major auction firms now schedule regular specialty sales of the furniture and other decorative arts of the 19th and early 20th centuries.

Interest in furniture made between 1820 and the First World War has been sustained by a number of precedent-setting museum exhibitions that have whetted collectors' appetites for objects made during these years. The Metropolitan Museum of Art in New York City presented its great "19th Century America" exhibition in 1970. This was followed by a rapid succession of other major scholarly museum shows throughout the country, most of them accompanied by catalogues that document specific design movements and substyles within the general period: "The Arts and Crafts Movement in America" (Princeton University, 1972); "Eastlake-influenced American Furniture" (The Hudson River Museum, 1973); "The Gothic Revival Style in America" (The Houston Museum of Fine Arts, 1976); "The American Renaissance" (The Brooklyn Museum, 1979); "The Furniture of John Henry Belter and the Rococo Revival" (The Museum of Our National Heritage, 1980) and "Innovative Furniture" (The Cooper-Hewitt Museum of the Smithsonian Institution, 1981). Several of these exhibitions travelled to additional museums in still other American cities, sparking further public interest in what had been heretofore considered a period unworthy of serious attention. The decorative arts scholarship represented by these exhibitions, and by many smaller shows and individual publications during the past decade, has cast new light on the stylistic trends, designers, and makers of 19th century furniture.

Art & Antiques magazine has been in the forefront of the movement to disseminate this new information to wider audiences of collectors. Many of the foremost curators and scholars working in the field have contributed articles, backed by original research, to its pages. The purpose of the present volume is to bring together these groundbreaking articles in a convenient, roughly chronological format that provides a comprehensive picture of changing patterns of furniture design, manufacture and use from about 1820 to 1915.

The 19th century in the United States, as in many parts of Europe, was a time of industrialization and technological innovation—trends that often ran counter to those underlying intellectual currents of romanticism and historicism that dominated the literature, influenced the aesthetics, and forged the ideals of the century. In the fine and decorative arts, America's trendsetters reflected the dynamic opposition of these movements, yet they remained very much under the influence of things European. Styles in furniture, as in clothing, changed from decade to decade throughout the period, often in response to the swinging pendulum of European fashion. Design trends were transmitted to this country both indirectly, through pattern books and trans-Atlantic consumer publications, and directly through the importation of finished European goods and the immigration of European craftsmen to these shores—first the English, Irish, and French, then the Germans. But America's artisans and designers, whether native-born or naturalized, soon shaped each successive new fashion to satisfy the unique imperatives of the American economy and marketplace.

Throughout much of the 19th century, opposing themes of revival and reform persisted, constituting the major, often contrary, currents in furniture design. Beginning with the classical revivals of the federal period, and continuing in an eclectic welter of historical styles throughout the century, furniture makers looked to the decorative vocabularies of past civilizations for inspiration. Too often, this resulted in slavish imitation of the ancient or the merely antique. In reaction to this enthusiastic and affected manifestation of historicism, design reformers in England—led by John Ruskin and Augustus Welby Northmore Pugin—urged close attention to the integrity of materials, and to the functional qualities of form and decoration. The polarity of the reformist and the revivalist viewpoints continued throughout the entire period under discussion in this book.

1820–1850

By 1820, the United States was well established—economically, politically, and culturally—as an independent young republic. In cities along the Eastern seaboard, notably Boston, New York, and Philadelphia, there was growing evidence of the nation's gradual shift from an agrarian/craft economy to one based on industry and mass production. As Kathleen Catalano explains in "Furniture Making in Philadelphia," the years between 1820 and 1840 witnessed slow but sweeping change in that most cultured of cities: handwork still figured prominently in the decoration of furniture, but steam powered lathes, saws, and veneer cutters were in common use. Trade specialization took hold. The autonomous cabinetmaker who formerly made everything from seating to case furniture to coffins, was replaced by the specialist—the turner, carver, gilder, or pianoforte maker—who dealt in only one product or skill. Changing technology affected style, as well. Those forms and motifs of the classic revival that had dominated the first quarter of the 19th century were now expressed in bulkier American Empire (or "Restauration" or "pillar and scroll") pieces that showed wide expanses of flame-grained mahogany veneer, cut on the new saws, to good advantage.

Concurrently, in New England, enterprising Yankees like Lambert Hitchcock were quick to see the economic advantage in the technological revolution. As Ruth Berenson points out, Hitchcock served the traditional cabinetmaker's apprenticeship in Litchfield, Connecticut making hand-turned Sheraton style chairs; but by 1830, he had organized a factory in a country hamlet northwest of Hartford to mass-produce these pieces with interchangeable parts on machinery powered by water from the nearby Connecticut River. Hitchcock was probably the first American to apply mass-production methods and labor-saving devices to cabinetmaking.

By the time of Queen Victoria's coronation in 1837, revivalism was a well-established phenomenon in the decorative arts. In both England and America, the classicism that carried over from the 1700s, especially in furniture design, became more literal during the second and third decades of the 19th century. Thomas Hope's *Household Furniture and Interior Decoration*, published in London in 1807, was one of the stylebooks that emphasized archaic Egyptian and Greek forms and ornamentation. Cabinetmakers in major American cities, including Anthony Quervelle and Michel Bouvier in Philadelphia and Charles-Honoré Lannuier and Duncan Phyfe in New York, incorporated classical Greek, Roman, and archaic Egyptian forms and motifs into their designs. Klysmos and curule chairs abounded; lyres, winged griffins, urns, columns, pilasters, anthemia, lotus capitals, and hoof or paw feet were common to furniture of the period. In her article on "Egyptian-inspired Furniture," Carol Bohdan notes that the Egyptian influence carried over into the remaining decades of the 19th century, and on into the 20th, forming one of the most persistent of the revival modes.

Like neoclassicism, the Gothic revival was born in the 18th century, celebrated by such architectural extravagances as Horace Walpole's mansion, Strawberry Hill; but it survived as an influence on the decorative arts well into the 19th century. By 1835, thanks to the efforts of such English architects and designers as Augustus Welby Northmore Pugin, who urged a return to the indigenous English medieval style, the Gothic enjoyed a fashionable resurgence in both England and America. (Pugin was the first of a group of prominent arbiters of design—among them John Ruskin, and decades later, William Morris—to urge a return to the aesthetic precepts of the Middle Ages with emphasis on the integrity of materials and craftsmanship, thus sowing the seeds of a design reform movement that would come to full fruition in the last quarter of the 19th century. There is a bit of a paradox in this, as the design reformers generally opposed the furniture revivals as "debased," although they themselves drew philosophic sustenance from the Gothic.)

Still other revival styles were spawned in the 1840s: the so-called Elizabethan style (its elements were rather more Jacobean) with characteristic spiral turnings was popular; and by 1845, elements of the rococo began to be seen. In the United States, sophisticated city cabinetmakers attempted to satisfy the changing tastes of their wealthy and well-travelled customers by working in a variety of revival styles during the decades just before and after the turn of the century. Many of these craftsmen, like Alexander Roux and Leon Marcotte of New York City, were of French descent.

1850-1875

At London's great Crystal Palace Exposition of 1851, the most prominent of the furniture fashions on display was that of the French antique, or Louis Quinze—an exuberant and often florid variation of 18th century design, with extravagant curves, a wealth of naturalistic carving, S and C scrolls, and cabriole legs. In the United States, this rococo revival mode was taken up by many of the best furniture makers, among them John Henry Belter of New York City, whose name has become synonymous with the style itself. As Ed Douglas cautions in his article on "Belter and the Rococo Revival," however, there were other cabinetmakers working in this mode, including Joseph Meeks and Alexander Roux. Their work is often undistinguishable from Belter's.

Significantly, Belter exemplifies three important aspects of the American furniture industry at mid-century: like many other cabinetmakers of the 1850s and 1860s, he was born and educated in Germany, emigrating to the United States to make his fortune; he found the rococo style congenial; and technologically speaking, he was an important innovator, best remembered for his patented method of laminating many thin layers of wood and shaping them in a steam mold or caul.

Technological innovation, as well as the innovative use of materials, figured strongly in furniture making by the end of the 1850s, as Page Talbott explains in her article on "Innovative Furniture." One particularly inventive genius, Michael Thonet, was a native of Germany, like John Henry Belter. Like Belter, too, he experimented with laminating thin layers of wood to achieve distinctive furniture forms. Christopher Wilk tells how Thonet and his sons eventually moved to Vienna, where they patented a method for bending wooden saplings to mass-manufacture the distinctive low-cost chairs that were soon sold all over the world.

Among the materials that were inventively used to make furniture at mid-century were cast-iron, wicker, and papier maché. In the 1850s and 1860s, cast-iron garden seats, embellished with naturalistic grape leaves or ferns, were made at Coalbrookdale, England and in several American foundries, as explained by Esther Mipaas in her study of this material. Katharine Menz reveals that although wicker was particularly well suited to translate the graceful curves and flourishes of the rococo revival, furniture in this medium continued to be made—in a variety of popular styles—for literally every room in the house throughout the remainder of the 19th century. By the mid-1860s, the rococo began to fall from fashion; it was replaced with several other revival styles including "neo-Grec" with its ebonized, polychromed finishes and Egyptian-inspired ornament; and Louis XVI, a rather faithful reproduction of the original 18th century mode. Most popular during this decade was the architectonic, ponderous, bilaterally symmetrical Renaissance revival style, so named for its ornamental details which borrowed heavily from the vocabulary of classic architecture—decorative cartouches, caryatid supports, pendant finials, and portrait medallions. An early and very successful exponent of the Renaissance revival style was Daniel Pabst of Philadelphia. David Hanks, in his monograph on this artisan, explains that Pabst succeeded by catering to the needs of wealthy clients in Philadelphia and elsewhere. He opened shop in 1854 and eventually employed 50 workers, turning later in his career to the "modern Gothic" mode.

Yet another German-born cabinetmaker of the period following 1860 was George Hunzinger of New York City, whose patented folding chairs combined constructional innovation with some whimsically-interpreted decorative trappings of the Renaissance revival style. Richard Flint observes that Hunzinger's distinctive furniture, characterized by machine-like cog and wheel shapes, continued in demand through much of the 1890s.

In the decade following the Civil War, the nature of the furniture-making industry changed rapidly. New factories were constructed in towns considerably to the west of the traditional seaboard cabinetmaking centers and convenient to river or rail transport—towns like Williamsport, Pennsylvania; Jamestown, New York; Cincinnati, Ohio; Muscatine, Iowa; and Grand Rapids, Michigan. Machines for sawing, planing, turning, mortising, carving, and decorative incising encouraged the mass production of all the latest styles produced in Europe and on the East coast. Much of the factory-produced furniture was in the Renaissance revival style. Some of it was attractive and well-made; some was shoddy and in poor taste. All of it was sold at moderate to low prices, meeting the growing middle class demand for fashionable home furnishings. Traditional cabinetmakers in Philadelphia, New York, and Boston were hard put to compete with these cheap western products. Some of them became merchants as well as producers, buying stock from the western factories and selling it to their old customers at attractive prices.

1875-1890

By 1875, in reaction to the revival styles of the preceding decades, which many critics considered to be excessively derivative and therefore debased, the movement for reform in furniture design became well-established in the United States. This trend had originated in England around mid-century, following the publication of John Ruskin's *Stones of Venice*, which urged a return to the principles of "honest" Medieval design and straightforward construction. The extreme ostentation of much furniture displayed at London's Crystal Palace Exhibition of 1851 further exacerbated the distaste of many young designers for the curving forms of the rococo, encouraging the development of the so-called modern Gothic style, based on indigenous English forms of the middle ages. Charles Locke Eastlake, an English architect, was largely responsible for disseminating this influence to the United States, through the publication of his best-selling book, *Hints on Household Taste*, the bible of the design reform movement in both Britain and America.

Eastlake's book encouraged the design and production of a wide range of reform styles in furniture in the United States. Some of the most distinctive of these Eastlake-influenced pieces were made by the New York City firm of Kimbel and Cabus, whose rectilinear, ebonized, modern Gothic pieces were decorated with geometric motifs, inset tiles, and ornamental strap hinges. In his study of this important cabinetmaking and decorating firm, David Hanks notes that Kimbel and Cabus was one of two American manufacturers who displayed modern Gothic at the Philadelphia Centennial Exhibition of 1876, thus helping to disseminate the taste for reform styles across the United States.

International pavilions—especially those of Turkey and Japan—in the Centennial Exhibition also whetted America's appetite for oriental and middle-Eastern design, contributing to the exoticism and eclecticism that characterized much furniture made in the late 1870s and 1880s. As a patriotic celebration, the Centennial Exhibition also rekindled public interest in the aesthetics of the colonial and revolutionary eras, encouraging the sometimes mannered reproduction of 18th century American styles in what was loosely termed the Colonial Revival.

By 1890, more furniture was being manufactured in Chicago than in any other American city. As David Hanks points out in his study of Chicago's furniture industry, there were interesting links between reform designers in England, Philadelphia and Chicago during the period from 1875 to 1895. Chicago architect Louis Henri Sullivan, for example, had worked as a young man for Frank Furness of Philadelphia, whose modern Gothic furniture designs with their delicately conventionalized floral motifs are believed to have been executed by Daniel Pabst's firm. And Isaac Scott, a Chicago furniture designer working in the same genre, learned his trade in Philadelphia, where he quite possibly came under the influence of Pabst and Furness.

1895-1915

Toward century's end, many English

and American interiors were furnished with bulky examples of so-called "Beaux Arts Revival" pieces, loosely based on Jacobean, Italian, and French design and notable primarily for their weighty carving in oak. Counter to this trend, some of the most interesting furniture of the 1890's was designed by architects in the reform spirit to bring aesthetic unity to their plans for residences and public buildings. Henry Hobson Richardson was a decade or so ahead of the pack. The spiral-turned red oak chairs he designed for the Court of Appeals chamber at the State Capitol in Albany, New York in 1884 combined the characteristic Romanesque elements of his architecture with Byzantine ornamentation—ram's heads and swirling spiral bosses. During the 1890's in Chicago, George Maher and Frank Lloyd Wright created strong, simple rectilinear chairs and tables compatible with the Prairie School style they favored. In Pasadena, California, brothers Charles and Henry Greene planned elegantly inlaid pieces for their Gamble house commission that reflect both concern for the natural beauty of the wood and appreciation of oriental design elements. In Scotland, Charles Rennie Mackintosh sketched spare, angular furniture in what has since come to be regarded as the style of the Glasgow School of Design. And in England, as Marian Page explains, Charles Francis Annesley Voysey created furniture so simple and perfect in its conception, utility, and intent that it has been compared to the work of the Shakers.

Like many of his fellow architect-designers, Voysey was greatly affected by William Morris's Arts and Crafts philosophy, which constituted the single most important influence on furniture design in the decades just before and after the turn of the century. Like other exponents of the reformist movement, Morris stressed the importance of hand craftsmanship and believed that honestly constructed furniture, simply designed and functional, possessed an inherent morality. Morris's social philosophy was also reformist: he glorified the concept of the guild, or craft cooperative. His ideas found many adherents in the United States.

A leading American proponent of Arts and Crafts philosophy was Gustav Stickley, who started a craft cooperative in Eastwood, New York, where he made simple, sturdy, rectilinear oak furniture in a distinctive style dubbed "Mission". Other designers quickly took up the fashion, among them Stickley's brothers, whose look-alike pieces were not so well constructed as Gustav's, according to author Barry Sanders. Another well-known Arts and Crafts community, Roycroft, was founded by charismatic journalist and philosopher Elbert Hubbard at East Aurora, New York. Robert Edwards describes the Roycroft furniture, which was plainly constructed of fumed oak and embellished only with the characteristic Roycroft insignia.

So great was the success of the so-called Mission style in the decade or two after the turn of the century that it precluded widespread American acceptance of Art Nouveau furniture. Named for the Paris shop opened by art dealer Samuel Bing in 1895, art nouveau was probably the most important influence on continental European decorative arts during the last decade of the 19th century. Its free-flowing, undulating lines, based on organic structures and incorporating graceful floral motifs, lent distinction to some furniture masterpieces turned out by Emile Gallé—who also designed glassware in the Art Nouveau mode—and by Louis Majorelle, both of Nancy, France. Katharine Morrison McClinton differentiates between the work of these French cabinetmakers, explaining that Majorelle—who embellished his pieces with remarkable cast brass mounts—was ultimately concerned with fine proportion, while Gallé emphasized delicate floral marquetry ornamentation, inspired by plant life of his native Lorraine.

Furniture in the Art Nouveau mode was manufactured and sold in the United States after 1895 by such firms as the Tobey Furniture Company and Karpen Brothers of Chicago, and by George C. Flint of New York. But as Betty Teller points out in her article on "Art Nouveau Furniture in America," these factory-made examples cannot be compared to the handcrafted, often one-of-a-kind pieces created by Gallé or Majorelle for an elite group of wealthy, sophisticated customers.

No discussion of turn-of-the century furniture would be complete without mention of the trend toward the rustic. As urbanization spread across the American continent, people of means sought escape from the noise, bustle and pollution of industrial cities by retreating to lavishly appointed hunting lodges, summer camps, and country homes in remotely located mountain areas. By the mid-1880s, there was a brisk demand for horn chairs to furnish hunter's lodges in both Europe and the United States. In the Adirondacks, where some of America's richest tycoons whiled away the summer months, local guides and outdoorsmen spent long winters fashioning artful furniture from bent twigs and saplings, still sheathed in bark. This elaborate "rustic" furniture was destined for the living rooms and bedrooms of their warm weather employers. Mass manufacturers began turning out rustic-looking chairs and rockers of sturdy hickory saplings to meet the demand for special furniture for summer cottages across the United States. As Craig Gilborn points out, this factory furniture was dubbed "Adirondack Hickory" because so much of it was shipped via rail to hotels and summer residences of that resort region. But most of it was made in Indiana factories, from the late 1890s right through the early 1940s.

In its exhilarating variety, the polyglot of 19th century revival and reform furniture styles speaks eloquently of the ideals and aspirations of a golden age, now lost—an age of vibrant energy, romantic dreams, and unshakable faith in man's progress. In part, it is the seductive charm of this tantalizingly recent era that encourages decorative arts scholars to sidestep traditional limitations of period and standard definitions of craftsmanship; and to reassess the furniture of the 19th century according to the values of its own time. It is hoped that by bringing together some of the best recent writings on furniture made between 1820 and 1915, this volume will encourage further study and collecting activity in a field richly deserving of such attention. ■

The Empire Style: Philadelphia

Philadelphia's cabinet-making business in the 1820s and 1830s was both popular and prosperous. Changes in style and technique helped sustain the city's status as an American furniture center.

BY KATHLEEN M. CATALANO

Considered "elegant" by some and "monstrous" by others, American furniture of the 1820s and 1830s has evoked strong reaction. Less controversial is the cabinet industry itself, which then witnessed a period of unprecedented growth and change. Nowhere is the vitality of the time more evident than in the Philadelphia trade, whose expanded market, high quality of goods, and effective method of operation sustained the city's long-established reputation as a furniture manufacturing center.

The Philadelphia shop system

Between 1820 and 1840, over 1,600 cabinet craftsmen were working in Philadelphia, many in the traditional furniture-making district around Second, Third, and Front streets. Just prior to the Revolution, in comparison, there had been only 100 cabinetmakers in the city. The size and nature of the individual shops varied greatly. Some were small and cramped, consisting of little more than one room, while others were relatively spacious, with several work areas and perhaps a wareroom or two where completed goods could be stored and viewed. Among the smallest cabinetmaking shops were those of William B. Fling and Abraham McDonough, who each employed only three apprentices. John Jamison, on the other hand, employed eight journeymen and four apprentices, while Robert West kept three apprentices, one woman (presumably engaged in upholstery work), and six journeymen, of whom one worked part-time.

Apprentices worked not for money, but to gain technical training and a rudimentary education. Journeymen, in contrast, received a salary, calculated upon a piecework or day basis that differed from employer to employer. When British traveler Harriet Martineau visited the United States in the 1830s, she noted that "the wages of labour are so good . . . there is less cause for discontent on the part of the workmen than elsewhere." Philadelphia's journeymen apparently did not agree, for they constantly complained of being underpaid. To remedy the situation, workmen attempted in 1828 to establish a uniform and "just" system of wages in their *Book of Prices*, a revision of the Philadelphia price books of the mid-1790s. This volume listed suggested wages to be paid journeymen cabinet- and chair-makers on a piecework basis, set the length of the working day at 11 hours ("employers to find candles"), and fixed the daily journeyman's wage at $1.33⅓, an increase of one-third over the going rate in 1795. Since its provisions were negotiated by a committee of both masters and employees, the 1828 *Book of Prices* was an early type of labor contract. While not all masters followed this guideline in calculating wages, there is some indication that this and other price books were used. When advertising for workers in 1826, for example, Isaac Pippit made this announcement in *The Freeman's Journal:* "I wish to employ four first rate journeymen, and will pay the prices established by the Society of Journeymen Cabinet-makers and the cash paid on demand."

In general, cabinetmakers enjoyed a moderate degree of economic success. Probate records show most were members of the middle class, with estate values ranging between $350 and $2,500. Some were even more prosperous.

Above: Mahogany and mahogany veneer center table with marble-inlaid top, labeled by Anthony Quervelle. The table's carved paw feet, heavy gadrooning, triangular platform and pedestal with foliated bud may have been inspired by the designs of George Smith, first seen in his *Collection of Designs for Household Furniture.* The Metropolitan Museum of Art; The Edgar J. Kaufmann Charitable Foundation Fund 1965.

> "Empire pieces often have heavy proportions, bold forms, animal-paw feet, and an abundance of carved decorative detailing—anthemia, acanthus leaves, dolphins, cornucopias, and gadrooning."

Thomas Whitecar, for example, had $9,000 worth of possessions at his death, while Lawrence Sink had $12,000 worth. The better-known makers also fared well. Anthony Quervelle owned houses on Locust, Pine, and Lombard streets and was a partner in the Bristol Iron Works. Michel Bouvier, who held several pieces of property throughout the city, accumulated over 157,000 acres of West Virginia coal fields, which he sold for a great profit.

At the other end of the scale were the inevitable economic failures. Some were sent destitute to the almshouse, while a number of others applied for insolvency, especially after the Panics of 1819 and 1837. Considering the large cabinetmaking population, however, the percentage of bankruptcies was small, perhaps because the craftsmen were a versatile group. Besides making

Above: The Loud Brothers worked here ca 1820. From Thomas Porter's *Picture of Philadelphia from 1811 to 1831*; Winterthur Museum Libraries. Below: Drop-leaf extension table of mahogany and pine. The Henry Francis du Pont Winterthur Museum; gift of the Aetna Life & Casualty Insurance Company.

furniture, cabinetmakers in the 20s and 30s often did repair and carpentry work. They made cornices and Venetian blinds, mended casters, "took down and put up" bedsteads, repaired steps, and hung doors. Most could furnish utilitarian items like knife and clothesline boxes, or mend and repaint old furniture. Some cabinetmakers engaged in totally unrelated sidelines. They performed as innkeepers, grocers, distillers, stonecutters, booksellers, coachmakers, lumber merchants, and undertakers.

This diversification enabled craftsmen to adjust to changing economic conditions. When one phase of business was adversely affected, they concentrated on another to supplement their income and sustain the general prosperity of the cabinetmaking community.

Woodworking machinery in Philadelphia

In the 1820s and 1830s, new labor-saving woodworking devices were introduced. These did not replace man, but foreshadowed the industrial age to come. Patents were granted for many machines that planed and grooved lumber, reeded table legs, and cut the angles of any desired circle or square. The circular saw, first made in upstate New York around 1814, was offered for sale in Philadelphia as early as 1825. New types of saws unrolled veneers in a continuous sheet, permitting up to ten cuts of wood per inch, as compared with the seven or eight layers produced by the hand method.

Many of these new machines were run by steam, which eventually would become the prime power source in Philadelphia. Between 1820 and 1840,

there were at least 16 sawmills in town, including one operated by cabinetmaker Michel Bouvier at 9 South Second Street. Despite the advent of steam power and the spate of new inventions, reliance on hand tools continued throughout the period. With the exception of steam saws, lathes, and veneer cutters—owned only by the large operators—woodworking machinery was not in general use in Philadelphia until after 1840. Not one of the cabinetmakers questioned in the 1820 Census of Manufacturers reported using any machinery in his operation; and Edward Hazen's book *The Panorama of Professions and Trades*, published in several editions in the 1830s, describes cabinetmaking solely in terms of manual production. Inventories of the period also show that cabinetmakers' shop equipment did not differ significantly from inventories of previous years.

Why were Philadelphia's cabinetmakers reluctant to accept machines? Perhaps because they were not produced on a large scale, or because Pennsylvania and West Virginia coal fields—and the rail transportation from these fields—were not sufficiently developed to make steam power economical. Or perhaps it was just plain pride in the traditional methods of handcraftsmanship. Whatever the cause, Philadelphia furniture continued to be handcrafted until much later in the 19th century.

Furniture-making specialists

Industrialization fostered specialization. Although furniture makers had specialized previously, greater numbers of workmen now concentrated on

President Andrew Jackson purchased Philadelphia furniture for use in the White House as well as in his Tennessee home, the Hermitage. (Above): One of "6 Mahogany Bedsteads" supplied by Philadelphia merchant George W. South in January, 1836. Barry and Krickbaum, also of Philadelphia, made the ca 1837 mahogany wardrobe below, now on view in a bedroom of the Hermitage. Both, Ladies' Hermitage Association, Hermitage, Tennessee.

producing specific types of furniture. Sometimes a number of specialists worked together in the same shop, but more often they maintained independent workrooms. Between 1820 and 1830 there were ten major craft divisions in the Philadelphia furniture trade. Cabinetmakers provided case pieces, tables, desks, sofas, and sometimes chairs and coffins. Carvers and gilders worked on furniture, looking glasses, and frames, as well as on stove patterns, railings, houses, ships, and steamboats. Pianoforte makers sometimes produced both the case and the works for the instrument but generally depended on the cabinetmaker for the case. Clockmakers, too, usually relied on the cabinetmaker to produce their cases. Portable-desk makers created gentlemen's dressing cases and ladies' workboxes, as well as portable writing desks. Turners made bedposts, chairs, and drawer knobs; frame and looking-glass specialists manufactured frames for paintings, prints, and mirrors. There were both "fancy" and "Windsor" chairmakers. Chair painters busied themselves exclusively with chair ornamentation. Upholsterers sometimes made their own chair and sofa frames, but often received their stock from cabinetmakers.

A typical specialist-craftsman, Thomas Loud, emigrated from England to establish a pianoforte manufactory in Philadelphia about 1816. Within several years he was joined by his brothers John, Joseph, and Philologus. Loud & Brothers became one of the largest and most prominent businesses of its kind in America. The firm made both the works and the cases of their stylish pianofortes at their three-building headquarters on Chestnut Street.

Style and decoration

Philadelphia furniture makers in the 1820s and 1830s offered their clientele an extensive range of goods. Besides the more common forms, craftsmen made bidets, hat stands, butler's trays, cellarets, bed steps, and tray stands. The 1828 *Book of Prices* reveals a wide difference in cost, depending upon the type of wood, finish, and decoration selected by the customer.

Furniture made of mahogany and other expensive woods usually was varnished. In *The Panorama of the Professions and Trades,* Edward Hazen describes the painstaking process:

> To give the work a complete finish, four coats of varnish are successively applied; in addition to these, a particular kind of treatment is used after the laying on and drying of each coat. After the application of the first coat, the surface is rubbed with a piece of wood of convenient form; after the second, with sand-paper and pulverized pumice-stone; after the third, with pumice-stone again; and after the fourth, with very finely powdered pumice-stone and rotten stone. A little linseed-oil is then applied, and the whole process is finished by the application of flour, and by friction with the hand.

Less expensive woods sometimes were painted in imitation of more costly materials. Various trade encyclopedias provided excellent instructions on how to mix paint colors to copy mahogany, rosewood, and satinwood. Brass or bronze mounts and gilt stenciling were also used to decorate furniture. Philadelphia stenciling tended to be flat and lacking dimension, as compared with the heavily shaded gilding preferred by New York City craftsmen. A pianoforte made by Loud & Brothers around 1826, now in the collection of the Chester County Historical Society, bears characteristic decoration. It has shallow-

Above right: Mahogany and bird's eye maple *secrétaire à abbatant,* made by Michel Bouvier around 1820 for Point Breeze, Joseph Bonaparte's country home near Bordentown, N. J. Its flat surfaces, sharp angles and pillared facade are characteristic of French Empire design. The Athenaeum, Philadelphia.

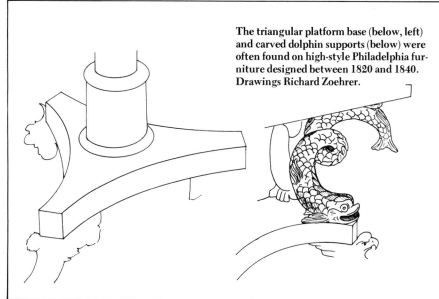

The triangular platform base (below, left) and carved dolphin supports (below) were often found on high-style Philadelphia furniture designed between 1820 and 1840. Drawings Richard Zoehrer.

carved scroll brackets with anthemia and cornucopias, features often seen on Philadelphia sideboards and sofas of the period.

For covered furniture, upholsterers and cabinetmakers could choose from a variety of goods. Hair cloth, the most common furniture fabric in the late 18th and early 19th centuries, continued in use, although inventories and bills of sale indicate a number of other textiles were also employed. For heavily trafficked areas such as dining rooms and libraries, strong materials like leather, plush, and wool were popular. In the more elegant houses, damask and silks were fashionable for drawing rooms. Slipcovers customarily were made of chintz and holland—a closely woven linen—while cane and rush were used for the seats of fancy chairs and settees.

Written descriptions and surviving examples indicate that furniture produced in Philadelphia between 1820 and 1840 was in the Empire fashion. A more literal and archaeological phase

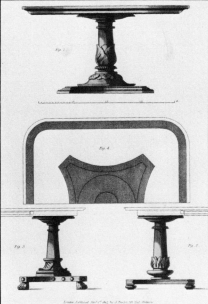

Designs for a "Pillar and Claw Table" from George Smith's *A Collection of Designs for Household Furniture* (London, 1808, Plate 69). Winterthur Museum.

of the neoclassicism that preceded it, this style employed the actual forms of ancient furniture, especially from Greece and Rome. Empire pieces often have heavy proportions, bold forms, animal-paw feet, and an abundance of carved decorative detailing—anthemia, acanthus leaves, dolphins, cornucopias, and gadrooning. In Philadelphia such carving tended to be shallow, as opposed to the more plastic, dimensional variety found on New York City pieces. (This is a turnaround from the mid-18th century, when Philadelphia carving

was noted for its depth and plasticity and New York carving was considered shallow and "stringy.")

At times, Empire furniture seemed excessively ponderous, a tendency noted in the Franklin Institute's catalogue for their Seventh Annual Exhibition of Domestic Manufactures. "Even now," notes the catalogue, "we occasionally observe forms too massive, or inappropriate to the uses expected of the goods—gaudy or inharmonious colors—gildings too lavishly spread upon objects of furniture."

By the end of the 1830s, the fashion for ornately carved detail was replaced by the late Empire or French Restoration style with its cabriole legs, large pillars and scrolls, and broad expanses of veneers.

Throughout the period, Philadelphia craftsmen endeavored to keep abreast of the latest fashions, boasting furniture "in the latest improved European patterns." Because British and French pattern books often were used, many pieces of Philadelphia's finest furniture

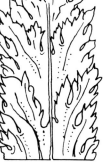

To accent the heavy forms of Empire furniture—a dominant style in Philadelphia after 1820—an abundance of carved detail was employed. Favored motifs included the cornucopia (shown at far left, this page, in bracket form) and the acanthus leaf (extreme right)—an ornamental detail often found on classic architecture. Gadrooning (left of center, below) was used on the baluster-like supports of pedestal tables as well as on the sturdy legs of case furniture. The animal-paw foot (right of center, below) appeared primarily on pier and pedestal tables and sideboards. Drawings Richard Zoehrer.

Sideboard of mahogany veneer over pine and poplar made by Anthony Quervelle between 1825 and 1835. Pressed glass knobs, mirrored panel and inset white marble slab lighten its ponderous lines. Note characteristic paw feet and shallowly carved cornucopias bracketing the mirrored crest. Winterthur Museum.

can be traced to a definite design source. Then, too, some of Philadelphia's finest furniture makers emigrated from France or England in the early 19th century. Michel Bouvier, for example, had served in the army of Napoleon I before coming to America in 1815. He eventually established a flourishing business on South Second Street, where for 30 years he made furniture, operated a steam sawmill, and sold lumber, veneers, marble, and upholstery supplies. He died in 1874, a wealthy and respected man.

The furniture of Bouvier's cabinet shop reflected his French heritage. For example, a mahogany and bird's-eye maple *secrétaire à abattant* made for Joseph Bonaparte—the brother of Napoleon, who lived near Bordentown, New Jersey—has the flat surfaces, sharp angles, and pillared facade characteristic of French Empire design. It is reminiscent of similar pieces illustrated by the Parisian designer Pierre de la Mésangère in his book *Collection de Meubles et Objets de Goût.*

Another prominent Philadelphia cabinetmaker of French origin was Anthony Quervelle. Born in Paris in 1789, he was working in Philadelphia by 1817, and by 1835 had a successful "Cabinet and Sofa Manufactory" at 126 South Second Street, not far from Michel Bouvier's shop. The quality of Quervelle's work attracted a wide and prestigious patronage. In 1829, for example, he was commissioned to make seven mahogany tables for the White House.

Despite his French upbringing, Quervelle—like other Philadelphia craftsmen—was much influenced by British design sources. The most important of these was George Smith's *A Collection of Designs for Household Furniture,* first published in London in 1808 and reprinted 18 years later in a revised edition as *The Cabinet-Maker and Upholsterer's Guide.* These two editions popularized such motifs as the lion's-paw foot, the hollow triangular and rectangular table platform, gadrooning, and the pedestal that rises from a foliated bud. Quervelle, in fact, gathered many of the elements for his individualized furniture designs from illustrations in Smith's books.

Marketing the furniture

The Philadelphia craftsmen's concern for style promoted the city's reputation as a fashion leader. Together with improved transportation systems, the growth of the West, and the rapidly increasing national population, this stylish reputation expanded the market for Philadelphia furniture. Growing demand encouraged large-scale production and new merchandising methods.

In preceding periods, most craftsmen were content with the two common forms of selling: custom-order or "bespoke" work and, by the late 1700s, "shop work" or the retail wareroom marketing of ready-made furniture. As sales increased, furniture makers adopted a third sales technique: wholesale or "order" work. Wholesale production grew more popular between 1820 and 1840, but most cabinetmakers continued also to accommodate the retail and—to a lesser extent—custom-order trade.

During this time, over 128,000 pieces of Philadelphia-made furniture were shipped to over 50 American cities and 20 foreign ports. Although chairs were by far the most popular export, virtually every other furniture form, including billiard tables, left the city. Most of the domestic trade involved cities south of Washington, D.C. In the foreign commerce, favorite markets were the West Indies, Mexico, Argentina, Venezuela, Uruguay, and Brazil. Sales to Philadelphians and residents of western and northern Pennsylvania—particularly in the region of Chester, Carlisle, Pottsville, and Pittsburgh—also constituted much of the business.

Some of America's leading citizens patronized Philadelphia cabinet shops. Shipping merchant Stephen Girard was prominent among the local clientele. Although much of Girard's house was furnished before 1820, he continued to buy chairs and small pieces of furniture exclusively from Philadelphia craftsmen until his death in 1831. He also retained several of the city's cabinetmakers for doing repairs. For example, he engaged Michel Bouvier on several occasions for repairing, polishing, and fastening the knobs on a secretary; "renewing" the base of a bedstead; repairing a sofa; and "taking down and putting up" bedsteads.

Bouvier also worked for Joseph Bonaparte, the ex-king of Spain. As early as 1818, the craftsman performed some unidentified work for Point Breeze, Bonaparte's country estate. Shortly thereafter, Bouvier took charge of major construction work for the

Card table of rosewood and mahogany veneer with pine, tulip, birch and chestnut. Made by Michel Bouvier, whose shop stencil it bears, ca 1830. Private collection; photograph by George J. Fistrovich.

monarch's house. When Point Breeze burned down in 1820, Bouvier was employed to refurnish it. At this time he created the well-known mahogany and bird's-eye maple *secrétaire à abattant*.

Philadelphia furniture makers also sold their wares to prominent people in other parts of the country. In 1826, for example, Anthony Quervelle shipped two boxes of furniture to the Secretary of the Navy, Samuel L. Southard, in Washington, D.C.; and two years later he supplied President Andrew Jackson with the previously mentioned mahogany tables—two round center ones with black and gold marble slabs, another similar but slightly larger table, and

four pier tables with white Italian marble tops. For his Tennessee home, the Hermitage, Jackson later purchased several pieces of Philadelphia furniture from the firm of Barry and Krickbaum and from merchant George W. South. Such prestigious patronage demonstrated a preference for the city's wares among people of fashion and bolstered the success of its furniture trade.

Operated by a versatile and conscientious group of men, Philadelphia's cabinetmaking business in the 1820s and 1830s proved both popular and prosperous. Relying on traditional methods of handcraftsmanship, furniture makers fashioned large quantities of goods for an ever-growing market. Patterned in the latest styles, these cabinet wares were succinctly described by a critic writing for the *United States Gazette* in 1826 as "highly creditable to the workmen engaged, and . . . additional proof that Philadelphia stands unrivalled in this species of manufacture." ∎

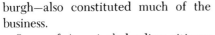

Above: Illustration from Edward Hazen's *The Panorama of Professions and Trades* (1837). Winterthur Museum Libraries. Right: Mahogany pianoforte made by Loud Bros. ca 1826. Scroll brackets with anthemion petals and cornucopias are characteristic Philadelphia decorations of the period, as is the stenciling with its distinctively "flat" quality. The Chester County Historical Society, West Chester, Pennsylvania.

Hitchcock Furniture

In the 1820s, 30s and 40s, Lambert Hitchcock manufactured turned Sheraton-type chairs with interchangeable parts in his precedent-setting factory in northwestern Connecticut. His was truly the first factory furniture.

BY RUTH BERENSON

No article of American furniture has proved more popular than the gaily decorated Hitchcock chair, both in its own time—the 1820s, '30s and '40s—and today. Yet few realize that its maker, Lambert Hitchcock, merits an honored place in American industrial history, not just because of his chair's distinctive appearance but because, as

the first person to apply mass-production methods and labor-saving devices to cabinetmaking, he was the progenitor of Grand Rapids.

Hitchcock is best viewed in the context of an era of rapid industrialization that produced Eli Whitney and the cotton gin, Isaac Merrit Singer and the sewing machine, and Eli Terry, who substituted wooden parts for the metal works that made clocks so expensive—as well as many other American tinkers. Like Whitney and Terry, Hitchcock was a real Connecticut Yankee.

He was born in Cheshire, Connecticut in 1795 to a family whose ancestry reached back to the 17th century and included numerous carpenters, joiners and the like. Nothing is known of his early years, but it is thought that he served his apprenticeship in Cheshire,

for, by 1814, he was already a journeyman in the chair and cabinet manufactory of Silas E. Cheney of Litchfield. There he remained for four years, becoming adept at fashioning the elegant Sheraton-type furniture that, if we are to judge from Cheney's signed pieces in the Judge Tapping Reeve House in Litchfield, was his master's specialty.

Litchfield today looks much as it did when Lambert Hitchcock lived there, a typical quiet New England village centered on a tree-shaded green. During the 1820s and '30s, however, it hummed with industry. According to John Tarrant Kenney, the latter-day Yankee who revived the Hitchcock Chair Factory in the 1940s and whose book, *The Hitchcock Chair*, is a mine of information, Litchfield, with a population of around 1000, produced "fur

Opposite: In its day this was a very popular type of Hitchcock chair with its cornucopia back and bolster top painted black and decorated with typical Hitchcock stenciling. It was made between 1825 and 1832 and signed "L. Hitchcock, Hitchcocks-ville, Conn. Warranted." Note the front legs turned with a tulip shape at the point where the stretcher joins the legs, and the unturned and slightly bent back posts; features which characterize Hitchcock chairs. Left: Because of the stencil decoration also found on his chairs, this yellow dressing table is believed to have been made at Hitchcock's factory at Unionville, Connecticut around 1845. The piece features green striping, a tilt mirror, sandwich glass pulls and a draw-out shelf for a candle. Above: This black settee made in the mid-19th century was found near Riverton (formerly Hitchcocks-ville) in excellent condition. Although unsigned, it has been attributed to Hitchcock because of the stenciling and the inter-changeable parts also typical of his chairs: the ring turned front legs, the bolster top, cornucopia back and the bent, unturned back posts. All courtesy The Hitchcock Chair Company Collection, Riverton, Connecticut.

hats, palm-leaf hats, clocks, clock dials, flutes, fifes, tinplate ware, cloth garments, woolen cloth, cabinet furniture, veneering stuffs, pleasure carriages, saddles and harnesses."

Elsewhere in Connecticut, too, the whir of machinery filled the air. In a flourishing firearms factory near New Haven, founded in 1798, Eli Whitney pioneered the use of standardized parts as well as the division of labor—methods which were basic to Hitchcock's venture into furniture production. We do not know if he saw Whitney's factory in operation, but he was almost certainly acquainted with Terry's clock works, located next door to Litchfield in what is now Thomaston, and with other small factories in northwestern Connecticut which were turning out such diverse objects as friction matches, telescoping fishing rods, steel fish hooks, and spectacles. Invention and innovation were so much in the air that it seems a plausible assumption that if Hitchcock had not conceived the idea of mass-producing furniture, someone else in the area would have done so before long.

Hitchcock was 23 years old when he decided to leave Litchfield and go into the chair-making business by himself. It was a crowded field: in New York there were enough such craftsmen to organize the Master Chairmakers' Society which mustered several hundred members to march in the parade celebrating the opening of the Erie Canal in 1825. But fear of competition did not deter Hitchcock. In 1818 he found what he thought would be an ideal location for a factory: the tiny hamlet of Fork-of-the-Rivers in Barkhamsted Township, Connecticut. Its location at the junction of the Farmington and Still rivers meant there would be the necessary water power. Surrounding forests ensured a plentiful supply of hardwood—

birch, maple, tulip, cherry—and also pine. Cattails for rushing grew on the river banks. Only 30 miles from Hartford, the state capital, and on the main stagecoach road to Albany, the village boasted an inn (which, as "The Old Riverton Inn," still prospers), a brickyard, three blacksmith shops, a grist-and-sawmill where Hitchcock's raw lumber was cut, and a woodworking shop owned by William Moore, Jr., who, in years to come, would be Hitchcock's friend and competitor.

That he had chosen well must have seemed obvious to him, since, not long after his arrival, the village became known as Hitchcocks-ville; it did not assume its present name, Riverton, until 1865, long after Hitchcock was dead and his factory, though still standing, had stopped making furniture.

Unfortunately there were two drawbacks to the location which plagued Hitchcock throughout his career and which, in the end, proved fatal to his business. The first was the village's isolation in the northwestern corner of the state, making both skilled and unskilled labor hard to come by. This is attested by his frequent advertisements in the *Connecticut Courier*, Hartford's most important newspaper, for "young men . . . of industrious and correct

habits who will abstain from ardent spirits" to learn the furniture-making trade. The second was the deplorable condition of the road to Hartford, where the furniture had to be shipped. Badly rutted, it was hazardous to heavily loaded wagons at all times and was impassable in winter, so that in cold weather his operations either slowed down or stopped altogether.

All this only slowly became evident. Hitchcock started out modestly making chair parts—legs, stretchers, slats, and seats to be assembled by do-it-yourselfers. He sold these parts to local dry-goods stores, and, eventually, farther afield. In the South, where there were few cabinetmakers, they seemed to have been especially popular. But Hitchcock's aim was to manufacture complete chairs out of interchangeable parts which could be assembled in a variety of ways and which, once they were painted and decorated, could be sold so cheaply that everyone could afford them. And, only four years after settling in Hitchcocks-ville, he was doing precisely that. By 1822 the *Connecticut Courier* was carrying his advertisements for "chairs of every description . . . on low and accommodating terms"—which meant from $.45 to $1.75, retail; his wholesale prices were even lower.

By 1825 Hitchcock had built a handsome brick factory on the bank of the Still River. Its roof gaily sported a cupola and a weathervane. The dam across the river assured a power source even in dry summers to propel the giant water wheel and thus turn the lathes, boring tools and other machinery that occupied most of the building's ground floor. Here the green lumber was processed, and the chair posts and backslats were steamed and bent. The second floor housed the "driving room" where the parts, still green, were bonded to-

gether at their tenons—or "driven up," as the phrase went—with glue made of animal hide. These fused parts were then placed in the drying kiln where the joints became firm. Rushing, caning, painting, striping, banding, and stenciling was done on the top floor, mostly by women. Legend has it that when the chairs were finished, they were dropped out of the windows onto wagons waiting to make the trip to Hartford. If they didn't break—and if the story is to be believed—then Hitchcock was certainly entitled to the signature he stenciled on the back of the seats: "L. Hitchcock. Hitchcocks-ville. Conn. Warranted."

Unfortunately for the connoisseur, many, but by no means all the chairs Hitchcock made between 1825 and 1832 bear this signature. In that year, pressed for cash, he went into partnership with his brother-in-law, Arba Alford. From then to 1843, when the partnership was dissolved and Hitchcock moved to Unionville, Connecticut, the signature read: "Hitchcock. Alford. & Co Hitchcocks-ville. Conn. Warranted." with the Ns in "Conn." usually, though not always, reversed.

There is disagreement as to whether Hitchcock made and signed any furniture in Unionville. Ethel Hall Bjerkoe claims to have seen chairs signed "Lambert Hitchcock Unionville Connecticut" but Kenney, the recognized authority, is doubtful, believing that furniture sold in Unionville originated in the Hitchcocks-ville factory; he does not cite any examples of a Unionville signature.

The ultimate source of Hitchcock's chair shapes were the designs for chairs contained in the pattern books of the English cabinetmaker, Thomas Sheraton, which were well known in America, especially the first, *The Cabinet-Maker and Upholsterer's Drawing Book*, published in 1797. Sheraton-influenced chairs were first advertised in America in 1797 and proved enormously popular with the finest cabinetmakers, among them Duncan Phyfe, Samuel McIntire, and John Townsend. But, because they called for precious, highly polished woods like mahogany, rosewood, and satinwood for inlays and gilding, bronze mountings, delicate carvings, and hand-painted decorations, they were very expensive. Hitchcock's mass-produced adaptations thus met a real demand, and it was not long before he was producing 15,000 chairs a year!

Contrary to general belief, not all Hitchcock's chairs were painted and stenciled: those advertised as "curled maple" were given a natural wood finish and at least one signed set of six has come to light. But the typical Hitchcock chair was lavishly decorated. First it was painted a solid color—black, ocher, dark green, or red. Sometimes it was grained to resemble the mahogany, rosewood, or walnut of more expensive furniture, an effect achieved by applying black paint over a red undercoat and then partially removing it with a streaking comb, sponge, or crumpled cloth. Afterward the chairs were striped and banded in yellow or gold; on a genuine Hitchcock piece the banding appears only on the fronts of the turnings—after all, no Yankee wastes good paint.

Doubtless what accounted for Hitch-

How to know the real Hitchcock

A typical example of a Hitchcock Chair (slat back, bolster top with turning on front legs)

☐ Usually signed with a stencil on the back of the chair seat or the back of the rocker top: **L. Hitchcock. Hitchcocks-ville. Conn. Warranted.** or **Hitchcock. Alford. & Co Hitchcocks-ville. Conn. Warranted.** Often, when chairs were rerushed, the side and back cover pieces were replaced, thus removing the portion with the signature.

Seats:
☐ Shapes are straight, rarely curved.
☐ May be caned, rushed, or planked.
☐ Rush seats are nearly always woven directly onto the kiln-dried, mortised-and-tenoned rails. However, some examples have been found in which the rush seats were woven separately and slipped into the seat frame. These, J.T. Kenney speculates, may have been woven by convicts at the Wethersfield Prison near Hartford. The prison had a chair-making shop which Hitchcock is known to have patronized.

Legs:
☐ Tapered front legs turned in the form of a tulip or 18 to 25 rings.
☐ Back posts usually bent, not sawed, and unturned.
☐ Striping and banding only on the fronts of the turnings, never all the way around.

Stenciling:
☐ On back slats; on crest rail and side-posts. (Only special order pieces were not stenciled).
☐ Fruit and flower motifs are most frequent. (A good discussion of Hitchcock stenciling can be found in Janet Waring's *Early American Stencils on Walls and Furniture*, Dover, 1968.) Designs are more stylized than naturalistic.
☐ Far more rare are simple geometric designs, sometimes found on plank-seated chairs.
☐ As many as five stencils were often used on a single chair.

Crest rail:
☐ Must be all in one piece; not in three parts glued together.

The crown-top Hitchcock rocker in the Boston style, left, is signed *Hitchcock. Alford. & Co Hitchcocks-ville. Conn. Warranted.* and was made between 1832 and 1843. Hitchcock's signature on rockers appears on the back of the top as shown in the example of the crown top below. These Boston-style rockers made by Hitchcock feature a heavy three piece planked seat and, often, this stencil design of basket of fruit and leaves, probably the most popular stencil decoration ever created by Hitchcock. Note the reversed *N*s in *Conn.* in the Hitchcock signature on the actual crown top and in the example at the bottom of the page. All, including the signed bolster-top, slat-back chair opposite, courtesy The Hitchcock Chair Company Collection.

L. HITCHCOCK. HITCHCOCKS-VILLE. CONN. WARRANTED.
HITCHCOCK. ALFORD. & Co HITCHCOCKS-VILLE. CONN.
WARRANTED.

Variations in form

Chairs having the characteristics outlined in the box "How to know the real Hitchcock" may be found in a variety of forms, since one of Hitchcock's innovations was the use of interchangeable parts. The most common variations of form are listed here, and some of Hitchcock's most notable interchangeable parts are illustrated.

Side chairs, the most common form, are found in the following variations: pillow-topped, bolster-topped, crown-topped, and roll-topped—all with rectangular slats that were easy to saw, bond, and stencil. Hitchcock also combined these tops with fancier back slats: button backs, turtle backs, eagle backs, and cornucopia backs.

Rocking chairs produced by Hitchcock usually were of the Boston or the Salem type. In some instances, bottoms were intentionally sawed off the legs of side chairs during production and rockers were attached. A few rocking benches were produced.

Armchairs were also made at the factory, usually with pillow tops, rush or cane seats and arms.

Other, rare Hitchcock furniture forms are bureaus, dressing tables, washstands, bedsteads, (advertised, but no documented examples known).

Chairs are again being made; those after 1950 have a registered ® with the signature.

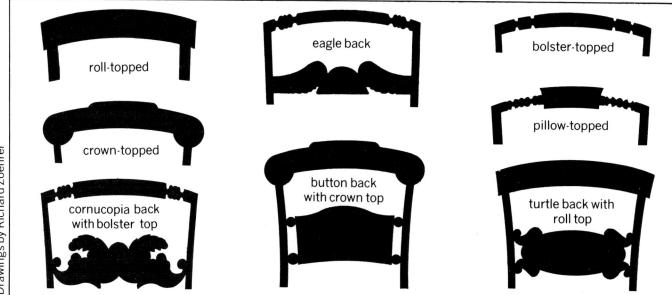

Drawings by Richard Zoehrer

roll-topped

crown-topped

cornucopia back with bolster top

eagle back

button back with crown top

bolster-topped

pillow-topped

turtle back with roll top

cock's immediate success was the lavish stenciled decorations on his chairs. Furniture stenciling, an English innovation, was first advertised in a New York newspaper in 1818, the very year Hitchcock started his business. It was quickly taken up by master craftsmen as an economical, easily executed, and attractive substitute for the painstaking carving or hand painting on more costly Sheraton chairs. Hitchcock's speedy adoption of stenciling when it was still very much of a novelty is yet another mark of his acumen. Typically, his stencils consist of stylized fruit or flowers in a basket or framed by leaves; a lyre motif is also frequent. The process, which could involve as many as five different stencils, consisted in rubbing multicolored bronze powders through

the stencil openings while the varnish on the chair was still tacky. Generally applied with a finger, these powders had burnished tones of gold or bronze, and a skilled operator, using repeats and overlays, could achieve complex tonal effects. (Unfortunately only a few signed their work.)

Inevitably, Hitchcock's success engendered considerable competition, especially among his neighbors. We have already mentioned William Moore, Jr., whose shop was already operating when Hitchcock started out in Fork-of-the-Rivers. Several chairs signed by Moore are known; since they omit the word "Hitchcocks-ville," Kenney assumes that they were made before Hitchcock's arrival, and certainly before the village changed its name. They

closely resemble Hitchcock's, and one is stenciled with an exact duplication of a signed Hitchcock design, raising the question of who copied whom. Close examination reveals that Moore's chairs were cruder than Hitchcock's; their legs are more widely splayed and the rush seats were woven separately, a practice Hitchcock seldom followed. Unquestionably Moore and Hitchcock were personal friends, for when the latter was threatened with bankruptcy in 1829 and was forced to put his factory under assignment, Moore was one of those who came to the rescue by lending money. Sadly, a year later Moore himself was forced into bankruptcy—and unlike Hitchcock, who managed to work his way out, he had to abandon his business in 1832 and died the next year.

Other Connecticut competitors, like Moore, used stencils which closely resembled Hitchcock's: Seymour Watrous of Hartford—who, however, may have been an old-fashioned cabinetmaker, working by hand; James L. Hull of Killingworth (now Clinton); T.N. Hodges of Hitchcocks-ville whose trade signature omitted the *s* and the hyphen in the town's name; and the Holmes & Roberts Company in nearby Colebrook. Holmes & Roberts may have supplied Hodges with chair parts, at least until 1839 when H&R was bought up by Hitchcock, Alford & Company.

Around 1845, when the Hitchcock-Alford partnership was dissolved, and Lambert moved to Unionville, Alford sold Holmes & Roberts to a group of its employees who continued to operate it as the Still River Manufacturing Company. They are believed to have produced some 300 chairs per week. Later, this firm metamorphosed into the Union Chair Company of Winsted, Connecticut and continued to manufacture furniture somewhat in the Hitchcock manner down to the 1870s.

There were more distant imitators as well. Allan Holcomb of New Lisbon, New York produced Hitchcock-type chairs, according to Robert Bishop, as did others in Rhode Island, Massachusetts, and as far west as Ohio.

Though the Hitchcock signature may be taken as a guarantee of a chair being a genuine product of the Hitchcock factory, many chairs and other furniture made there remained, for unknown reasons, unsigned. Thus the problem of identifying a genuine Hitchcock from the many contemporary imitations is a vexing one, as is clear from a visit to the charming Chair Museum in Riverton, which, with its varied display of Hitchcock and other furniture of the period, is a must for anyone interested in the subject.

Hitchcock's go-getting salesmanship accounted for both his success and for his eventual failure. As we have seen, even when he was only making chair parts, he was selling them not only locally but in the south. After his partnership with Alford freed him from the entire responsibility of running the factory, he traveled widely to capture other markets. In 1835 he visited Detroit, Chicago, Saint Louis, Cincinnati, Pittsburgh, and Philadelphia, and in 1841 he went to Baltimore and Washington. Incredibly, he also found time to serve two terms in the Connecticut legislature.

It was one thing to sell his furniture, but it was quite another to be paid for it. Because he sold on credit, he was continually short of ready cash. This was why, in 1829, he had to put the factory and other assets under assignment. Happily, he was able to work his way out and his partnership with Alford doubtless helped him financially. But he was not content to sit back and enjoy his prosperity. Instead, he went right on expanding, opening a retail store in Hitchcocks-ville and, in 1834, the New Chair Store in Hartford.

Two years later, Hitchcock, Alford & Company bought the sawmill which had been cutting Hitchcock's lumber since 1818, and in 1839, as already noted, they took over the Holmes and Roberts Chair Company.

By 1841, Lambert Hitchcock was once more in financial hot water: the Hitchcock-Alford partnership was dissolved and replaced by a new firm, The Hitchcock Company, in which Lambert held only a one-third interest, the other two thirds belonging to Alford and to Josiah H. Sage of Sandisfield, Massachusetts (whose house, incidentally, contains some of the best-preserved wall stenciling in New England).

Though this new infusion of capital put the business on a sounder footing, the transport difficulties that had plagued Hitchcock from the beginning showed no sign of improvement, and Hitchcock decided he must move his factory elsewhere. In 1844 he bought land in Unionville, a few miles from Hartford, and built a new factory there. The move turned out to be a terrible mistake. Though railroads were then beginning to spread all over New England, Hitchcock put his faith in the future of water transport; recalling how the Erie Canal had opened up the whole former Northwest Territory to trade with the East Coast, he was convinced that the New Farmington Canal, on whose banks his new factory stood, would do the same for western Connecticut. But in 1847, work on the Farmington Canal (which was supposed to go from New Haven to Northampton, Massachusetts) was halted. Gradually it silted up and Hitchcock was left literally high and dry.

Even worse, the New York, New Haven & Hartford Railroad bypassed Unionville for Plainville, which, though only eight miles distant, was difficult for heavily loaded wagons to reach. His brother-in-law Arba Alford helped him out with a loan and continued to supply him with furniture made in Hitchcocks-ville, but sales must have been few. Apparently little or no furniture was made in the new Unionville factory, and the end of his life found Hitchcock trying to eke out a living by using his turning machines to make spools for Connecticut's new silk industry.

Hitchcock died in 1852, insolvent. After an active, creative career spanning 34 years, his assets came to $12,420.54, his liabilities to $13,758.02. It was a sad, not to say ignominious end. Yet Hitchcock must have experienced many satisfactions. He saw his dream—to bring beautiful, well-made furniture within the reach of nearly everyone—come true. He saw his name bestowed, if only temporarily, on the village he chose to work in, and, more importantly, he saw the name become a generic term for the chairs he designed and made. Those who bought his chairs treasured them, preserved them, and often had their portraits—by Erastus Salisbury Field, Noah North, Sheldon Peck, Ammi Phillips and others—painted in them. Unfortunately no portrait of Lambert Hitchcock himself appears to have survived. But in the afterlife reserved for honest, hardworking craftsmen, he must reflect with pleasure on how his work has endured, still popular more than a century after his death, in the painstaking reincarnations manufactured by John Kenney and sold at the old brick factory, which still stands in Riverton. ■

Rococo Revival: John Henry Belter

German-born craftsman John Henry Belter's name became the generic designation for all Rococo Revival furniture of the mid-19th century.

BY ED POLK DOUGLAS

In his 1850 book, *The Architecture of Country Houses*, tastemaker Andrew Jackson Downing observed: "Modern French furniture . . . stands much higher in general estimation in this country than any other. Its union of lightness, elegance, and grace renders it especially the favorite of the ladies . . . [The style is] characterized by greater delicacy of foliate ornamentation, and greater intricacy of detail." In Downing's time, this style was whimsically called "antique French," "modern French," "Louis XIV," "Louis XV," or "florid Italian." Today it is known as ro-

coco revival. In 19th century America, its foremost maker and exponent was the German *emigré* cabinetmaker John Henry Belter, who lived from 1804 to 1863.

Origins of the rococo revival style

Like most 19th-century furniture revival styles, rococo revival originated in Europe. It began in England in the 1820s and flourished during the 1830s at the court of Louis Philippe of France. By the late 1840s its popularity was worldwide. With its profusion of "ruffles and flourishes," rococo revival was an obvious reaction to the comparative simplicity of the preceding regency and restoration periods. It drew upon the baroque and rococo elements of 18th-century design during the reigns of Louis XIV and Louis XV: the

Rococo revival furniture had become a feature of American parlors by
the mid-1850s. John Henry Belter, a master cabinetmaker in the style,
produced a large number of pieces during his relatively short career.
The rosewood *meridienne* above, 1850-1860, is attributed to Belter and
is 42″ long. One of a pair, it is a rare, highly sought after furniture form.
Both courtesy Joan Bogart, Rockville Center, New York.

curving silhouette, cabriole leg with scroll foot, balanced—but frequently asymmetrical—S and C scrolls, and naturalistic carving of fruit, flowers, and foliage. In the 19th century, to suit a different artistic milieu, these forms were refashioned with different proportions and materials, using methods that reflected the new interest in uphol-

stery and in greater comfort.

Sociologically, the rococo revival style expressed the self-conscious desires of a nouveau riche middle class and a shaky aristocracy for the legitimacy and grandeur of the *ancien régime*. At its most elaborate, the style was one of glittering opulence and unabashed delight in decoration. On a simpler plane, it was comfortably appropriate to middle-class sensibility, prosperity, and taste.

The style comes to America

The revived rococo style was perfect for mid-19th century America, bursting with confidence and just coming into its own as a world power. From the townhouses of Boston's Beacon Hill, to Mississippi River mansions, to the miners' shanties of Sacramento, rococo revival was definitely fashionable in 1850. Once again, Paris set the pace for the rest of the world.

The fashion traveled in several ways. European-trained cabinetmakers emigrated to America, bringing copybooks and actual pieces of furniture. Native-

born cabinetmakers found inspiration in the increasingly available European design books and periodicals. The great international fairs of the 1850s and 1860s provided other trans-Atlantic links in the diffusion of taste. Though the rococo-revival style had figured prominently in the national fairs held in England and France in the 1840s, its influence was paramount at the international expositions held in London in 1851, New York in 1853, and Paris in 1855.

At New York's Crystal Palace Exhibition of 1853, American taste presumably was elevated by exposure to quality objects from foreign countries. The display of carefully chosen American goods was calculated to show the world that the United States had come of age. Both foreign and domestic critics were amazed at the American-made furniture exhibited. Their favorable comments were well publicized. For example, in *The World of Science, Art, and Industry Illustrated from Examples in the New-York Exhibition, 1853–54* (G.P. Putnam & Co., 1854) Prof. Benjamin Silliman wrote that in the rococo revival, "we have a furniture style of our own, which, though not original, bears yet the marks of our utilitarian age." The graceful attributes of the style's 18th-century models were reduced "to greater simplicity," he explained, and molded into "forms more consistent with comfort and constructive truth."

Furniture manufacture in America

By mid-19th century, the American furniture industry was at a crossroads. Many small cabinetmaking shops using 18th-century methods were forced out of business by larger establishments that employed more men and used steam-powered woodworking devices —specialized planing and grooving machines, lathes, jig saws, and veneer cutters—to turn out great volumes of furniture with little skill required. Furniture warerooms, comparable to today's retail stores, were run by middlemen who bought from a number of cabinetmakers, resold under their own label, and understood little of the manu-

facturing process. Competition for customers led to energetic merchandising of mass-produced furniture.

For those with taste and means, however, custom-ordered handmade furniture was still available. A Philadelphia furniture maker, George J. Henkels, wrote in *Household Economy* (1867) that: "Hand-made work is much better than machine-work, and all cabinetmakers of reputation have their own designs, so as to have a pattern exclusively to themselves. The machine-work is sold mostly by those who have no factory, but merely keep the furniture stores. Persons who understand this prefer to pay the price for good hand-made work." Many such "cabi-

The rosewood "slipper chair" at left, 44″ high, was made between 1850 and 1860 and is attributed to Belter. It is among the more ornate of his forms. Above: Rosewood and ash armchair in a variation of the so-called "Rosalie" pattern. Attributed to Belter, ca 1855. It is restrained in its decoration, with a close-carved seat frame. The Western Reserve Historical Society, Cleveland, Ohio.

net-makers of reputation" and their skilled employees were foreign-born—German or French. Of the 193 cabinetmakers and furniture dealers listed in *Trow's New York City Directory* of 1854–55, 131 have German surnames. Though outnumbered by the Germans, the French owned the best-known shops. Similar demographics existed in other cities having a developed furniture industry.

Most of these cabinetmakers retained some Old World ties in matters of design inspiration and in the importation of foreign goods, materials, and workmen. A real or imaginary "French connection" was thought to be a major selling point in advertisements of the period. Many such foreign-born cabinetmakers became prominent, successful members of their local communities.

John Henry Belter

Among these "citizens by adoption" was John Henry Belter. Today, as in his own time, his name is synonymous with certain furniture forms employing carved, pierced, and laminated woods. Beginning in the mid-19th century, the name *Belter*, like *Chippendale*, was used generically to describe anything resembling his distinctive furniture. Today we've learned that other cabinetmakers used similar methods, and the term *Belter-type* is now used to more accurately describe such furniture.

Johann Heinrich Belter was born in southern Germany, possibly Ulm, in 1804. He spent part of his youth at Stuttgart in the province of Württemberg, apprenticed to woodworkers and cabinetmakers there. Seeking opportunity, he arrived in New York City in the late 1830s or early 1840s. Only a few facts are known about his life in the United States. He is first listed as John Henry Belter, cabinetmaker, at 40½ Chatham Street in *Doggett's New York City Directory*—which also lists his address at 372 Broadway from 1846 until 1852.

Trow's New York City Directory of 1853 cites Belter at 547 Broadway. In 1854 the address is unchanged, but Belter's shop has evidently grown, for it

appears as "J. H. Belter and Company." The opening of a factory at Third Avenue near East 76th Street is also mentioned. A new address for the warerooms, 522 Broadway, is listed in the 1856 directory, and the association of a J. H. Springmeyer, a brother of Belter's wife, Louisa, is noted. Two more Springmeyers, William and Frederick, were a part of the business by 1861, when the firm moved to 722 Broadway. A majority of its employees were German.

Belter died in 1863, supposedly of influenza. According to an apocryphal story, he destroyed all his patterns and designs just before his death. The Springmeyers continued the business under the old name until 1865, when it became Springmeyer Brothers. They went bankrupt two years later, possibly because of the uncertain economic conditions of the post–Civil War years, lack of business acumen, or the inability to adapt Belter's characteristic forms to changing tastes.

Dating and chronology of Belter furniture

Apart from showing Manhattan's relentless growth "uptown," the city directories' description of Belter's various business locations is rather dry. However, these facts have helped furniture historians assign an approximate date of manufacture to a given piece of furniture based on the address shown on its label—when there is one. This dating method is not foolproof. You must ask: Is the directory listing accurate? Did a furniture maker label an object when it was made or when it was

The laminated rosewood armchair and settee here and opposite are part of a suite of furniture made in New York ca 1850-1860. These pieces are attributed to the firm of J. and J.W. Meeks because of their close similarity to documented pieces. While related to Belter-attributed work, the specific details of the forms are quite different. The Metropolitan Museum of Art, gift of Mr. and Mrs. Lowell Ross Burch and Miss Jean McLean Morron, 1951.

sold? If the latter, does the piece of furniture typify the most recent production, or was it held in stock for years before being sold?

Stylistic chronology is also important. Though 20th-century scholars do not accept the previously popular theory of "growth, maturity, and decline" in the arts, they remain interested in design development. In the forms attributed to Belter, there is a great deal of variety in design. Belter's work differs considerably from that of his counterparts in Europe and America, so there is speculation about his sources. Are his ideas unique? Did he move from an awkward, earlier period to one of complete sophistication? Do light, delicate forms precede those of baroque robustness, or is it the other way around? Which of his works are "most typical" or "most original"?

Belter research is in its youth and often presents special problems, for Belter did not label many pieces in a permanent manner. The variety of designs attributed to Belter indicates that during his relatively short 20-year career in America, he frequently introduced new forms while continuing to manufacture old ones. Though stylistic chronologies of American furniture are often assisted by patent dates, in Belter's case several patented innovations were used for years before he registered them.

When present, however, labels can be very revealing. One laminated rosewood table is labeled

J. H. BELTER & CO.

FACTORY WAREHOUSE

3rd Avenue   76th St.   522 Broadway

MANUFACTURERS OF

ALL KINDS OF FINE FURNITURE

NEW YORK

From information in City Directories, this seems to be Belter's label between 1856 and 1861. Several interesting things may be inferred from the wording. As this label implies, and as Claire Vincent points out in her essay in *Technological Innovation and the Decorative Arts* (Winterthur, 1974), "Belter is an example of a genuinely creative cabinetmaker content to be known to his patrons and to posterity as a manufacturer." Belter's obvious pride in his technologically advanced factory, however, is belied by the hand-carved ornamentation that imparts the individual stamp of the designer and craftsman to many of his pieces.

The Belter label of 1856 also suggests that this factory produced a variety of furniture types. While seat furniture is most commonly seen today, other identified Belter forms include tables, *étagères*, cabinets, beds, bureaus, and firescreens. One may also assume that he produced sideboards, desks, secretary-bookcases, mirrors, commodes, wardrobes, and other furniture forms common to 19th-century life.

Belter's four patents

There are four Belter patents of importance. The first, dated July 31, 1847, is for "Machinery for Sawing Arabesque Chairs"—a jig saw and clamp to hold a laminated wood chair back in place while a pierced design was cut into it. In a succeeding process, carved decoration could be added for a more plastic effect.

Belter's second patent, for a "Bedstead," is dated August 19, 1856. It registers a flowing form constructed with two pieces of laminated wood, held together by a notched internal frame that could be disassembled easily in case of fire. Such a bed had no "intricate recesses about the joints and fastenings," which were "difficult of access and no-

torious as hiding places for bugs." In an era when fastidious personal hygiene was neither possible nor expected, this point was well taken.

In this patent application, Belter carefully stated that he was not attempting to register the centuries-old process of lamination, only this specific application of it. Fortunately for later scholars, he described the process in detail.

After several unsuccessful attempts the previous year, on February 23, 1858, Belter registered a third patent, probably his most important, for "Improvement in the Method of Manufacturing Furniture." Thin layers of various woods—oak, ash, walnut, and rosewood—were glued together, then bent under steam pressure in specially designed molds or cauls. These thin, curved surfaces were incredibly strong and could be carved, perforated, or decorated with applied ornament. While the patent was meant for seat furniture, the application notes that by changing the forms of the clamps and cauls used to build the laminated

frames, the same process could be employed for any furniture form. Belter did use laminated sections on objects other than chairs. It is also evident that he was using this process of construction some years before he was granted the patent. Perhaps the patent was an attempt to thwart competition from other manufacturers.

Types of Belter furniture

Seat furniture attributable to Belter's shop is the type most commonly seen today and exhibits the greatest variety of forms. Two categories may be arbitrarily assigned, based on the design of the seat backs. "Pierced-carved" chairs and sofas have curved, laminated backs that are perforated and carved or have applied carving; in "closed-carved" pieces, the decorative carving is similarly placed—or entirely absent—but there is no openwork. A logical supposition is that the closed-carved forms were developed first. Surviving documentation indicates both types were available from the mid-1850s.

Belter continued the 18th-century custom of offering pieces *en suite* as well as individually. His parlor suites were especially popular. A typical grouping is described in a Belter invoice of September 1855:

2 Arabasket Rosewood Sofas			175	$350.00
2	"	"	Arm Chair	80	160.00
4	"	"	Parlour Chair	45	180.00
1	"	"	Centre table		175.00
1 Fine	"		Etagère		300.00

Along with some of the objects it lists, this invoice is in the collection of the governor's mansion, Austin, Texas.

Larger "double parlor suites" were also available to furnish the connecting drawing rooms found in many 19th-century homes. Rosalie, a house museum in Natchez, Mississippi, owned by the Daughters of the American Revolution, still has its original 21-piece Belter double parlor suite purchased in New York about 1857.

Belter employed an almost unbelievable variety of designs in his seat furniture. Fifteen patterns have been identified in the closed-carved class, while there are around 20 pierced-carved patterns. Others will surely emerge as Belter research continues. In several

A label used by Belter between 1856 and 1861 is affixed to the underside of this rosewood center table. The curving legs exhibit expertly-carved floral brackets, and the laminated, pierced apron is decorated with flowers, fruit, and vegetation. The oval top is of marble. Museum of the City of New York, gift of Mr. and Mrs. Ernest Gunther Vietor.

cases, Belter's own name for a pattern can be identified with specific examples, such as the "Arabasket" suite. Recent scholars have named some patterns after the collections in which they are housed, as in the case of "Rosalie."

Belter made many variations of the "slipper chair": a high-backed seat used in the parlor, boudoir, or bedroom as an accent piece displaying virtuosity of design, decorative carving, or unusual upholstery—like needlework. Each slipper chair is a tour de force of carved openwork, often unique. The slipper-chair patterns are in addition to those of the pierced-carved variety.

For other furniture forms, Belter employed the same processes, materials, and details but used fewer patterns. Tables were available in many specific patterns, such as the "Arabasket Rosewood Centre table," but an *étagère* might be designed to complement several patterns. Labeled Belter bedsteads vary from the simple to the elaborate, with the price set accordingly. Rosewood and rosewood veneers were the favored materials, but he also used oak and walnut; secondary woods such as oak and ash gave strength to the lamination process.

Belter's competitors: Meeks and Henkels

During the 1850s, when rococo revival was at its height, Belter was one of several furniture makers using laminated woods with decorative carving. Among his competitors were J. and J. W. Meeks of New York City, working from 1836 to 1868; and the Philadelphia firm of George J. Henkels, operating from 1843 to 1877. Meeks was a family establishment, founded in the late 18th century by Joseph Meeks, that made quality furniture in the various revival styles popular until 1850. Meeks's technical expertise was equal to Belter's, although the firms employed different vocabularies of form and detail. Because Belter's name was remembered—and the Meekses' overlooked—in the intervening years, much Meeks furniture has been attributed to Belter. Today's scholars are correcting the confusion by publishing documented work by both firms.

The identified work of George Henkels differs substantially from both Belter's and Meeks's; although tame in comparison, it is not without merit. Other names—Badouine and Klein of New York and Lutz of Philadelphia—also have been mentioned in the context of laminated furniture, but they have yet to be associated with specific characteristics. Furthermore, a large group of odd patterns of varying quality are known which have no maker's attribution.

How to identify a Belter piece

What are the characteristics of Belter's work? How is a Belter-made chair distinguished from one by another manufacturer? Are there guidelines for identifying his other furniture forms? Which pieces might be labeled?

In many cases, identifying Belter's work is an intuitive process, the fruit of observation and study of documented works. There are as yet no concrete "rules"; no Belter pattern book or catalogue has been discovered. Even the self-styled Belter experts sometimes disagree on attribution.

In general, Belter's work has a bold, robust quality tempered by an excellent sense of proportion and a sophisticated use of decorative ornament. Seat furniture frequently displays fluid tendril or sausagelike scrolls that form the silhouette of the chair back and encircle pierced-work ornament. Seats usually have serpentine fronts, carved seat rails, and cabriole front legs with French or scroll feet, sometimes decorated with a carved leaf. Back legs are plain and usually rectangular in section. (Rear legs on Meeks-attributed furniture are usually circular in section.) Belter's rich vocabulary of carved fruit, flowers, and foliage, seen in many variations throughout his work, has a vigorous naturalism coupled with the pleasant irregularities of hand carving.

In the past it was thought that Belter's work could be positively identified by the number of laminations used on a chair back and by the absence of a seam in the middle of the back. We know now that Belter used from four to 16 layers of laminate, with eight being an average. Depending on the size of a

chair back and the available curved wood from the caul or mold, Belter-made chairs often have seams on the outer layer of wood.

Because characteristics of Belter's furniture other than chairs are difficult to pinpoint, intuition gained from careful study is important. Such pieces have the same bold fluidity as his seat furniture, modified accordingly. Laminated wood, plain or pierced, is used for table aprons, shelf brackets, cartouche cresting, or decorative edging. Marble or wooden tabletops project over their supporting frames. Stretchers between the legs usually are composed of vigorous scrolls. Dressers or worktables often have compartmentalized interiors of laminated wood. Belter's bed form is so distinctive that his workmanship is

This rosewood armchair, probably made in the 1850s, is attributed to Belter. The laminated back has seven layers, bent in a caul and carved in an elaborate pierced design. Surviving sofas in a related pattern with a gilt finish were probably among the most expensive Belter products. The Metropolitan Museum of Art, gift of Mrs. Charles Reginald Leonard.

obvious, although there have been crude copies.

Like many of this contemporaries, Belter rarely labeled his work in a permanent way. No piece of seating furniture attributed to Belter has a surviving label. There are a few tables with paper labels and some objects with painted inscriptions. Besteads are usually stamped with the patent date. Several invoices can be linked with specific objects. In other cases, facts of provenance fill in gaps that visual observation might not.

What were Belter's sources?

Belter's design sources can only be guessed, for little is known of his early training or of the specific influences to which he was subject during his career. His furniture forms are generally variations of French rococo revival, no doubt transmitted through pattern books, periodicals, and the observation of foreign-made furniture. The bold naturalism of his ornament has an 18th-century precedent, but it is more characteristic of English and German mid-19th-century design. Similarly decorated objects are extensively illustrated in the catalogue of London's 1851 Crystal Palace Exhibition. Certainly the predominantly European-born craftsmen in Belter's factory kept these transatlantic links strong.

Belter's experimentation and his use of laminated woods is not unique, but his stylistic development seems to be. Although scholars see a possible connection between Belter and his fellow German Michael Thonet, who was working at the same time on his Bentwood process, the American production of Belter and his competitors has no real foreign analogy.

A possible influence on Belter, never properly investigated, is that of papier-mâché furniture, widely exported from Britain after 1830. Papier-mâché furniture in the rococo-revival style has a combination of strength and lightness that is structurally and visually similar to Belter's work. Its painted decoration might be seen as a two-dimensional counterpart to Belter's relief carving.

Other interesting contemporary furniture types which, seen in retrospect,

Two mid-1850s rosewood sofas. Belter's Arabasket pattern, below. Museum of Fine Arts, Houston; Bayou Bend Collection. Sofa above is attributed. Metropolitan Museum of Art, gift of Mrs. Charles Reginald Leonard.

are similar to Belter's work are objects of cast iron—particularly those using naturalistic motifs—and elaborately pierced Oriental teak, ebony, and rosewood furniture made for export.

Appreciating Belter

Unlike much American furniture of the middle and late 19th century, Belter-type rococo-revival furniture was not strictly mass-produced and has always been recognized for its special qualities. But after 1870 it grew unfashionable and was moved from drawing room to attic. Bulkier pieces such as beds and cabinets were often discarded altogether. But Belter's reputation as "New York's most fashionable cabinetmaker after Duncan Phyfe" endured through this decline, assuring survival of representative examples of his work.

In the early 20th century, a few far-sighted museums and individuals, willing to reject the dictum that anything made after 1830 was significant solely for *lack* of taste and craftsmanship, fostered a new interest in Belter. The 1930s witnessed a more popular revival of things Victorian, culminating in such extravaganzas as the motion picture *Gone With the Wind.* Belter-type furniture was carried along on this wave of antebellum enthusiasm, and many early Southern homes newly opened to public "pilgrimage" tours were furnished in the rococo-revival style. Nevertheless, Belter's work was still viewed as "the best of a terrible period," hardly comparable to the work of 18th-century American cabinetmakers.

Today, more than a century after the rococo-revival style came to America, the work of Belter and his contemporaries is experiencing a boom that shows no sign of abating. The early-20th-century "Victorian lovers" have been vindicated, for Belter-type furniture has increased many times in value, particularly in the late 1970s. Collectors, dealers, and museums are avidly vying for quality examples, and "Belter-mania" is a recognized affliction throughout the United States. A varied selection of Belter furniture may be found on today's market, but those who aspire to own it must have well-filled purses. ■

Daniel Pabst

Working in the Renaissance Revival and modern Gothic styles, German-born Pabst created fashionable furniture for an elite Philadelphia clientele.

BY DAVID HANKS

Fiske Kimball, director of the Philadelphia Museum of Art, challenged the museum's decorative arts curator, Calvin S. Hathaway. "Find us a cabinetmaker in 19th-century Philadelphia comparable to those master Philadelphia cabinetmakers of the 18th century," he is said to have asked Hathaway. Hathaway's discovery was Daniel Pabst.

Much that is known about Pabst comes from the cabinetmaker's granddaughter, Edna Reisser Shenkle, whose recollections were recorded by Calvin Hathaway in 1969. The most important document in the study is a list of customers that the cabinetmaker recounted from memory at the request of his daughter, Emma Pabst Reisser, Edna's mother. The list is hardly complete. Pabst omitted a number of prominent clients for whom he is known to have worked, such as the Henry Charles Leas and Edward Ingersolls. Nevertheless, by tracking the names of customers who appeared on the list, Hathaway discovered some furniture once owned by Pabst's clients.

Born in Langenstein, Hesse-Darmstadt, Germany, on June 11, 1826, Pabst was educated in a technical (trade) high school. The curriculum included freehand and mechanical drawing and modeling in addition to standard courses in arithmetic, German, English, and geography.

Although Pabst learned the cabinetmaking trade in school, he probably also served an apprenticeship. Upon graduation he planned to practice his art in Langenstein, but he soon learned that he would have to remain in that small town for the rest of his career because "the laws compelled a man who had a trade to practice forever in his own village," and, said Pabst, "what place was there for me in that little town?" Therefore, despite his love of all German things, after five years of travel in his native country he emigrated to America, settling in Philadelphia in 1849. Until he was able to go into business for himself, Pabst worked as a journeyman-furniture maker. On July 4, 1854 he opened his own shop at 222 South Fourth Street and moved to 269 South Fifth Street 16 years later. There he remained until retirement in 1896.

In Philadelphia, Pabst joined a community of German furniture craftsmen numbering about 725 in 1850. The majority of German-born furniture makers in the city were, like Pabst, from the same general area in southern Germany—Hesse, Bavaria, and Württemberg. In addition to these craftsmen, another 1,545 furniture makers worked in Philadelphia in 1850; by 1880 the total number of cabinetmakers was 3,698.

Throughout his life, Pabst felt a strong attachment to Germany and was dedicated to helping other German émigrés establish themselves in Philadelphia, "taking them into his household while they were studying and learning their way in the new country." In 1877 he joined the German Society of Philadelphia. Pabst wrote and published poetry in German about his native village, and clung to the artistic traditions that were a part of his heritage. "I brought all of Germany here with me, in my inward eye," he reminisced. "The tall towers of Cologne, the wonders of Frankfurt-on-Main, the old grey castles perched in mid-air along the Rhine—they all were part of my work."

Pabst's wife, Helena Gross, was also German-born. Of the seven children born to the Pabsts, only three—Emma, Laura, and William—survived to adult-

hood. Most of Pabst's married life was spent in a typical Philadelphia row house at 264 South Fifth Street, a few doors from his shop.

When Pabst first arrived in Philadelphia, however, he was merely one more foreign-born worker with few connections in the city and little potential for success. Yet out of these insignificant beginnings, he became "one of the leading and most successful designers and manufacturers of artistic furniture in Philadelphia," according to a 19th-century newspaper account. Although the precise reasons for Pabst's success are unknown, the quality of his furniture and nature of his clientele are probably high among them. Pabst made only the finest furniture "that does not come out for the glue like your poor modern machine stuff." Such objects were necessarily expensive because they required skilled workmanship and a great deal of time. As Pabst later admitted, "If I tried to earn my living that way today I would starve. There would be no great ladies with carriages as they used to arrive before my factory at 5th and Spruce Streets." These "great ladies" included, among others, Mrs. Henry Disston, Mrs. Thomas McKean, and Mrs. John C. Bullitt—all wealthy members of Philadelphia society. Other names on Pabst's list of customers included Furness, Parry, Wyeth, Newbold, Wistar, Harrison, Welsh, Preston, Doyle, and Roosevelt. Another customer was the Pennsylvania Railroad. How Pabst attracted the interest of such customers is not known, but according to *Illustrated Philadelphia: Its Wealth and Industries* (1889), "the palpable merit of his productions soon [attracted] the attention of the public, until now he receives customers from all parts of the United States."

Top left: Black walnut extension dining table, ca 1868. Pabst combined incised and relief carving on this piece made for historian Henry Charles Lea. Left: This symmetrical, restrained walnut sideboard, ca 1868, was also made for Lea. Both Philadelphia Museum of Art, bequest of Arthur H. Lea. Opposite: Dining room of Theodore Roosevelt's house at 6 W. 57 St., New York City. Attributed to Daniel Pabst and Frank Furness, after 1876. Photo courtesy Sagamore Hill National Historic Site, Oyster Bay, New York.

Pabst's active career can be divided into two parts. Six years after opening his shop he entered into a ten-year partnership with Francis Krauss, probably another German émigré, about whom little is known. In 1871 a Francis Krauss was listed in Gopsill's city directory as a confectioner, which leads to the speculation that Krauss may have been Pabst's financial partner rather than a furniture maker. During the second half of his career, Pabst was in business for himself at 269 South Fifth Street.

Because specific documentation is missing, we attribute the body of works associated with Pabst to his workshop, rather than to him specifically. During the course of his career the shop employed up to 50 men. Both provenance and the list of customers mentioned previously are strong evidence for establishing Pabst as sole designer of the identified pieces. Furniture which is ascribed to Pabst shows a coherent style

with recognizable techniques of craftsmanship and use of ornament.

One of the earliest objects Pabst signed is a small sewing box with fitted compartments and a mirrored lid. He made it for his wife, whom he affectionately called Salina. Glued to the inside are two small sheets of paper decorated with watercolor floral designs, bearing the following inscription in flowing script: "Daniel Pabst gbr(born) Im 11 June 1826. Philadelphia 11th of June 1850. Remember me Salina Gross 1850."

Probably the earliest group of furniture which can be attributed to Pabst's shop was made for the noted historian Henry Charles Lea (1825–1909). Made about 1868, the year the Lea house at 2000 Walnut Street was built, the furniture is attributed to Pabst on the basis of family tradition. The group consists of a walnut cabinet from the Leas' northwest parlor and a walnut dining-

room suite containing a pedestal dining table, sideboard, ten side chairs, and two armchairs. There is no reason to question the use of Pabst's name in connection with this furniture since at the time it was so identified, little attention has been focused on 19th-century furniture. Pabst's name was not well known among antiquarians, so little if any monetary value was associated with his name.

The Lea sideboard is based on earlier prototypes such as those by 19th-century designers Rochefort and Skaaren and cabinetmaker Alexander Roux of New York that were exhibited at the New York Crystal Palace Exhibition of 1853. In general they reflect the style then fashionable on the Continent and featured in European design books. Pabst was undoubtedly familiar with them. But the Pabst sideboard is a much-simplified version. He replaced rococo tendency toward hyperbole and

Cabinet, ca 1868. Black walnut and poplar with bird's-eye maple.
Carving on this cabinet made for the Leas has decorative motifs similar to those on the sideboard shown previously, but is finer and more
elaborate. Philadelphia Museum of Art, bequest of Arthur H. Lea.

use of extravagant floral festoons popular from 1850 to 1860 with the then new preference for linear and geometric ornamentation and increased symmetry and restraint typical of the Renaissance revival style.

The walnut cabinet made for the Leas' northwest parlor has contrasting burled walnut panels, Renaissance pilasters, incised ornament, and a vine-wreathed carved head in the center of the door. The richly varied ornamental details used in the two pieces intended for the same house show Pabst's imagination and creativity. For example, the classically inspired carved head on the cabinet refers to the object's function: storing the literature of Greece and Rome.

Also among the Lea furniture attributed to Pabst is an extension dining table with "massive Baroque scrolls decorated with 16th-century motifs like the boxes and pyramids and the garlands." Accompanying dining chairs, including ten side chairs and two armchairs, also combine characteristic Pabst elements—carving, from incised to relief, and a variety of surface treatments. The chairs have incised lines accented with an infilling of gold paint.

Pabst made two matching cabinets for the Ingersoll family. Like the Lea sideboard, the Ingersoll cabinets were monogrammed in the cartouche, in this instance with the initials EI for Edward Ingersoll. Epicurean subjects were commonly employed on dining-room furniture of the period. A pair of cabinets, made about 1865–1870, was intended for the Ingersoll dining room. Roundels on the base of the cabinets depict fish in one and birds in the other. A contemporary photograph shows one of the cabinets in the dining room of Fernhill, the Ingersoll house in Germantown.

Pabst's reputation as a fine cabinetmaker even gained the attention of the White House. According to Pabst's grandson, S. William Reisser, Pabst "made mantels for the White House and furniture for three Presidents."

Another group of furniture which can be attributed to Pabst with certainty—a three-piece bedroom suite made about 1875—marks a change in his style from Renaissance revival to "modern Gothic." The latter style is characterized by overall patterns of conventionalized floral motifs and adaptations of medieval or Gothic ornament. Architectonic Renaissance revival forms such as plinths, pediments, and cornices are retained in these pieces. According to Pabst family history, this bedroom suite was part of a set Pabst made for his daughter Emma in 1878, when she was 18.

Pabst achieved ornamental details of stylized floral designs with a cameo technique. He cut through bird's-eye maple veneer to the walnut underneath. The result is a striking design of contrasting light and dark woods, seen in Federal furniture and characteristic of Philadelphia cabinetwork throughout the century. Careful attention to detail, such as the cut veneer which outlines the chamfered edges of the night table, reflects Pabst's high standards of workmanship. The overall effect of the suite is powerfully architectonic. He achieved this feeling through the bureau and bed's scale and through use of architectural details—engaged columns with fanciful capitals and a steeply angled pediment. The pediment has a keystone in the form of a conventionalized floral design.

Whereas the prevailing style in America in the 1870s was Renaissance revival, Pabst favored the modern Gothic style of the English reformers such as Bruce Talbert. This preference identifies Pabst as innovative and progressive. Talbert's *Gothic Forms Applied to Furniture, Metalwork, and Decoration for Domestic Purposes* (London, 1867) was published in Boston in 1873. In all likelihood Pabst knew about it. He also would have become familiar with the new style through periodicals such as *The Workshop*, published in New York, and from furniture of foreign manufacture displayed at Philadelphia's 1876 Centennial Exhibition.

Perhaps the most important design source for Pabst was Christopher Dresser's work. Dresser was one of the most original and influential English designers of the late 19th century. Pabst undoubtedly knew of Dresser through his books, published in London and available in Philadelphia. Dresser also visited Philadelphia on the occasion of the 1876 Centennial Exhibition and was invited to lecture at the newly formed Pennsylvania Museum and School of Industrial Art. In his first lecture, Dresser reiterated his esthetic theory, which reflected typically Victorian moral overtones: ornament must go beyond external beauty and "may express the knowledge and refinement of its producer, or his coarseness, ignorance and vulgarity." Dresser called for a national style of ornament which would compare to that of great past civilizations. For example, the Egyptians developed ornamental forms "expressive of national peculiarities of character, of religious faith, of wants and of feelings as well as of individual idiosyncrasies." Dresser's own ornamental style, based on the work of Owen Jones and other English reform designers of the 1850s, refers to past styles—Egyptian or Greek. It was fundamentally based on a conventionalized interpretation of nature in which natural floral and plant motifs were reduced to basic geometric patterns. Pabst follows these same principles in his ornamentation.

In his book *Principles of Decorative Design*, Dresser also set forth rules for constructing furniture which Pabst applied to the pieces he designed in the modern Gothic style. Wood was to be used in a natural manner—that is, worked with the grain to achieve the greatest strength with the least expenditure of material. Furniture was to have "simplicity of structure and truthfulness of construction." The easiest mode of constructing should be used, and the creator should "think first of what is wanted, then of the material at command."

The same principles of simplicity and truthfulness of construction were advocated by Charles Locke Eastlake, whose *Hints on Household Taste* was published in London in 1868 and made its first appearance in America in 1872. So successful was Eastlake's book (reprinted numerous times in England and America) that his own name was often given to the style, although Eastlake himself protested this practice. His book was intended as a guide for popular taste rather than for cabinetmakers, and its influence was primarily in shaping the taste of the client for a new style of furniture.

In comparison with Pabst's Renaissance-revival furniture made for the Lea and Ingersoll families, the bedroom suite for his daughter represents a new manner of design. The ornament on the Pabst-Lea cabinet emphasized ornate carving and has an "applied" quality. By contrast, on the bedroom suite, the strong, incised linear patterns show more integration to the overall form. The effect is of greater unity.

The new ideas propounded by the English reform designers and popularized by Eastlake found their most vivid expression in furniture designed

niture and interior woodwork following Furness's designs is surmised because Theodore Roosevelt, Sr., was also listed as a Pabst customer.

The form and proportion of the Furness-designed dining room chair executed by Pabst for the Roosevelt house are very close to a chair shown in Dresser's *Principles of Decorative Design*. The built-in dining room mantel/sideboard is reminiscent of the bureau and mirror Pabst made for his daughter. The dining table is supported by a substantial base that includes sculptured pelicans.

Although the present location of the dining room furniture is not known, other pieces of furniture were removed by the Roosevelts to Sagamore Hill, Oyster Bay, Long Island, in the late 1880s. These included a settee and a

Hudson River. Although only the base of the black-walnut sideboard has survived, its execution attests to the high quality produced in Pabst's shop. Particularly fine are the door panels carved in relief with scenes from Aesop's "Fox and Crane" fable which, according to research by Mary Jean Madigan, are very similar to a design for embroidered curtains by C. Heaton that appeared in Eastlake's *Hints on Household Taste*. Rather than the conventionalized floral ornament on the Pabst family bedroom suite, where an intaglio technique was used, the buffet here employs more naturalistic ornament, carved in relief.

Until recently no labeled examples of Pabst's furniture were known. Now four pieces documented by Pabst's signature—a cabinet, tall clock, and two

by Philadelphia architect Frank Furness. Pabst's work shows many similarities to Furness's. And it seems they worked together. Furness's name was on Pabst's customer list and Pabst made furniture for Furness from the architect's designs. Further evidence of an important working association is that Pabst and Furness had many of the same clients.

The most notable commission that can be attributed with some certainty to Furness and Pabst was for the furniture and interior woodwork in Theodore Roosevelt, Sr.'s house at 6 West 57th Street in New York City. A contemporary photograph of the Roosevelt dining room shows an exuberant and electrifying interior. The design can be attributed to Furness on the basis of very close similarity in form and the exact repetition of Furness motifs, such as the pelican, used in other pieces. That Pabst's shop made the fur-

bedroom suite consisting of armchairs, table, bed, and wardrobe. According to the Roosevelts the bedroom furniture composed a master bedroom suite that won first prize at the Philadelphia Centennial Exhibition. The Roosevelts visited the exhibition and undoubtedly saw the sideboards that Pabst made and designed. One of the sideboards won an award at the Centennial Exhibition and was "commended for utility, durability, and beauty." The location of this award-winning piece is not known. It was undoubtedly a Pabst masterpiece.

Pabst's award-winning sideboard was similar in style to another important sideboard that he designed shortly after the Centennial Exhibition. According to a newspaper account, John Bond Trevor of Yonkers, New York, commissioned Pabst's Philadelphia firm to design a "buffet" to fit a niche in the dining room of Glenview, the house Trevor was building on the banks of the

bookcases—have been discovered. The first one to be identified is a cabinet found by Pennsylvania furniture dealers Robert Edwards and Kenneth Jones. In it they located a fragment of Pabst's letterhead with the inscription, "Daniel Pabst, Philadelphia." The cabinet is unusual for an American piece. It incorporates a tile motif that is more typical of modern Gothic English furniture designed by Bruce J. Talbert, William Burgis, and others. With the exception of pieces manufactured by the New York firm Kimbel and Cabus, such ornamentation was rarely made here. The Pabst cabinet does not feature typical ceramic tiles, but a substitute simulating tiles and ribbed glass. The centralized floral design was inspired by a Christopher Dresser design. So are the Furnessian capitals above the turned columns. Designs are achieved by cutting through the walnut burl veneer to the darker walnut beneath.

Opposite page: The ornamental designs on much of Pabst's furniture and woodwork, shown in the drawings here, are floral and plant motifs reduced to basic geometric patterns. They are similar to the decorations used by English reform designer Christopher Dresser. Drawings Richard Zoehrer. Above: This handsome Pabst cabinet, ca 1885, was discovered by a Pennsylvania dealer at a flea market where it was being used to display beer cans. Wurts House Collection; photo Peter Lester.

Also labeled by the cabinetmaker is the only tall clock known to be made by Pabst. An inscription engraved at the top, inside the door, reads: "Travis Cochran & Wife. From Henry Seybert." Inside the door at the bottom appears an engraved signature: "Daniel Pabst Artist. 1884." The clock dial is marked "J. E. Caldwell & Co. Philadelphia." Relief carving on the clock front is particularly fine, as are the carved lions above canted corners. The clock resided with one family until it was recently acquired by a private collector.

A third example of Pabst signed furniture is a bookcase that was originally part of the library in the home of Frank Furness's brother, Horace Howard Furness.

Maria Thompson (Mrs. Radcliffe Furness Thompson) discovered a remarkable document in the Furness family records, signed by six Furnesses, which reads: "These bookcases were placed in position this day—February 18th 1871. They were designed by Capt. Frank Furness, and made by Daniel Pabst—. . ." That they should so record the event indicates how important the furniture and the event of installation must have been to the Furnesses. The bookcases were moved to the family house in Wallingford, Pennsylvania, in 1896.

According to city directories, Pabst took his son into his business in 1894. Although he continued to work until 1896, his shop must have been much reduced in size. He is last listed in the directories in 1896.

Pabst continued to make furniture after his retirement, although probably mostly for family and friends. A desk dated 1901 shows, in its form and decoration, the influence of earlier styles in which he had worked so successfully. According to family tradition, this desk was exhibited at the St. Louis World's Fair of 1904.

Daniel Pabst died on July 15, 1910, honored, as we have seen, throughout a life that spanned much of the 19th century. His finely crafted work and avant-garde designs place his furniture among the best in Philadelphia in the second half of his century. ■

Egyptian Revival

In America, the so-called *Egyptian Revival style was a variant of the Renaissance Revival, popular after the Civil War. But other Egyptian-inspired pieces were made from 1800 to 1922.*

BY CAROL L. BOHDAN

Egyptian forms and symbols influenced American furniture design throughout the 19th century and again briefly in the 1920s. But they appeared before that in mid-18th-century English and European furniture. Ornaments such as the palmette, anthemion, lion mask, and above all the sphinx were revived as early as Greek and Roman times. The application of sphinx heads to a table in the boudoir of Marie Antoinette at Fountainbleau was probably inspired by contemporary excavations at Herculaneum from 1748 to 1780 and at Pompeii beginning in 1763.

The *ancien régime*'s casual interest in Egyptian ornament was intensified greatly by reports of the Napoleonic expedition's discoveries in Syria and Egypt from 1798 to 1801. Napoleon employed over 100 scholars to study

Egypt. From 1809 to 1828 they produced a 10-volume epic, *Description de L'Egypte*, containing measured drawings of antiquities and a staggering amount of detail—an admirable first attempt at scientific documentation of the Egyptian arts. Napoleon appointed designers Charles Percier and Pierre Fontaine as his official court architects and decorators. Their *Recueil de Décorations Intérieures* (1801) was the first book to document French furniture forms in the new archaeological style.

The artist Baron Dominique Vivant Denon accompanied Napoleon on his campaign and a year later, in 1802, published his widely influential *Voyage dans la basse et haute Egypte*. Profusely illustrated with detailed sketches, Denon's volume, along with the work of Percier and Fontaine, provided both French and English designers with a rich repertory of Egyptian ornament. His own suite of bedroom furniture, commissioned in the Egyptian style, whetted fashionable interest.

Interest spreads to England

As the "Egyptian taste" developed in France, it began to find favor in England, particularly through the work of

designer Thomas Hope, who lived from 1769 to 1831. "The gentleman of the sphinxes" was a friend of Percier and an avid reader of the accounts of Denon. Hope traveled throughout the East for eight years, collecting vases and sculpture in Egypt, Syria, Spain, Turkey, and Greece. A virtuoso draftsman, he applied Egyptian and Greek ornaments to furniture of his design, including pieces for his London house at Cavendish Square and his Surrey home, Deepdene. One visitor described a bed at Deepdene as being

> made exactly after the model of Denon's Egyptian bed, a sofa-bed wide enough for two aldermen, embossed gold hieroglyphic frights all pointing with their hands distorted backwards at an Osiris or a long-armed monster of some sort who sits after their fashion on her hams and heels and has the likeness of a globe of gold on her lapetted, scaly-lapetted head.

In *Household Furniture and Interior Decoration* (1807) Hope illustrated many novel furniture designs influenced by Egyptian forms. But he warned other young artists against using the style indiscriminately on the grounds that hieroglyphics were unintelligible and that the impressive scale

Opposite: Boxwood and acadia chair from Egypt's XVIII Dynasty (ca. 1494 B.C.), Thebes, The Metropolitan Museum of Art, Rogers Fund, 1936. This page, left: American Empire armchair, maple, possibly made in New York or Philadelphia ca 1815-25. Courtesy the Henry Francis Du Pont Winterthur Museum. Above: Typical New York regency style pier table, perhaps from Duncan Phyfe's workshop, ca 1815. The Metropolitan Museum of Art, gift of John C. Cattus. Note variant of paw-foot on all three pieces.

of the originals could not be reproduced.

Hope's advice was not heeded. Throughout the Regency period, from 1810 to 1820, Egyptian elements are found in the work of many English designers, including Henry Holland and George Smith, whose book *A Collection of Designs for Household Furniture and Interior Decoration* appeared in 1808. In a fanciful spirit, Thomas Sheraton's *Cabinetmaker, Upholsterer and General Artists' Encyclopedia*, published between 1804 and 1806, presented designs for chairs having shaggy lion legs, backs formed of camels, and crocodile and sphinx-head ornaments. As Hope had predicted, these were quickly seized upon "as evidence of a disordered mind." In Sheraton's designs, however, there is a forecast of the way in which Egyptian motifs would be used on American furniture after 1830.

Egyptian taste in America

A succession of English design books and the migration of English and French cabinetmakers to America, particularly during the Napoleonic Wars (1796–1815), reinforced the classical taste that began to take root in the early Federal period. British-trained architect Benjamin Henry Latrobe's designs for the White House, circa 1809, typified furniture that used the archaic Greek and Egyptian forms pictured in Hope's book. Very quickly, the grace and restraint of the ancient style, as popularized by the esthetes Denon, Fontaine, Percier, and Hope gave way on both sides of the Atlantic to heavier and more complex forms. Just as the animal-related motifs on the furniture of Pharaonic Egypt reflected an egoistic concern with power, the sphinx seemed to be appropriate symbol for Napoleon's new military order. Similarly, animal-inspired furniture, incorporating legs of lions, birds of prey, the winged sphinx, animal heads, and paw or claw feet symbolized a vigorous young America whose national identity was reconfirmed in the joyful aftermath of the War of 1812.

French émigré cabinetmaker Charles-Honore Lannuier, active in New York City from 1803 to 1819, and Duncan Phyfe, a native of Scotland who worked in New York from 1792 to 1847, were progenitors of the Empire or "late classical" style in America dur-

ing its seminal period around 1815. Both borrowed freely from Greece, Rome, and Assyria as well as from Egypt, articulating what would become, in the next several decades, a rich American interpretation of the Empire style. In its heavier forms and use of gilding, Lannuier's work generally reflects his French background. But Phyfe's approach is more akin to that of English Regency designers in its lighter and sensitive use of such Egyptian motifs as paw feet and beautifully carved lotus leaves.

Egypt romanticized

The scientific, archaeological aspect of Egyptian design quickly became diluted through combination with other sources, but French literature revitalized both European and American appetites for things Oriental. Just as the last volume of Napoleon's scientifically accurate *Description de L'Egypte* was printed in 1828, Victor Hugo's novel *Les Orientales* was published. It described a romantic and exotic Egypt— "palms powdered by the winds of the desert, cities with metallic domes and minarets of ivory," in the words of one 19th century critic. *Les Orientales*

transformed the basis for Egyptian taste from scientific appreciation to romantic "Egyptianizing." To Americans, the Egyptian style was soon considered as picturesque as that of the Greek temples, "rustic" cottages, Gothic ruins, and Chinese pagodas that inspired the eclectic architecture of the day. Many Egyptian-style structures were erected in the United States. In 1832 an "Egyptian" gateway—the prototype for many others—was constructed in Mt. Auburn Cemetery, Cambridge, Massachusetts. The following year Robert Mills designed America's very own obelisk: the Washington Monument. In 1835 the most important "Egypto" structure—the New York Halls of Justice and House of Detention, better known as the Tombs, was conceived by architect John Haviland.

By the 1840s mummy displays, lectures, and books fed the American hunger for Egyptian things. In 1842 George Gliddon offered a lecture series based upon his experiences as one of the first American consuls in Cairo. Published in book form in 1843, Gliddon's lectures sold an extraordinary 24,000 copies. The earliest American history of Egyptian architecture, *Monuments in Egypt* by F. L. Hawks, appeared in 1849. Several collections of Egyptian antiquities, including a group of 680 objects donated to Johns Hopkins University, were given to American institutions.

Such activities probably did not pro-foundly influence American furniture design. As the major Egyptian tomb excavations were yet to be undertaken, early collections probably included no examples of furniture. And there is little to suggest that American furniture makers of the period found inspiration in Egyptian-style American architecture, unlike Thomas Hope who derived ideas for sideboards from architectural forms. Instead, Egyptian elements were used casually and at random. They formed a large, if eclectic, part of the working vocabulary of American furniture designers and cabinetmakers.

Although Egyptian symbols were absorbed into 19th-century American styles, a distinct Egyptian-revival style did not exist in the same sense as the other historic revivals: Gothic, renaissance, and rococo. Rather, several decidedly Egyptian elements, such as the sphinx, formed parts of the Victorian composite style known as "neogrec." Often Egyptian symbols were juxtaposed with Gothic and Renaissance elements in such furniture.

In *Upholstery and Furniture Bazaar* (1854) Charles H. White cited the popularity of such decorative motifs as the palm, water lily, Eastern star, beetle, spiral, zigzag, fret or labyrinth, wave, scroll, and fan. In the 19th century any motif that seemed even vaguely Eastern was apt to be labeled "Egyptian." The reverse was also true: forms indigenous to Egypt were rarely recognized as such. Many, like the anthemion, were associated with the Greeks.

Later 19th-century developments

Throughout the second half of the 19th century, the major inspiration for Egyptian-related design continued to be the geographic lure of Egypt itself. Published journals of French Orientalist painter and sculptor, Jean-Léon Gérôme, who visited Egypt in 1856 and 1867, as well as the opening of the Suez Canal in 1869—celebrated by Verdi's opera *Aida*, performed in New York in 1873—and significant archaeological findings at such sites as Giza drew unprecedented numbers of American curiosity seekers to the East. Contemporary reports stirred popular interest. Lady Duff-Gordon related a talk with the peasants near Thebes:

> One of them had droll theories about "Amellica"—as they always pronounce it; e.g. that the Americans are Fella'heen [peasants] of the English; "they talk so loud." "Was the king very powerful that the country was called El Melekeh" (the queens)? I said, "No, all are kings there; you would be a king like the rest." My friend disapproved of that utterly; "If all are kings, they must all be taking away the other's money"—a delightful idea of a king's vocation.

The great monuments at Giza, Karnak, and Sukkarah were photographed in 1857 by Francis Frith and by others. The work of American visionary and Orientalist painters like Elihu Vedder, Edwin Blashfield, Frederic Bridman, and Charles Allan Winter gave life to the literary tales and verbal reports of Egypt. Work by such sculptors as William Wetmore Story did the same. Story was noted for the archaeological exactitude of his props and costumes. His marble *Cleopatra* (1869) rested upon an Egyptian chair probably modeled after an original.

In the late 1850s, 1860s, and 1870s fashionable cabinetmakers and decorating firms applied Egyptian-inspired ornament to American furniture. The parlor suites made by the New York firms of Pottier and Stymus, Alexander Roux and Leon Marcotte consisted of cabinets, settees, and chairs with ornate decorations, much of it in the form of elaborate mounts. Bronze and brass castings of sphinx heads, plaques of carved mother-of-pearl, and porcelain polychromed with Egyptian-style figures were common on such furniture. Carved anthemions, palmettes, and incised Egyptian scrolls were also plentiful. Of Pottier and Stymus, the rival cabinetmaker Ernest Hagen wrote:

> ... their work was nearly all done in the "Neo Grec" most awfull gaudy style with brass gilt Spinx head on the sofas and armchairs, gilt engraved lines all over with porcailaine painted medalions on the backs, and brass gilt bead moldings nailed on. Other wise, their work was good; but the style horrible.

The British occupation of Egypt, beginning in 1882, gave added impetus to the tourist trade. By 1881, Thomas

In America, the so-called Egyptian Revival style was a variant of the Renaissance Revival, popular after the Civil War until the late 1870's. The New York-made armchair, seen with a detail of its carved arm support on this page, is part of a four-piece parlor suite of cherry wood, ebonized and gilded with decorative ormolu mounts. The Margaret Woodbury Strong Museum, Rochester, New York. Opposite page, top: One of a pair of ivory-inlaid fruitwood armchairs, ca 1930, carries the winged Egyptian god Anubis on its back splat and stiles. Egyptian taste persisted well into the 20th century. Courtesy Sotheby Parke-Bernet.

The gilded blue porcelain bust of Cleopatra on the opposite page, designed by Isaac Broome for the Ott & Brewer Company of Trenton, ca 1876, attests to the 19th-century appetite for Egyptian-inspired decorative objects. New Jersey State Museum, the Brewer Collection. Egyptian taste prevailed in Regency England, as the sphinx-carved detail of the painted and gilded armchair, ca 1800–1825, this page, shows. Morton's Auction Exchange, New Orleans.

Cook's steamers carried 800 tourists a year to Luxor. Newly built railroads dramatically eased access to fabled sights. Visiting Americans began to acquire bits and pieces of Egyptian material culture. On January 22, 1881, the obelisk nicknamed Cleopatra's Needle, erected by Thutmose III at Heliopolis circa 1455 B.C., was removed to Graywacke Knoll in New York's Central Park, behind The Metropolitan Museum of Art. In 1884 an Egyptian newspaper reported that a California engineer named Sutro "astonished Luxor today by buying a room of antiquities for 2500 francs of Mohammed Mohassis, much good, much bad. Today everybody is agog to sell him. He took three mummies yesterday. ..." By 1886 The Metropolitan had purchased 29 objects from the Nineteenth Dynasty tomb of Sen-nedjem at Thebes. (Items from an earlier excavation there had received considerable attention at the 1862 exhibition in London. A widespread demand for the "Thebes stool" was satisfied by Liberty of London and several American makers who reproduced this popular item until the turn of the century.)

Copies of Pharaonic furniture

In the 1880s original Pharaonic furniture inspired several English designers to make close copies, although these are often embellished with other ethnic motifs. An Egyptian-style couch, attributed to artist William Holman Hunt, for example, was inlaid with Assyrian figures. Innovative British designer Christopher Dresser created furniture based on original pieces exhibited in London. Carved with animal heads and paw feet, Dresser's couches, chairs, and cabinets represent a historical revival in the spirit of earlier designers Denon and Hope. Using inlay of ivory, ebony, and other exotic woods, and painted panels and tiles, Dresser created a rich surface quality emulating the jewel-like ornamentation of the originals. (Because good timber was in short supply in Egypt when the original Pharaonic furniture was made, inlay, gesso, and polychrome decoration were often used to mask flaws in the wood. Necessity inspired

beautifully patterned surfaces.)

Lawrence Alma-Tadema, perhaps the most esteemed painter of classical antiquity in his time, was also deeply involved in furniture design. In the 1870s Henry G. Marquand, an American collector and the second president of The Metropolitan Museum, commissioned Alma-Tadema to design a suite of twenty pieces, including a spectacular grand piano for the music room of his New York mansion. These are resplendent examples of the so-called art style with eclectic ornamentation, some of it Egyptian-inspired. At least two armchairs decorated in a similar spirit, with inlay of mother-of-pearl and colorful woods against a ground of ebonized rosewood veneer, were made about 1875 by an unknown cabinetmaker for James Lenox, a philanthropist and collector of books and art, and Dr. I. Wyman Drummond, both of New York City.

An outstanding period collector with an avid and refined taste for the Egyptian style was entrepreneur Jay Gould, who purchased the Hudson River mansion, Lyndhurst, in 1880. To Andrew Jackson Davis's Gothic-revival setting Gould added some superb "Egyptian" objects, including furniture, bronzes, and mantel sets composed of clocks and miniature obelisks. Probably all of these were of American origin, though only a few—such as the Tiffany and Company mantel sets—are documented as such.

The "Moorish" vogue

In the decades of the 1880s and '90s America experienced a "Moorish," or "Turkish," vogue. These terms were used to describe any exotic middle Eastern effect, but much of what was called Moorish was actually contemporary—in contrast to ancient—Egyptian furniture. This fad was precipitated in England by "Moorish" furniture, newly made in Egypt and imported in large quantities from Cairo. Small, hexagonal occasional tables, chairs, and benches were popular, especially those ornamented with panels of "Musharabyeh" turning, a distinctive woodcarver's device that was copied and applied to the paneled interiors of many American

mansions of the period. "Mooresque" furniture, copied by Liberty of London, found its counterpart in countless "Turkish corners," "Moorish dens," and smoking rooms in America. These were popularized by the Philadelphia Centennial Exposition of 1876, which featured a Turkish bazaar and café, "where one could savor rich Mocha coffee, as 'fragrant as the perfume of Araby the Blest.' " The Centennial also featured a display of contemporary Egyptian furniture, including "a superb stand constructed of ivory and mother-of-pearl blocks ... one of the most striking art objects."

From Tutankhamen to art deco

The rage for the Moorish style continued unabated in America into the 1890s. However, in 1903, when Howard Carter discovered the tomb of Thutmose IV with its fine furniture, interest was once again directed toward the archaeological rather than the romanticized type of Egyptian-inspired furniture. Theodore M. Davis, a Newport, Rhode Island copper magnate, financed Carter's diggings. In 1922 Carter made his most celebrated find: the Tomb of Tutankhamen. The young king's throne of wood overlaid with sheet gold, in particular, captured the world's imagination. Reproductions of Tutankhamen's tomb furniture appeared in British stores; some were made in England but many were copies

The ormolu and marble mantle set above, made by Tiffany and Company around 1885, represents a popular, romanticized notion of Egyptian design rather than one which is archeologically correct: the heiroglyphs on the obelisks, for example, are meaningless. Elements of the Egyptian design vocabulary were used fancifully, not to say indiscriminately, through much of the 19th century on American-made furniture and decorative objects. The polychromed wood stool below, labelled by New York cabinetmaker Alexander Roux about 1865, has "Egyptian" hocked feet and spindled palmettes. It exemplifies the eclectic style characterized as "neo Grec" by contemporary furniture maker Ernest Hagen, who thought it "most awfull gaudy." Both pieces, The Metropolitan Museum of Art, Edgar J. Kaufmann Charitable Foundation Fund.

by Egyptian craftsmen, who were eager to capitalize on the archaeological find of the century.

Tut's tomb furniture had many characteristics common to the prevailing 1920s art deco style. In particular, it was made from luxurious materials: ivory, bronze, silver, and decorative woods such as purple amaranth, violet wood, zebra wood, palisander, and ebony. Soft curves and straight lines predominated in both Tutankhamen and deco furniture. The massiveness of many art deco pieces, especially cabinets, aligned with Egyptian taste. A number of magnificent pieces of Egyptian-style furniture were made into the

early 1930s. Without wood analysis, it is often impossible to determine whether these were made in England, France, Egypt, or the United States. Such late examples of the Egyptian Pharaonic style are among the most intricate ever created, and seat furniture often bears upholstery embroidered with signs, symbols, and hieroglyphics, many of which were believed to contain prophecies for the future. ■

In the 1870's, Henry G. Marquand, the second president of the Metropolitan Museum of Art, commissioned British painter Sir Lawrence Alma-Tadema to design a 20-piece suite, of which the grand piano on this page is part, for his New York mansion. The piano's imaginatively eclectic decoration derives from many historical sources. Egyptian influence is apparent in the feet and legs of the stools and in the incised variations of lotus and papyrus forms. Sotheby Parke-Bernet.

Eastlake-influenced Furniture

More than any other individual, Charles Locke Eastlake was responsible for introducing the principles of the English design reform movement to the American public. His influence led to a broad demand for relatively simple, clean-lined "art furniture" between 1870 and 1890.

BY MARY JEAN MADIGAN

By 1876, America's centennial year, a revolution in taste was sweeping the country. The intimate dramas of Victorian family life were no longer played out against the red plush, white marble, and extravagantly curved and carved rococo furniture that graced America's stylish antebellum parlors. Now the nation's most elegant homes were decorated in subdued "artistic" tones, set off by rectilinear furniture of rich bird's-eye maple or elegantly ebonized cherry wood—simple of line and delicately ornamented. The new designs, broadly categorized as "art furniture," were sometimes called "modern Gothic'" or "Queen Anne Revival" depending on stylistic inspiration. They were also referred to as the "Eastlake" after the English architect whose best-selling book *Hints on Household Taste* created a popular demand for simple, tasteful "reform" furniture in America between 1870 and 1890.

To the modern eye, such furniture—with its intricately stylized marquetry, gilded incised designs, spindled galleries, inset tiles, richly grained woods, and decorative turned elements—hardly seems "simple." But in contrast to the heavily carved furniture of preceding decades, embellished with naturalistic roses and bunches of grapes imposed on the elaborate rococo shapes that we now regard as the embodiment of Victorian design, Eastlake-inspired furniture was remarkably functional and clean-lined.

Eastlake: The forgotten reformer

More than any other individual, Charles Locke Eastlake was responsible for bringing the principles of the English design reform movement to the attention of the American public. Born to an affluent Devonshire family in 1836, Eastlake was named for an uncle, Sir Charles Lock Eastlake, a prominent painter who eventually became keeper and then director of Britain's National Gallery. Under the guidance of his illustrious uncle—with whom he is still confused, despite the different spelling of their middle names—Eastlake was

trained in architecture. As a young man, he traveled widely in Europe, writing articles related to architecture and the arts. Though he never practiced the profession, Eastlake was appointed secretary of the Royal Institute of British Architects in 1855. In this capacity he published *A History of the Gothic Revival* (1872), an enduring work of scholarship that documents the design origins of many English structures built between 1820 and 1870. In 1868, capitalizing on his growing reputation as an astute design critic, Eastlake wrote his magnum opus, *Hints on Household Taste.* In 1878, following the footsteps of his uncle, he was appointed keeper of the National Gallery and for 20 years worked to classify and conserve the extensive painting collection there. He then retired to "Terra Cottage" (a characteristic pun on the favored building material of the Eng-

lish Art Movement) at Bayswater, where he died in 1906.

As propagandist for design reform, Eastlake was a product of his times. A clamor over esthetic standards in art, architecture, and "household manufacture" echoed through the upper reaches of English society in the mid-19th century. Architect Augustus Welby Northmore Pugin and painter John Ruskin led a national movement for reform, urging a return to the "honest" principles of Gothic design and to the careful workmanship of the medieval period. Such reformers felt that the poorly constructed, tastelessly ostentatious "French Antique" furniture displayed at London's Crystal Palace Exhibition of 1851 revealed the stagnation of English design. More than any other factor, this exhibition turned young English designers away from French rococo forms then dominant, encouraging a reformist trend toward the revival of indigenous English medieval styles. This later was expressed in the work of such designers as William Burges, Bruce Talbert, and Alfred Waterhouse, who looked to the Gothic for inspiration. It also moved William Morris, progenitor of the Arts and Crafts movement, to found a trend-setting decorating firm that made wholly handcrafted furniture, stained glass, and embroidered textiles in the medieval manner for a wealthy group of patrons. Morris now occupies a prominent place in the history of Victorian decorative arts, while Eastlake—who

Above, left: The relatively simple lines and straight spindled crest of this walnut side chair, ca 1880, embody Eastlake's ideas of good design. The patented E.W. Vail folding chair (1875), opposite page, has overtones of the Renaissance revival. Right: Eastlake-inspired walnut bookcase with sawtooth molding, bail handles, and incised design. All, courtesy of the Margaret Woodbury Strong Museum, Rochester.

Left: Night stand, bird's eye maple veneer by Daniel Pabst of Philadelphia, 1875. Note the incised foliate ornament. Philadelphia Museum of Art; given by Charles T. Shenkle in memory of his mother, Mrs. Edna H. Shenkle. Right: Renaissance revival-style easel with Eastlake-influenced decoration: pierced quatrefoils and gilded incised ornament. Ebonized walnut, ca 1875. The Strong Museum. Below: Ebonized cherry secretary, 1882, made by Herter Brothers of New York for Jay Gould. Marquetry rose branches are gracefully deployed over the surface of the front drop panel and drawers. Brass bail handles accent this simple rectilinear piece. The Metropolitan Museum of Art; gift of Paul Martini.

was perhaps better known in his day—has until recently been nearly forgotten. (Morris's first lecture on the decorative arts was given in 1877, long after Eastlake's *Hints on Household Taste* achieved best-seller status on both sides of the Atlantic.)

Hints on Household Taste: Eastlake's "Bible"

Hints on Household Taste first appeared in England in 1868, an expanded version of a series of articles Eastlake had previously published in *The Queen* and *London Review*. Written to instruct the masses in the principles of tasteful home decoration, *Hints* achieved immediate popularity. It was reprinted four times in England and, after 1872, six times in America. The book expressed Eastlake's view that furniture should be functional, simple and rectilinear in form, honestly constructed without "sham or pretense," and ornamented with respect for the intrinsic qualities of the wood as well as the intended function of the furniture. It offered specific advice on the design, construction, ornamentation, and manufacture of many other household articles including wallpaper, metalwork, ceramics, draperies, clothing, and jewelry.

Though Eastlake included some of his own sketches among the illustrations of well-designed furniture chosen for *Hints*, he was primarily a critic of taste, not a furniture designer. (Some of his ideas, sketched out for friends, were ultimately translated "in the wood" by the London decorating firm of Jackson and Graham, but it should be stressed that actual pieces of furniture designed by Eastlake himself are exceedingly rare.) The furniture illustrated in *Hints* had ornamental features including shallow carving, marquetry, incised or pierced geometric designs, rows of turned spindles, chamfered edges, brass strap hinges, bail handles, and keyhole hardware inspired by Gothic forms. Every decorative device, according to Eastlake, also had to fulfill a useful function.

Although a few of the sketches used to illustrate early editions of *Hints* disclosed his preference for medieval design, Eastlake had no desire to impose his personal stylistic preferences on the public. Rather, he stressed the importance of "the spirit and principles of early manufacture"—that is, of the Middle Ages—and not "the absolute forms in which they found embodiment." Eastlake intended his ideas on tasteful form and ornament to be generally applicable to a wide range of "art furniture" styles, not just to those in the Gothic mode. This is confirmed by his elimination of several medieval-looking designs from later editions of *Hints*, replaced with pictures of more up-to-date Queen Anne-style furniture.

Eastlake considered simplicity the key to beauty. "The best furniture of all ages has been simple in general form, never running into extravagant contour or unnecessary curves." He especially disdained the "shaped" forms of rococo revival, which he thought "ensured the greatest amount of ugliness with the least possible comfort." These curved forms, counter to the "nature" of the wood, he regarded as "always rickety" and "constructively weak." To relieve the simplicity of rectilinear forms, Eastlake advised using turned legs or spindle supports. Where an "effect of richness" was desired, he suggested restrained, conventionalized carving, inlay, and sometimes even veneer. Ornament, he felt, should be stylized rather than naturalistic, for it is "this difference between artistic abstraction and pseudo-realism which separates good and noble design from that which is commonplace and bad." A functionalist, Eastlake cautioned that carved decoration should always be shallow and never "inconveniently" located, as were the "knotted lumps" of grapes or roses decorating rococo-revival chairs that often stabbed the sitter between his shoulder blades.

Hints further suggested that furniture be made of such solid, strongly grained woods as oak, walnut, or mahogany. "Deal," or soft pine, was fine for inexpensive pieces if painted or darkly stained. Oil-rubbed finishes were preferred to "French-polished" ones, and varnish was taboo: "The moment a carved or sculpted surface begins to *shine*, it loses interest." Eastlake urged that furniture be obviously and honestly constructed, and "sham" decoration avoided, but he was realistic about the common practice of veneering: "If we are to tolerate the marble lining of a brick wall and the practice of silver-plating goods of baser metal—now too universally recognized to be considered in the light of a deception—I do not see how veneering is to be rejected on moral grounds."

Though some later historians believed that Eastlake held—with William Morris—that furniture was "good" only if handcrafted, this assumption is not confirmed by *Hints*. Eastlake thought machine-carved, glued-on ornament—commonly found on cheap Renaissance-revival furniture—was "egregiously and utterly bad," but he did not disdain all machine work. "The division of labor and perfection of machinery have had their attendant advantages," he wrote. "It cannot be denied that many articles of ancient luxury are by such aid now placed within the reach of the million. It would be undesirable and indeed impossible to reject in manufacture the appliances of modern science." Nor was he an elitist. "Good artistic furniture ought really to be as cheap as that which is ugly," he believed. "The draughtsman and the mechnaic must be paid, whatever the nature of their tastes may be."

Eastlake's ideas in America

Though *Hints on Household Taste* was well received in England, Eastlake's was but one of many voices crying out for design reform there. In the United States, however, his words took on the special distinction Americans had always reserved for European arbiters of taste. In affluent post-Civil War America, energies were redirected from belligerency to the establishment of a new industrial and social order. The somberness of the war years persisted in America's parlors, where massive walnut Renaissance-revival furniture—monuments to historicism and reminders of the dignity of the newly unified American nation—shared space with the light-hearted curving rococo-revival forms of the 1850s that Eastlake

so detested.

As newly rich Americans traveled abroad or browsed through English periodicals, they encountered the new movement for design reform, creating an enthusiastic audience for the "professors of taste," led by Eastlake. According to the contemporary writer Harriet Prescott Spofford, when *Hints on Houshold Taste* was first published in Boston in 1872, "the book met a great want. Not a marrying couple who read English were to be found without *Hints on Household Taste* in their hands, and all its dicta were accepted as gospel truth." Between 1873 and 1890 the book was reprinted five times in America. Eastlake's ideas were echoed by a spate of authors who repeated—often verbatim and without credit to Eastlake himself—his major themes of "honesty in construction," simplicity, and functionalism, as well as his specfic suggestions for decoration and household ornament. Henry Hudson Holly, for example, cribbed entire passages from *Hints* in a series of articles published by *Harper's Monthly Magazine* in the mid-1870s.

Eastlake's ideas were further popularized by the Philadelphia Centennial Exhibition of 1876. British furniture on display there reflected the precepts of "good taste" already prevalent in England. Rectilinear form, simplicity of outline and detail, turned balusterlike supports and rows of spindles, shallow carving, and inlaid ornamentation characterized the furniture of Cooper and Holt of London, and that of Collinson and Locke. Though Renaissance-revival pieces continued to dominate the American displays, at least two manufacturers exhibited pieces "in the Eastlake manner." Kimbel and Cabus of New York City showed an entire drawing room of ebonized cherry—dado, mantel, cornice, sideboard, pedestal, and spindle sofa—in "modern Gothic" style similar to Eastlake's own sketches. Mitchell and Rammelsburg of Cincinnati, Ohio, showed a sideboard and mirrored hall stand with chamfered corners and metal strap hinges described by a contemporary reviewer as "rigidly after the canons of Eastlake."

Although—as these examples indicate—Eastlake's ideas had made considerable headway by 1876, the Centennial Exhibition itself had a ripple effect on American design, particularly in the Midwest. George W. Gay, president of Berkey and Gay, a Grand Rapids furniture company, recalled that the exhibition "had a far-reaching influence, expecially on western manufacturers who until then had not had occasion to compare their products with those of the best manufacturers of America and Europe. The Eastlake style was quickly taken up by the manufacturers of cheaper furniture, who until then had given very little attention to artistic form."

Some factory owners feared that Eastlake's ideas, stressing simplicity of form, would hurt the market for their products. One tradesman wrote in the *Cincinnati Trade List*: "We hope the fashion won't live very long or extend to this city. Of all the clumsy, ugly inventions, or rather copies, the sort ad-

vocated with bigoted zeal by Eastlake deserves to be most condemned." Other manufacturers, however, tried to capitalize on the new demand for Eastlake-inspired furniture by rushing into production some dubiously designed "Eastlake" articles hardly representative of the reform spirt and design principles expounded in *Hints on Household Taste*. These debased designs were immediately criticized by the Americans tastemaker Clarence Cook, who observed in *The House Beautiful* (1878): "The 'Eastlake' furniture must not be judged by what is made in this country and sold under that name. I have seen very few pieces of this that were either very well designed or well made. None of the cheaper sort is ever either." That year, in a revised British edition of *Hints*, Eastlake tried to disassociate himself from "What American tradesmen are pleased to call 'Eastlake' furniture, with the production of which I have had nothing whatever to do, and for the taste of which I should be very sorry to be considered responsible."

American furniture manufacture after 1870

Despite these criticisms, by the late 1870s a number of American furniture makers were producing high-quality pieces unquestionably in keeping with Eastlake's standards. As the author has noted in her definitive analysis, "Eastlake's Influence on American Furniture" (*Winterthur Portfolio X*, 1975), Eastlake's ideas were quite compatible with the system of production then developing in America. By 1870 the center of furniture manufacture had moved from the Eastern seaboard to the river and rail-line towns of the Midwest. Factories in Williamsport, Pennsylvania; Jamestown, New York; Cincinnati, Ohio; Grand Rapids, Michigan and many other towns were amply supplied by native ash, oak, cherry, and walnut to keep their foot-and steam-powered machines humming. New inventions—such as Blackman's steam-powered woodcarving machine, which employed a pantographlike device to reproduce designs in wood—afforded the swift and inexpensive reproduction of furniture designs illustrated in the latest art periodicals and books. The furniture produced in these factories ranged from excellent to shoddy, depending on the grade of lumber used, how well it was seasoned in the drying kilns appended to the larger factories, and upon the skill of each machine operator throughout the manufacturing process. At its worst, factory furniture was poorly designed and rickety. But with careful specifications, good materials, well-trained machinists, and sufficient time allocated for finishing, it was entirely possible to produce factory furniture that upheld Eastlake's standards of sturdiness, utility, and good design.

Not all American furniture of this period, of course, was made in factories. In organizing the first exhibition of Eastlake furniture at the Hudson River Museum in 1974, the author found that the demand for Eastlake-influenced reform furniture cut across lines, encouraging a large American output of four general types: very expensive custom-made furniture turned out by individual East Coast cabinetmakers and a few exclusive decorators such as Herter Brothers of New York; moderately expensive furniture made to order in multiples from stock designs by maker-retailers (for example, Kimbel and Cabus of New York, whose 1876 photograph catalogue of stock designs is now held by the Cooper-Hewitt Museum); moderately priced but well-constructed factory furniture produced in the Midwest for wholesale shipment to Eastern retail outlets; and cheap—often flimsy—factory goods produced at very low cost for a working-class market, often sold on credit in the factory's own retail warerooms in Eastern cities. It was the last category of manufacture that gave much "Eastlake" furniture a bad name in subsequent years, for the truly cheap pieces were often gross misinterpretations of Eastlake's ideas. The Brooklyn Furniture Company, for example, touted itself as "the largest,

Herter Brothers of New York City specialized in marquetry ornament, as seen on the crest of the ebonized cherry side chair, opposite page top. Philadelphia Museum of Art; given by Mrs. William T. Carter. Opposite, below: Walnut sideboard with mirrored panels and spindled crest rail. The Metropolitan Museum of Art; gift of Mr. Richard T. Button, 1970. Above: Kimbel and Cabus drawing room display at Philadelphia Exhibition, 1876. This New York City firm made ebonized furniture with gilded, incised geometric patterns and inset tiles. Henry Francis du Pont Winterthur Museum Libraries. Left: This Kimbel and Cabus cabinet is illustrated in the 1876 catalogue, The Hudson River Museum, Yonkers, New York.

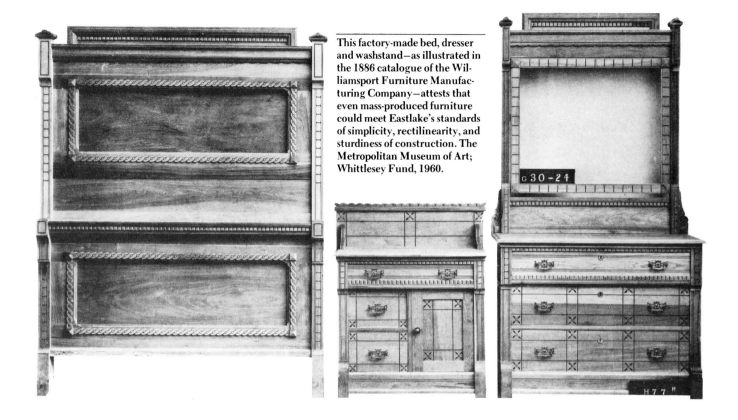

This factory-made bed, dresser and washstand—as illustrated in the 1886 catalogue of the Williamsport Furniture Manufacturing Company—attests that even mass-produced furniture could meet Eastlake's standards of simplicity, rectilinearity, and sturdiness of construction. The Metropolitan Museum of Art; Whittlesey Fund, 1960.

cheapest, and most reliable furniture-maker in the world," but the suites that appeared in its 18 warerooms—selling for as little as $55 for seven pieces—did little justice to Eastlake.

Stylistic trends in Eastlake-influenced furniture

Whether mass-produced or custom made, Eastlake-influenced furniture of the 1870s and 1880s followed several concurrent stylistic trends that were variously named. But they all adhered to his general precepts of rectilinearity, simplicity, and stylized flat or low-relief surface decoration. In the early 1870s there appeared a transitional style in which Eastlakian decorative devices—incised gilded geometric designs, stylized marquetry, and medieval-looking pierced work—appeared on forms that were basically Renaissance revival. Within a short time the raised central pediments, heavy molded cornices, pendent aprons, and finials of these transitional pieces gave way to simpler, more rectilinear shapes closely aligned to Eastlake's ideal.

By 1876 some individual craftsmen, limited-stock producers of fine furni-

ture, and a few of the better factories were turning out pieces with a markedly medieval appearance, sometimes called "modern Gothic." Kimbel and Cabus of New York, whose characteristic ebonized pieces had brass strap hinges, incised geometric designs picked out in gilt, and medieval-looking tiles, best exemplified this trend. The modern Gothic style may have been directly inspired by some of Eastlake's own sketches for the early editions of *Hints on Household Taste*, as well as by English architect Bruce Talbert's *Gothic Forms Applied to Furniture*, which was reprinted in Boston in 1873. By 1885 the rage for medieval shapes and decorations had run its course and was rarely mentioned in trade journals or maker's catalogues after that time.

A concurrent trend for Oriental decoration was first inspired by a display of Japanese arts at London's Exhibition of 1862. By the late 1870s the taste for Japanese design had reached America. Rectilinear Eastlake furniture of better quality was often given an ebonized finish reminiscent of Oriental lacquer, then inlaid with marquetry blossoms or

tiles painted in the Japanese style. Herter Brothers of New York City, a fine custom-furniture-making and decorating house, were the first and best exponents of this fashion. Their German-born craftsmen excelled in marquetry inlay, creating some exquisite one-of-a-kind pieces like the desk made for Jay Gould in 1882 for $550, now in The Metropolitan Museum of Art, or the wardrobe ornamented with inlaid cherry blossoms, made for Lillian Russell around 1880. Eventually the Japanese taste was adopted by lesser furniture makers, and by 1885 Oriental fretwork commonly replaced the spindle galleries of many factory-made pieces. Throughout the 1880s, Oriental motifs—cranes, rushes, butterflies, cherry blossoms, fans, chrysanthemums, and other devices—proliferated on furniture of every quality.

Yet another trend in furniture design migrated from England to the United States in the late 1870s. Loosely described as "Queen Anne" after the 17th- and 18th-century design principles it purported to emulate, this reform style had a profusion of turned elements and spindles, exemplified by the graceful Collinson and Locke sideboard displayed at the Philadelphia Centennial Exhibition of 1876. So-called Queen Anne was always more popular in England than here.

Surviving examples

Although it was once made in great quantity, by 1895 Eastlake-influenced furniture was no longer considered fashionable. Subsequent generations of homemakers were quick to relegate it to the barn or attic. As a result, except for bedroom furniture which continued in use long after it fell from fashion, few complete suites of "Eastlake" have survived. Even the finest pieces were subjected to careless use, unappreciated until recently.

Collecting considerations are complicated by the fact that American furniture of the 1870s and 1880s varied greatly in styling, quality, and method of manufacture. Much of it constituted a very free translation of Eastlake's ideas. The more hastily constructed factory pieces that often turn up in today's country auctions and antique shops almost always violate some aspect of Eastlake's principles. Machine-carved applied ornament is frequently used, and the pieces usually are varnished. Often there are unnecessary decorative details and excrescences which bear little relation to function and intrude upon the rectilinearity of outline.

For some reason, bedroom furniture of all qualities is nearly always designed in close accordance with Eastlake's precepts, whereas a wider—and usually less accurate—range of interpretation prevails for inexpensive parlor suites. Individual craftsmen and high-quality cabinetmaking firms also interpreted Eastlake broadly. The philosophical concepts of function and design expressed in *Hints on Household Taste* are adhered to but embodied in unique designs expressing the individual character of each craftsman or firm.

Today, major museums hold examples of Eastlake-influenced furniture by the finer makers including Herter Brothers, Kimbel and Cabus, Daniel Pabst, and others. With increasing frequency, signed or attributed pieces by

While Eastlake was basically a tastemaker and not a furniture designer, several sketches used to illustrate early editions of *Hints on Household Taste*—like the sideboard above—betray his fondness for medieval design. Winterthur Museum Libraries.

these makers turn up at the better auctions and shops at increasingly hefty prices. Even the factory-made pieces are commanding the close attention of museums, historic houses, and collectors who seek typical examples of late 19th-century, middle-class home furnishings.

Five years ago Eastlake-influenced furniture was unappreciated, but is now collected by those whose interest in Victorian decorative art reflects a growing trend. Eastlake himself is now lauded for his contribution to the evolution of design. *Hints on Household Taste* inspired a generation of Americans to critically appraise their surroundings; to be aware of design principles. Eastlake bridged the gap between William Morris' elitist philosophy of handcrafted furniture for the affluent few, and later expressions of the Arts and Crafts movement that were largely mass-produced. ■

Kimbel & Cabus

In the last quarter of the 19th-century, this New York firm produced some of the Victorian era's most distinctive furniture in the so-called modern Gothic style.

BY DAVID HANKS

While the study of late 19th-century American furniture is still in its infancy, serious collecting interest has developed following the pioneering work of Marilynn Johnson Bordes of The Metropolitan Museum of Art, who first described many major cabinetmakers of the period in the catalogue for the landmark exhibition *19th-Century America* (1970). As Bordes points out, there were many fine cabinetmakers at work in New York, Philadelphia, and other American cities in the latter half of the 19th century, including such major firms as Pottier & Stymus, Cottier & Company, and Herter Brothers. But some of the most distinctive furniture produced during this period in the modern Gothic style—richly ebonized,

tile-inlaid pieces profusely embellished with geometric gilt incising—was made by the firm of Kimbel & Cabus, which is first listed in an 1863 New York City directory at a Broadway address.

Early history of the firm

Before going into partnership, both Anthony Kimbel and Joseph Cabus had worked with others, as research by Richard McGeehan indicates. Kimbel, primarily a designer and furniture dealer, was in partnership with Anthony Bembe during the 1850s. Surviving examples of their work include furniture made for the United States House of Representatives in 1857, attesting to the firm's prominence, *Gleason's Pictorial Drawing Room Companion*, a popular ladies' periodical of the time, described Bembe and Kimbel as "having a manufactory at Mayenne in France, as well as in New York, and Mr. Bembe, the senior partner, has furnished many of the noblest palatial residences in western Europe. The branch of the concern in New York has therefore the advantage of an eminent European connection, and receives, as they

appear abroad, all the new models and designs in furniture. . . ." The same account, illustrated with a wood engraving of an elaborate parlor of Bembe-Kimbel furniture in the prevailing rococo-revival style, notes that Anthony Kimbel was "for several years principal designer in Mr. Baudouine's well-known furniture establishment in Broadway, and his unique styles appear to be American modifications of those now in vogue abroad." Charles A. Baudouine, a New Yorker of French descent, was widely regarded as one of the best local cabinetmakers of his day, so we may assume that through these distinguished associations Kimbel had attained an exceptionally high level of design competence by the time he entered into partnership with Joseph Cabus.

Kimbel & Cabus's most distinctive furniture was crafted in the so-called modern Gothic style. Many of their stock pieces from the Centennial year appear in a photographic record book. A page from this "catalogue" is shown right. Courtesy The Cooper-Hewitt Museum, the Smithsonian Institution's National Museum of Design.

Kimbel & Cabus also made Renaissance revival furniture, like the rosewood cabinet, above right. The Brooklyn Museum, gift of Susan Dwight Bliss. This cabinet, #4 in the Cooper-Hewitt design book, originally sold for $200. Note elaborate marquetry panels on the curved lower sections. The same marquetry design appears on the rosewood cabinet, left. Although this piece is not in their 1876 design book, it is similar to other Kimbel & Cabus furniture. Private Collection.

Comparatively little is known of Cabus, who had been working as a cabinetmaker. From a paper label found on a Renaissance-revival sideboard owned by a private collector, scholars deduce he was briefly in partnership with another more prominent New York cabinetmaker, Alexander Roux; however, this arrangement is not recorded in any New York City directory. By 1862 Joseph Cabus is listed alone as a cabinetmaker at 924 Broadway.

When Kimbel and Cabus joined forces in 1863, they initially worked out of Cabus's shop. Their early prosperity is indicated by the 1865 acquisition of an additional property at 136 East 18th Street. The following year, they moved to 928 Broadway, where they remained until 1874. That year Kimbel & Cabus occupied both 7 East 20th Street and 458 10th Avenue, where they stayed through what were apparently the firm's peak business years. Their partnership was dissolved in 1882. Cabus moved uptown to 506 West 41st Street, where he worked as a cabinetmaker until 1897, while Kimbel remained at the East 20th Street address in a new partnership with his sons Henry and Anthony. Although Kimbel and Sons continued to make furniture until 1941, this account is confined to pieces produced during the earlier Kimbel & Cabus partnership.

Stylistic development

The dry facts gleaned from city directories tell furniture historians the story of a given firm's evolution and relative prosperity. But contemporary illustrations of the furniture itself, together with surviving signed or labeled pieces, give us a better idea of a cabinetmaker's stylistic development. In the case of Kimbel & Cabus, a remarkable collection of photographs of the company's furniture survives, bound into scrapbooks at the Cooper-Hewitt Museum. Though it was not unusual for furniture makers and other manufacturers after 1870 to commission photographs of their "line," regrettably few of these valuable documents have survived. As Mary Jean Madigan conjectured in an article in *Winterthur Portfolio X* (1975), the scrapbooks at the Cooper-Hewitt Museum may actually have been working catalogues used in the company's showrooms, from which a client could order custom-made furniture. Price notations are recorded on many pages, giving some substance to

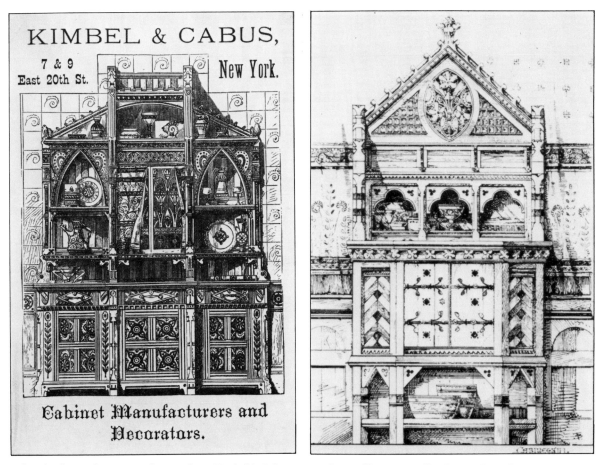

Like other late 19th century cabinetmakers, Kimbel & Cabus were influenced by Bruce Talbert's 1876 design book, *Examples of Ancient and Modern Furniture, Metalwork, Tapestries, Decoration, Etc.* Above right: A plate from that book displays a modern Gothic cabinet similar in feeling to the one appearing on a Kimbel & Cabus trade card from the same period. Courtesy, the New-York Historical Society, Bella Landauer Collection.

this theory. The earlier of the two scrapbooks dates from the mid-1870s, while the later book, compiled in the 1890s, shows furniture in a revival mode produced by Kimbel and Sons after the dissolution of the Kimbel & Cabus partnership.

The earlier of the scrapbook-catalogues shows that by the mid-1870s, Kimbel & Cabus were turning out a large and stylistically diverse line of furniture. Like their competitor Alexander Roux, they made both "plain" and "artistic" furniture—chairs, tables, sofas, hanging cabinets, and important case pieces. Furniture pictured in the mid-1870s book may be grouped into two broad categories: Renaissance revival and modern Gothic, Kimbel & Cabus's most characteristic style. (The furniture shown in the later 1890s Kim-

bel and Sons scrapbook is very different. It might be called "Beaux-Arts revival" and is strongly French in inspiration. Because it comes well after the period of Kimbel & Cabus' partnership, it is not further discussed or illustrated in this article.)

Renaissance-revival pieces

Some of the most elaborate and expensive Kimbel & Cabus furniture pictured in their mid-1870s scrapbook or catalogue is in the Renaissance-revival style that dominated American furniture design in the decade following the Civil War. Renaissance-revival furniture is massively architectonic. It expresses a strong bilateral symmetry; case pieces usually have a high crested central component flanked by lower elements. Medallions, roundels, pendant finials,

columns, and panels of marquetry typically ornament such pieces. Decorative details—palmettes, arabesques, and such—are incised and gilded or detailed with contrasting ebonized, polychromed, or grained woods in the so-called Neo-Grec manner. Some pieces of Kimbel & Cabus's Renaissance-revival-style furniture were further embellished with porcelain plaques.

Perhaps their most important Renaissance-revival piece, pictured in the early photographic catalogue and presently in the collection of The Brooklyn Museum, is a richly ornamented cabinet with marquetry panels and Neo-Grec detail. Its central roundel, enclosing a ceramic plaque painted with a classical scene, is a mannered tour de force, an unusual feature for a piece of American furniture at this

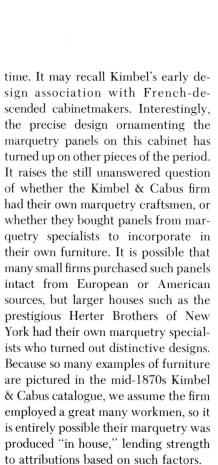

time. It may recall Kimbel's early design association with French-descended cabinetmakers. Interestingly, the precise design ornamenting the marquetry panels on this cabinet has turned up on other pieces of the period. It raises the still unanswered question of whether the Kimbel & Cabus firm had their own marquetry craftsmen, or whether they bought panels from marquetry specialists to incorporate in their own furniture. It is possible that many small firms purchased such panels intact from European or American sources, but larger houses such as the prestigious Herter Brothers of New York had their own marquetry specialists who turned out distinctive designs. Because so many examples of furniture are pictured in the mid-1870s Kimbel & Cabus catalogue, we assume the firm employed a great many workmen, so it is entirely possible their marquetry was produced "in house," lending strength to attributions based on such factors.

Modern Gothic-style furniture

While other contemporary cabinetmakers like Alexander Roux turned out look-alike furniture in the Renaissance-revival mode, no other firm approached Kimbel & Cabus's most characteristic style—a distinctive interpretation of the so-called modern Gothic. Because this style was very much in vogue in England by the mid-1870s, Kimbel and Cabus may have selected it to represent their line in the important Philadelphia Centennial Exhibition of 1876 that has been so thoroughly researched by Rodris Roth of the Smithsonian. The display—a well-intregrated room—attracted a gratifying amount of favorable attention. "The exhibit of Messrs. Kimbel & Cabus," observed one critic, "was of handsome and judicious design, one of the few attractive displays of drawing-room furniture, shown in a section with all the accessories of an harmonious

room." Singled out for special praise was the furniture "of ebonized cherry, richly carved, though not profusely so," especially "the cabinet or desk . . . of modernized Gothic form, and profusely gilt, the panels being figured with Cupids and exquisitely painted flowers; sofa and chairs richly upholstered in maroon satin, with gold cord and fringe." This same critic judged the total effect of the Kimbel & Cabus Centennial display as "rich and tasteful enough to rank it among the very best of the American exhibits in household art."

The modern Gothic fashion grew out of the English design reform movement led by Charles Locke Eastlake, whose name is the one most often associated with this style. Eastlake's book *Hints on Household Taste*, first published in England in 1867 and reprinted in America some seven times after 1872, created a strong demand for furniture in the modern Gothic mode. In catering to

Left: Ebonized cherry cabinet with inset Minton-Hollins tiles and incised gilded decoration. Courtesy the Hudson River Museum, gift of Susan Dwight Bliss; photo Thomas S. Berntsen. Except for the tiles, this cabinet is identical to design #331, priced at $75, in the 1876 design book at the Cooper-Hewitt Museum. Kimbel & Cabus's customers may have been able to select from a variety of tiles to be set into specially ordered pieces. Because much modern Gothic furniture was tall and unwieldy, few large pieces survived intact. For example, the ebonized cherry cabinet on the opposite page, left, has had its coved crest cut down, hardly detracting from the splendid effect of the incised gilded ornament, brass hinges, and inset tiles. Courtesy The Hudson River Museum, gift of Mrs. Joseph Lippman; photo Thomas Berntsen. The cabinet as it originally appeared is seen in the Kimbel & Cabus photograph, opposite page right, taken from their design book now in the Cooper-Hewitt Museum. This design was #262 and originally sold for $300. Note the different tiles on the Hudson River Museum's cabinet. Courtesy The Cooper-Hewitt Museum.

this demand, furniture makers like Kimbel & Cabus and the Cincinnati firm of Mitchell & Rammelsburg—who also showed modern Gothic pieces in the 1876 Centennial Exhibition—were probably guided by the detailed pattern books of another British reform designer, Bruce J. Talbert. Talbert's most famous works were *Gothic Forms Applied to Furniture, Metalwork and Decoration for Domestic Purposes* (1867), which was reprinted in Boston in 1873, and *Examples of Ancient and Modern Furniture, Metal Work, and Tapestries* (1876), also reprinted in Boston in 1977.

Modern Gothic furniture illustrations in Talbert's books expressed the principles of late 19th-century reform design, inspired by the craft traditions of the Middle Ages. Design reformers like Talbert urged a return to the medieval principles of simplicity, "honesty," or obviousness of construction, and sympathetic use of materials. These virtues had been ignored by England's mid-19th-century designers of revival-style furniture, who aped the florid rococo and baroque excesses of earlier periods. In contrast to these mid-Victorian revival designers, whose wares dominated Britain's Crystal Palace Exhibition of 1851, Talbert eschewed "an elaborate reproduction of the past." Instead, he tried to understand the principles behind Gothic design: "It is not Medieval furniture, confined to the antiquarian knowledge of the past, that is wanted, but a recogition of the more honest principles that governed them."

If Kimbel & Cabus's modern Gothic furniture is compared to the plates in Talbert's books, close parallels are seen. Like Talbert's drawings, Kimbel & Cabus's furniture is expressively architectural, with surmounting gables, coves, turned columns, and flying buttresses similar to detailing on houses of

Above: Library table, ebonized cherry, 1880. Affixed to the underside of the drawer is a paper label identical to the one inset on the opposite page. This simple table may be a later refinement of #430, pictured in The Cooper-Hewitt Museum's Kimbel & Cabus design book. Courtesy The Hudson River Museum; photo Thomas S. Berntsen.

Ebonized cherry music stand, ca 1876. Inset
composition panels printed with vignettes of
medieval musicians. Label, inset below, is
glued to underside. Courtesy Barry and Dee
Dee Wigmore. Nearly identical is design #
328 in the Kimbel & Cabus 1876 design book.

A. KIMBEL & J. CABUS.
Cabinet Makers and Decorators,
NEW YORK.

the period. Painted tiles—some imported from the Minton-Hollins works at Stoke-on-Trent, England—or inlaid wooden panels are often incorporated into these pieces. Such ornamental devices were considered typical of English furniture of the period, but apart from the Kimbel & Cabus furniture, they are rarely found in American work. Another characteristic—and functional—feature Kimbel & Cabus borrowed from Talbert is the use of elaborately shaped incised brass strap hinges applied to desks, sideboards, cabinets, and other case pieces. Particularly distinctive is the incised linear and geometric decoration that sometimes covers every surface of Kimbel & Cabus's furniture, picked out in gilt on

the ebonized cherry pieces, or left plain on those pieces where the wood—usually ash—is given a natural finish.

Identifying Kimbel & Cabus furniture

Because their designs in the modern Gothic mode are so distinctive, it is tempting to attribute certain pieces of American furniture to Kimbel & Cabus on the basis of style alone. But exercise caution in making such attributions, because pirating of successful designs was a common practice among American manufacturers. In some instances, attributions made primarily on the basis of style may be corroborated by comparing extant pieces of furniture to the photographs in the Kimbel & Cabus

scrapbook-catalogue in the collections of the Cooper-Hewitt Museum. Several pieces have come to light that are identical to the pictures in the catalogue, save for variations in the inset tiles. Madigan has conjectured that Kimbel & Cabus's customers who ordered pieces from the catalogue may have been able to "customize" their furniture by choosing special tiles from the wide selections available for inset.

Kimbel & Cabus also used paper labels on some furniture; and a piece bearing such a label is considered to be definitively documented. However, not all pieces retain such labels, which—if they were ever affixed—may have been removed by the original owners, their servants or their descendants. ∎

Opposite page: Illustration of Kimbel & Cabus's booth at the 1876
Philadelphia Centennial Exhibition. From Harper's Weekly. Courtesy,
author's collection. In its display Kimbel & Cabus showed a well-inte-
grated group of modern Gothic furniture in an appropriate room setting. Thousands of Americans passed through the exhibition hall, helping to spread the demand for furniture in this style. A contemporary
critic noted that "the effect of this section was rich and tasteful enough
to rank it among the very best of the American exhibits in household
art." This page: Hanging shelf of ebonized hardwood with a spindled
gallery and ornamental panel of a printed design or varnished paper.
Courtesy The Hudson River Museum, photo by Thomas S. Berntsen. Hanging shelves were popular pieces of art furniture in the late
1870s. This one is documented in the Kimbel & Cabus design book at
the Cooper-Hewitt Museum, as seen in the inset detail of a photograph
from that book. Note the design number, 423 and the price notation, 8
(for $8.) Courtesy The Cooper-Hewitt Museum.

Gallé and Majorelle

The designs of Majorelle and Gallé represent the height of the Art Nouveau movement. They both embellished their furniture with flowing organic decoration, but while Majorelle was ultimately concerned with fine proportion, Gallé believed firmly in the importance of the decoration itself.

BY KATHARINE MORRISON McCLINTON

Art Nouveau was a decorative movement that revolutionized the design of household interiors, architecture, and even fine arts in the last quarter of the 19th century. It was a free-flowing organic style with a swirling, undulating rhythm that drew its chief inspiration from nature. The roots of Art Nouveau can be traced not only to the teachings of English design reformers like John Ruskin and William Morris but also to the decorative flat patterns of Oriental designs and stylized medieval motifs that appealed to the eclectic, exotic tastes of the late 19th century.

The Art Nouveau style spread throughout Europe. It was seen in France as early as 1875 in the glass of Emile Gallé. Gallé had produced glass in his own distinctive style of Art Nouveau since about 1872. However, the name *Art Nouveau* was not coined until Samuel Bing opened his shop in Paris 23 years later. Gallé best expressed French Art Nouveau—its feminine beauty of flowing line, its motifs of flowers, birds, and insects such as the butterfly and the dragonfly, and its mystical naturalism.

Emile Gallé was born into the trade. His father, Charles Gallé-Riemer, operated a small ceramic factory in Saint Clement near Nancy. As a child Gallé had an obsession for flowers. He studied botany and plant drawing and began to draw designs for his father's pottery. In 1862, at 16, Gallé continued his studies in Weimar, Germany, and then went to the glassworks of Burgum, Schwerer & Co. at Meisenthal in the Saar, for training in the technique of glassmaking. Returning to France in 1870, Gallé worked in his father's factory but left to volunteer in the Franco-Prussian War. After the war, in 1871, Gallé spent some time in London studying in the South Kensington Museum and the Botanical Gardens at Kew. After he returned to Nancy, Gallé set up his small glassmaking studio. He soon began to exhibit his glass in the important salons in Paris.

Gallé was the founder of L'Ecole de Nancy, a cooperative organization for the production of the decorative arts of the city. Among its members were architects, painters, sculptors, cabinetmakers, and decorators. The group included Victor Prouvé, artist; Camille Martin, bookbinder; Jacques Gruber and Antonin Daum, glassmakers; and

Louis Majorelle and Eugene Vallin, cabinetmakers. Majorelle was an important member of L'Ecole de Nancy and in this way he came into close association with and under the influence of Gallé.

About 1885 Gallé became interested in furniture, leading to establishment of a cabinetmaking shop in his factory. Gallé himself was not a woodworker, but he gathered a group of carpenters, woodcarvers, cabinetmakers, and inlayers to produce the furniture. Although many pieces were made from designs Gallé initiated, the mass production was carried out by his workmen. However, Gallé soon learned the skills of woodworking from them and he often signed himself "Menuisier—ébéniste, céramiste-verrier." The made-to-order pieces were creations of his artist collaborators and himself. The most important artists who worked with Gallé were Victor Prouvé and Louis Hestaux, who often executed carving. A. Herbst, Paul Olderback, and Dubois, expert craftsmen, worked with Gallé on such pieces as the desk "La Forêt Lorraine." Louis Majorelle may have made the metalwork on the furniture, such as bronze key plates, but Gallé soon learned the techniques of metalworking. A sketch of a key lock for a table illustrated in *Revue des Arts Décoratifs* has the credit line "Dessin et fabrication d'Emile Gallé."

In 1889 Gallé first exhibited furniture at the Exposition Universelle in Paris. The pieces included the ponderous cabinet of bog oak "Le Chêne" and the huge table "Je Tiens au Coeur de France," both in the style of the French Renaissance with heavy moldings, pediments, and bases. The cabinet had panels of sculptured human figures after designs of Victor Prouvé, and the table had a stretcher with sculptured leaves and thistle blossoms carved by Louis Hestaux. Another huge oak cabinet, "La Montagne," also of Renaissance structure, was ornamented with panels of marquetry.

Also in the exhibit was the cabinet "Grand Meuble d'Appui." Its structure was derived from Louis XV style but its panels of marquetry had designs of orchids and exotic insects in Art Nouveau

curves.

Gallé exhibited a group of his furniture in the Exposition Universelle in Paris in 1900. The majority of these pieces were lighter in weight than the ones exhibited 11 years before and were made of walnut and ash. They combined rococo, Louis XV, Louis XVI, and Art Nouveau styles. Some pieces had slender, straight Louis XVI legs. Rococo pieces had curved structural outlines and modified cabriole-type legs with scrolled feet. Rococo also contributed the principle of asymmetry to the furniture, but in Gallé's work this asymmetry also reflects Oriental influence, most evident in small pieces such as occasional tables, vitrines, or *étagères*. The main structural lines of such a piece are often symmetrical, but the shelves are placed in stepped sequence similar to those in Japanese cabinets. Tri-legged gueridons have triangular top shelves with asymmetrically scalloped edges. The structural lines of the furniture were relatively traditional, yet the ornamentation—carving or marquetry—was Art Nouveau and the emphasis was on decoration rather than form.

Gallé believed that the form or structure of a piece of furniture should not be sacrificed to the decoration and that the decoration should not violate the structure, but that both together should form a unit. However, his theories are not often exemplified in his furniture. In the buffet "La Blanche Vigne" vines forming the structure culminate in a cornice of vines on a trellis, and the marquetry in the panels of the buffet depicts landscape scenes. While this buffet is esthetically pleasing, there's no question that the decoration dominates the structure. The huge dragonfly legs on later cabinets and tables also crowd out the structure.

An important characteristic of Gallé's furniture is his use of tree branches in the structure of tables and cabinets. In his article "Le Mobilier Contemporain orne d'après la Nature," in *Revue des Arts Décoratifs*, Gallé illustrates a table leg composed of the branches on the maple tree. On the desk "La Forêt Lorraine," the legs and structure lines are composed of carved

In Majorelle's cabinet above, ca 1904, the general structural outline is quite plain; it flows in simple lines characteristic of Majorelle's later works. Courtesy United Art & Antiques, Beverly Hills, California. Gallé's dessert buffet, opposite, 1901-1902, of walnut. Musée des Arts Decoratifs.

tree branches. But the most striking example of the use of the arboreal motif is seen in the tree branches and vines that cover the larger dresser "Chemins d'Automne." The branch motif fits into Gallé's theories regarding harmony between furniture structure and decoration. He envisions a smoking table that utilizes the various parts of a tobacco plant—stem, flower, and leaves—with marquetry based on spirals of cigarette smoke. Gallé recommended the poppy, which connotes sleep, as a suitable motif for bedroom furniture. The famous bed "Papillons" with the symbolism of dawn and twilight expressed this theory.

Many different woods were employed in the construction and ornamentation of Gallé's furniture. The majority of the woods used in furniture structure were indigenous to Lorraine. These generally were oak, walnut, and ash. Various other woods were used for veneers and marquetry, including native plum, chestnut, ash, sycamore, hemlock, and kingwood. Exotic woods included amaranth, amboyna, harewood, sabicu, and ebony, which composed various tones and colors of the marquetry. Gallé was fascinated by these woods, which provided color, texture, and grain in veneers and marquetry. He made beautiful wavy, *strié*, flecked, burl, and striped tiger effects. Gallé stocked several hundred different varieties of wood in his factory.

The fire screen of carved ash in the Victoria & Albert Museum incorporated several different kinds of wood, as many pieces did. It has oak, sabicu, and zebrawood applied in relief, and marquetry of amboyna and walnut. Its carved leaves and branches, ornamenting both structure and marquetry, carry out Gallé's leaf theme. Another piece—a small worktable of carved ash and walnut with a branched structure—has walnut, amboyna, harewood, and sycamore marquetry. A small commode of carved oak has a marquetry landscape and flowers executed in oak, walnut, maple, sycamore, harewood, and mother-of-pearl.

Gallé began to use marquetry in about 1885, and from then on it became his most important method of decoration. Marquetry was used on tabletops, commode doors, and cabinet and *étagère* panels. Victor Prouvé and Louis Hestaux generally created the marquetry designs.

Decorative motifs and themes on Gallé's furniture are drawn from three sources. Art Nouveau plants and flowers such as the poppy, water lily, and orchid were popular motifs. Flowers were enlarged beyond their natural size and stalks tended to eclipse the flower. Rushes and subterranean flora and weeds were often used as motifs.

From the Japanese came chrysanthemums, irises, butterflies, and dragonflies. Dragonflies were enlarged to form the legs of tables and cabinets. Gallé used a border of dragonflies at the top of a cabinet or around the edge of a tabletop.

But the most representative motifs were the native plants and flowers of Lorraine: the thistle, its emblem; *les ombelles* or cow parsley, which grew in abundance in its woods; the pine, banana leaf, wheat, and grapes. The *ombelle*, Gallé's special favorite, appeared on a bedroom suite and many small tables and cabinets. Another favorite was the poppy or *pavot* and its buds. Poppy buds were carved as finials on chairs and cabinets and in turned colonnade borders, on table and cabinet aprons, and chair stretchers. The leaves of the Lorraine thistle were also carved on table stretchers and legs.

Gallé's ornamentation honored all nature. He recreated forests, fields, flowers, and even fossils and insects. The subjects of marquetry designs were Lorraine's landscapes—fields, rivers, sky, distant horizons, flowers, and fruits. Gallé designed furniture ornamentation with the same subtle symbolism he used on glass. He inscribed religious and philosophical sentences, the verses of poets, and names of personages in Greek mythology. Furniture with marquetry inscriptions were called *meubles parlante*. Many small tables were inscribed with verses. The tea table "A Fleur d'Eau" is inscribed "La musique de l'eau, des feuilles et du ciel," from a verse by Maurice Boucher. The small cabinet "Les Fleurs du Mal" was named after the marquetry

Right: Inlaid cabinet, Majorelle, ca 1900. Walnut and mahogany. The iris marquetry woodland scene in the top panel reflects Gallé's influence. Decorative panels contrast with the simple flowing design and the delicate legs. Note Majorelle's signature, bottom left corner, scratched into the surface in ink. Courtesy Christie, Manson & Woods International Inc., New York. Far right: Vitrine of fruit woods, Gallé, ca 1900. This piece is highlighted by marquetry leaves and stylized carving, though for Gallé, the decoration is simple. Gallé's signature, bottom right, differs from Majorelle's—it is a marquetry inlay. Courtesy Macklowe Gallery, Ltd., New York. Left: *Grand meuble D'appui*, Gallé, 1889. The form of this transitional piece is traditional Louis XV, but the orchids and insects in the marquetry design are typical of the Art Nouveau movement. Courtesy Christie, Manson & Woods International Inc.

"In recreating forests, fields, fossils and insects, Gallé's ornamentation honored nature. Lorraine's landscapes were the subjects of his marquetry designs—its rivers, sky, distant horizons, flowers, and fruits."

Left: Vitrine, Majorelle, ca 1900. Zebra wood. This cabinet of striped wood is decorated with the wrought iron work that Majorelle used—as he also used ormolu—to embellish many of his pieces. Compare the flowing lines of the legs with the articulated legs on Gallé's piece to the right. Courtesy Macklowe Gallery, Ltd. Below: Cabinet, Gallé, ca 1900. The iris motif that dominates the ornamentation of this piece was a particular favorite with Art Nouveau cabinet makers, especially Gallé. The carving on the crest represents *les ombelles* (French for Queen Anne's lace or cow parsley). Gallé's signature appears bottom left. Courtesy Simon Lieberman, New York.

scene on the front panel which was inspired by Baudelaire's poem, the lines of which are in the marquetry. Inscriptions of verses of Symbolist poets like Baudelaire and Victor Hugo expressed exotic themes and induced an esthetic experience beyond that innate in the article of furniture itself. In an essay, "Le Decor Symbolique," Gallé explains the significance of Symbolism in his work.

In addition to large important pieces and bedroom and dining-room ensembles, Gallé produced a great many small occasional tables in imaginative shapes. Some are round and scalloped, others are triangular with star-shaped or kidney-shaped shelves, and some are in the form of *ombelle* blossoms. All these tables were ornamented with marquetry, and the majority of them have legs and stretchers with timbered carvings. These were among the pieces that Gallé produced for the trade. Other commercial pieces included small buffets, commodes, desks, gueridons, *étagères*, bookcases, fire screens, and small accessories such as trays, wastebaskets, and boxes.

Gallé produced great quantities of furniture. In addition to the display room at the Nancy factory, he had one shop in Paris and by 1889 one in Frankfurt, Germany. He opened a shop in London in 1904, the year of his death. After Gallé died, the factory continued to produce and sell furniture as well as glass until it closed in 1935.

Gallé signed his furniture in various ways—always inlaid in the wood, becoming a part of the marquetry design. Gallé was more artist than *ébéniste* (cabinetmaker specializing in veneered furniture), more the creator of ideas than the actual producer. Although he wanted his furniture to be available to the general public, it proved to be too precious and expensive.

Louis Majorelle (1859-1926) was the son of a Nancy cabinetmaker who reproduced antique furniture with lacquer *vernis Martin* (French japanning on wood). As a youth Majorelle showed talent in painting, and at 16 one of his pictures was accepted at the Paris Salon. In 1877 Majorelle entered L'Ecole des Beaux Arts in Paris, where he was a

Gallé created many small occasional tables in imaginative shapes. The water lily is the dominant motif of the table above. Marquetry designs include lilypads and flowers floating on the table top. Fruit woods. Courtesy Macklowe Gallery, Ltd.

pupil of the artist Jean Millet. After his father's death in 1879, Majorelle returned to Nancy and took over his cabinetmaking business, "Majorelle Frères et Cie, Meubles d'Art." At this time the Maison Majorelle included a workshop with 30 men skilled in cabinetmaking, marquetry, and bronze work. There was also a section called *Lunaire*, where metal lamps, lighting fixtures, and mounts for furniture and glass were made.

After a dozen years devoted exclusively to the reproduction of antique furniture, Majorelle began to produce furniture of his own design. In about 1890, through Gallé's influence, Majorelle adopted the Art Nouveau style. In this period the majority of Majorelle's furniture was slender, reminiscent of Louis XV pieces, ornamented with carving and marquetry in naturalistic floral motifs. Large panels of marquetry had scenes of flowers, birds, and landscape. (Victor Prouvé designed the marquetry. It is not certain whether

Majorelle executed it or whether it was done by Louis Hestaux or Camille Gauthier, artists known to have often worked for Majorelle.) Bronze mounts in graceful Art Nouveau curves often added to the surface interest. Many of the cabinets are similar to those of Gallé. His influence is also seen in the motifs Majorelle used in carved decoration such as the poppy head and colonnettes of plant stems and banana leaves.

Many of Majorelle's desks, cabinets, and *étagères* with marquetry and asymmetrical shelves are also similar to Gallé's. However, although Majorelle used naturalistic marquetry and occasionally used arboreal forms in the structure of his furniture, he usually emphasized fine proportion and elegance of line. And in this emphasis, Majorelle differed from Gallé. In both theory and practice he considered structure and proportion more important than ornament. The carving on Majorelle's furniture was naturalistic, but much of his furniture at this time

fied and used in a new way. From this time on Majorelle abandoned marquetry in favor of metal mounts and surfaces of dark, polished woods. There were exceptions. In the Salon of 1907 he exhibited a cabinet with carved roses and panels of marquetry decorated with climbing roses.

Some of Majorelle's chairs have rectangular backs with marquetry or upholstery panels. There is often a top crest of carving on the chairs. A carved walnut armchair now in the Victoria & Albert Museum has an open back—curves which form an interlacing pattern at the top. Characteristic of Majorelle desks and tables is the splayed leg with shaped feet and front legs dividing to form supports for the overhanging kidney-shaped extension. This flying-buttress support is also seen on legs of small gueridons or occasional tables. Other legs are reeded or twisted in beautiful flowing lines.

Majorelle made heavy furniture from about 1910 to 1914. In this period, furniture legs became massive, ending in huge elephantine club feet. The structure of these pieces is bound by heavy, curved moldings, although some are accented by carving. He made many sets of furniture at this time. After World War I his furniture became simple and sober with little ornament. Majorelle's attempts at Art Deco were not successful.

Majorelle's interest in metalwork was not confined to the bronze ornaments on his furniture. He also produced wrought iron and exhibited iron stair railings, lamps, and stands for vases at various Paris salons in early 1900. The stair rail in the Hotel du Secrétariat of the Faculté de Medicine at Nancy and the grand stairway for Galeries Lafayette (and its stair rail now in the Paris Musée des Arts Décoratifs) are examples of some of the finest ironwork of the era. Majorelle also produced iron and bronze lamps as well as mounts for lamps and vases by Gallé, Daum, and other Nancy glassmakers.

The Maison Majorelle was a large factory. It did an extensive business which was carried on in shops throughout France. In addition to the shop and

was of acajou and this was not as easy to carve as the soft woods Gallé chose.

Majorelle sought new forms and tried to liberate his furniture from traditional influences. At the Paris Exposition Universelle in 1900, he exhibited a cabinet of palisander and acajou with bronze mounts of *nénuphars* (water lilies) which attracted the judges' attention. For this piece, Majorelle was awarded the Légion d'Honneur, and from then on he became a well-known figure in the decorative arts world. Majorelle was invited to serve on juries of important exhibitions and he soon opened a Paris shop. This marked the beginning of his best period, which extended from around 1902 to 1906. He designed desks, tables, and bedroom suites with bronzes of the *nénuphar* and orchid motifs. These characteristic motifs were tantamount to his labels. A bedroom ensemble of mahogany and palisander ornamented with *nénuphar* bronzes was made for the German emperor Wilhelm. The ormolu mounts were placed on cabinet doors, at knees, and on feet. They often extend the full length of a leg or along the side of a cabinet. While the lines of this furniture were reminiscent of the Louis XV period, the pieces were marked with Majorelle's originality. The serpentine front and the cabriole leg were modi-

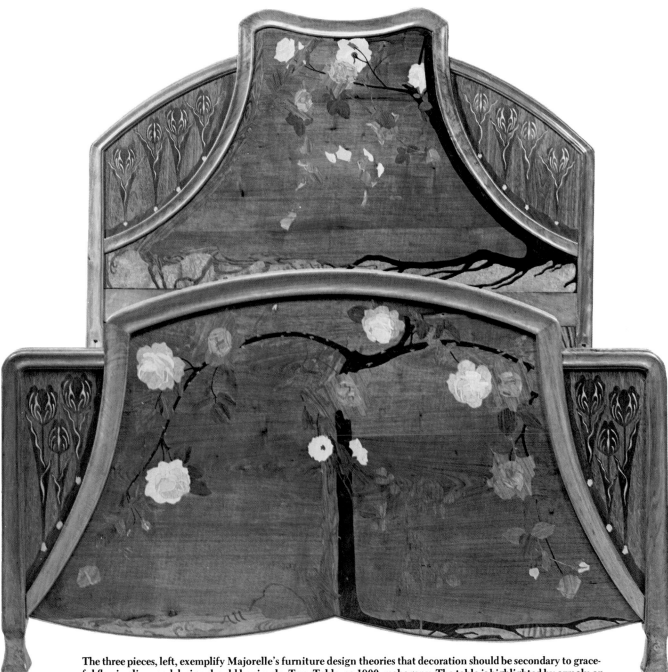

The three pieces, left, exemplify Majorelle's furniture design theories that decoration should be secondary to graceful flowing lines and design should be simple. Top: Table, ca 1900, mahogany. The table is highlighted by ormolu on feet and legs. The flying buttress line, on the right side, is purely decorative. Secretary, ca 1900, of various fruit woods. The marquetry panel opens into a writing surface. Mahogany chair, ca 1900. All: Courtesy Macklowe Gallery, Ltd. Above: Bed, Majorelle, ca 1899. Quite decorative for Majorelle, the backboard is inlaid with roses and falling petals. Courtesy Sotheby Parke Bernet Inc., New York.

factory in Nancy, Majorelle had a shop in Paris before 1900. He also had shops in Cannes and in Contrexeville, Voges. Majorelle was also an interior decorator, decorating the Café de Paris in 1898. Two years later he decorated the tearoom in Les Magasins Réunis, Nancy. Majorelle died in 1926, but his firm, in collaboration with the decorator Remon, decorated the apartment of the commandant of the *Normandie* in 1935.

In addition to Majorelle's personal creations, which were always expensive, the Maison Majorelle produced many small, less expensive articles of furniture such as tables, vitrines, ladies' desks, fire screens, and nests of tables and trays.

Majorelle signed much of his furniture "L. Majorelle, Nancy," scratched in the wood in paint or ink. He seldom signed in the marquetry design. The iron and bronze decorations are also signed, usually with the initials "L.M."

Majorelle was an accomplished cabinetmaker. Although trained in the traditional school, he acquired a mastery of new forms. His finest work ranks among the top achievements of French Art Nouveau furniture and he also occupies an important place in the history of furniture. Majorelle's best pieces have an undulating, dynamic flow of line. Of strong solid construction, they are set on firm bases. In contrast to Gallé's elegant decorative style, Majorelle's furniture forms are functional. ■

American Art Nouveau Furniture

Elaborate Art Nouveau furniture that gained popularity in turn-of-the-century Europe was successfully translated for an American audience by such firms as Karpen Bros. and the Tobey Company. But French-influenced forms were soon lost in sweeping enthusiasm for simpler mission styles.

BY BETTY TELLER

Recently, an upsurge of scholarly and collecting interest in American furniture design of the late 19th and early 20th centuries has been accompanied by a spate of exhibitions and publications documenting the styles, designers, and makers of this period. American Art Nouveau furniture, however, has attracted scant attention because relatively few pieces were made and even fewer have survived. Nevertheless, close study of American furniture manufacture at the turn of the century reveals that the Art Nouveau style enjoyed a brief vogue among American makers before succumbing to the broader middle-class demand for popular "mission" furniture.

Art Nouveau in France

The Paris Exposition was the main stimulus to American interest in Art Nouveau. Visitors to the 1900 exposition had ample opportunity to discover Art Nouveau at the height of its development. Evidence of the new style was everywhere in Paris—in the decorative railings, lamps, and entrances to the Metro designed by Hector Guimard, in the shops, and especially in Siegfried Bing's *Maison de l'Art Nouveau*—a pavilion on the exposition grounds, designed like a small house and completely decorated with Art Nouveau furnishings.

The term *Art Nouveau* originated as the name of Bing's Paris shop, which specialized in unique, artistic furnishings and artworks in the modern style. By 1900—four years after it opened—the phrase was commonly used to describe the work of individual designers and artists working in Paris and Nancy. Bing, a dealer in Oriental antiquities, was not a designer himself, but he attracted a coterie of artists, including Georges de Feure, Eugene Gaillard, and Eugene Colonna, who designed furniture for the shop. Until it closed in 1902, Bing's shop was the heart of the new design movement in Paris.

At the exposition, Bing's *Maison de l'Art Nouveau* offered a stunning realization of the decorative possibilities of Art Nouveau when applied to a complete environment. The dining room by Gaillard, the salon by Colonna, and the boudoir by de Feure each presented a total design concept. The *Maison* impressed visitors accustomed to unimaginatively arranged displays of individual pieces of furniture. Other fair buildings besides Bing's pavilion housed examples of the new style as well.

Many Americans in the furniture industry visited the exposition and returned home greatly affected by its splendors. During the summer of 1900, American furniture trade papers ran articles discussing the exposition and the new furniture displayed there. Almost overnight, the term *Art Nouveau* entered the American vocabulary.

But few Americans could define Art Nouveau precisely, and even today it is difficult to produce a workable definition. Art Nouveau was more a philosophy than a style—an attempt to create something entirely new and modern. Japanese art, rococo design, the English Arts and Crafts movement, and the

Gothic revival all influenced the Art Nouveau movement. Nature's motifs—stems, leaves, and flowers, both naturalistic and stylized—were perhaps the most important element. In some cases Art Nouveau designs were plastic and deeply dimensional; others had only surface ornament. National and personal temperaments affected the pieces produced: Austrian and Scottish versions of the style stressed geometric and stylized forms; Dutch works revealed the influence of Indonesian batiks; French works luxuriated in rich, sensual materials and craftsmanship.

American furniture manufacturers, unlike their Scottish or Viennese counterparts, were outsiders looking upon all the various manifestations of Art Nouveau. They did their best to define a style for their customers, but they never succeeded in articulating a successful and distinctive American variant. Although many American furniture makers trained in Europe and kept a watchful eye on European developments, their products show only passing enthusiasm for the style. Art Nouveau furniture produced in this country was a mass-manufactured, highly commercial product for the most part.

American demand grows

Press coverage of the Paris fair generated a wave of interest in the new art. Photographs of most of the furnishings in Bing's pavilion appeared in American magazines in 1900 and 1901, and manufacturers sensed a market for pieces in the French style. New York furniture trade papers began illustrating examples of American Art Nouveau. In November 1900, for example, *The American Cabinet Maker and Upholsterer* showed a mahogany chair with marquetry flower designs inlaid in its back and twisted carved legs, in the Philadelphia firm of Bodenstein and Kuemmerle. They called it "the newest fad" and commented, "It is styled as 'Art Nouveau' goods and the Paris Exposition is responsible for it being made in this country."

New furniture lines were displayed twice yearly, in January and July, at large exhibitions open only to dealers in

The Paris Exposition of 1900 introduced a new style of decorative art to the world. American manufacturers capitalized on the sudden popularity of Art Nouveau furniture, generally standardizing French motifs into simple, easily-identified designs. The mahogany side chair opposite, ca 1900, exemplifies this restrained interpretation of the French Art Nouveau style: the asymmetrical whiplash pattern tooled into the leather seat and the pierced foliate splat are modified versions of fluid and undulating Paris designs. Geoffrey N. Bradfield Collection; photo Mysak/Studio Nine. Above: This mahogany curio cabinet made by George C. Flint & Co. of Chicago ca 1910 is a simplified imitation of a Louis Majorelle piece. The Metropolitan Museum of Art, Edgar J. Kaufmann Charitable Foundation.

New York, Chicago, and Grand Rapids. In the January 1901 exhibition a few Art Nouveau pieces appeared in several manufacturers' lines. While no business risked more than a few items in the new "novelty" style, most manufacturers made at least a bow to the new designs.

Parlor suites, chairs, and odd pieces in imitation of the French were offered by these New York City firms: S. G. Estabrook, Palmer and Embury, C. H. Medicus & Sons, and the Schrenkeisen Company. F. H. Conant's Sons of Camden, New Jersey, H. M. Strausman and Company of Rochester, New York, and the Phelps-Vogler Company of Cambridge, Massachusetts, were other Eastern manufacturers who attempted the new style, while S. Karpen Bros. of Chicago and the Indianapolis Chair Manufacturing Company—large Midwestern makers—also showed a few pieces.

Structure and ornament

Perhaps because of the general confusion about the elements of the so-called Art Nouveau style, accuracy of design became a major selling point. As more and more manufacturers unveiled their lines in 1901, advertisements began to stress the "correctness" of their particular interpretation of Art Nouveau— that is, how closely their pieces resembled those designed in Paris. Advertisements lauded the "strict accuracy" of the designs offered. Pieces were said to be "correct" in finish and fabrics as well as in design. More often than not, however, the "correct" carving, fabric, and finish were merely superimposed upon the ponderous golden oak, mahogany, or walnut upholstered sofas, davenports, and armchairs already popular in America. On such pieces, basic form remained unchanged and did not often relate to the "new" surface decoration. (In general, side chairs and tables were more unified in total design than were upholstered pieces.)

Certain types of motifs were always "correct," no matter how awkward their execution. American designers tended to standardize Art Nouveau motifs into a simple vocabulary the public could understand and readily identify. Women with flowing hair and clinging garments, tulips, lilies, and undulating, twisting, stem-like lines already symbolized the modern style in graphics and were easily adapted by furniture designers. Realistic carving of vegetation of all types was also recognized as "Art Nouveau."

The structural forms of Art Nouveau were more difficult to standardize. Although the Art Nouveau movement in France was attempting to create a totally new style, many French designs derived their basic forms from the rococo Louis XV and more delicate Louis XVI styles. It is not surprising that American designers followed this lead and grafted Art Nouveau decoration onto forms that reflected the popular revival styles of the day.

Traditional French styles strongly influenced the design of high-grade American furniture in the 1890s. Re-

Left: Mahogany side chair, made by the Heywood-Wakefield Co. of Baltimore, ca 1900-1910. On French pieces, free-flowing forms often defined structure. In contrast, the Art Nouveau design on this mass-produced and medium-priced American chair is typically confined to a decorative element on the splat. Cal Schumann Collection; photo courtesy the Baltimore Museum of Art.

production designs dominated the market. Designers were accustomed to mixing and matching periods using an eclectic vocabulary of revival elements. Accordingly, Art Nouveau decoration showed up in some surprising places—inlaid in the tall Swiss-style back of a chair with Duncan Phyfe arms, or carved on the crest of an upholstered patent rocker. In structural form, American Art Nouveau furniture more often resembled the reproduction pieces of the 1890s than the Louis XV prototypes of French Art Nouveau.

Two American interpretations

Two distinct categories of Art Nouveau furniture emerged in America. One emphasized carving; the other, marquetry. Both were derived from French designs, which had often successfully employed both elements together.

Some of the most interesting French pieces expressed their organic motifs in fully realized sculptural carving, where the chair or table seemed to be rooted, plantlike, in the floor. A few American pieces imitated this sculptural style, but for the most part Americans relegated carving to a purely decorative role.

Carving on American pieces was often sculpted in deep relief, though not used to define a structural element, as it often had been in France. Samuel Karpen, senior partner of S. Karpen Bros., Chicago, reported on the French method of carving he'd observed at the exposition: "One thing, entirely new and unknown here [in the U.S.] is a style of carving that is beautiful. There are no sharp finishes, such as we are familiar with; that is to say, the carving or design sweeps off into the wood without even the slightest suggestion of a line to denote where the effect begins or ends." The Art Nouveau productions of S. Karpen Bros. featured deep-relief

Right: Charles Rohlfs utilized the curvilinear French idiom to create his handcrafted, one-of-a-kind pieces. This oak side chair, ca 1898, is considerably more opulent and closer to its European counterparts than the mass-produced examples of American Art Nouveau furniture. The Art Museum of Princeton University, Princeton, New Jersey; gift of Roland Rohlfs.

carvings of women in clinging robes with flowing tresses in this new, sculptural style. Karpen's 1901 catalogue boasted of a heavily upholstered parlor suite: "The fine relief carvings are a triumph of the artist's skill in wood craft; all of the carvings originally modeled in clay by our special artist and sculptor." Karpen was not the only manufacturer emphasizing carving of this type. The Tobey Company of Chicago advertised pieces in 1901 with "incut carving after the Nancy method." Several other manufacturers also showed carved designs.

A second major group of American Art Nouveau furniture designs employed marquetry. Some of the finest French designs by Emile Gallé included delicate inlays of natural woods. In America, plant and flower motifs were inlaid on pieces whose forms might not otherwise suggest Art Nouveau. Because such marquetry work was usually purchased ready-made from firms specializing in its manufacture, the design of the inlay was sometimes unrelated to the piece on which it was used. The quality of marquetry varied greatly. High-quality marquetry might be inlaid on a poorly made chair, or low-grade marquetry used on an otherwise well-made piece.

Inlays were also imported from France, causing confusion today as to the origin of pieces. Some New York

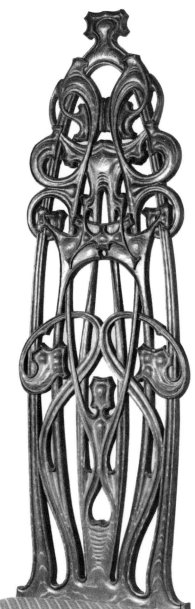

marquetry makers came from France; their work is nearly indistinguishable from that made in France.

Marquetry was used most often on side chairs and tables, although it had wide decorative applications. For example, a March 1901 issue of the *American Cabinet Maker and Upholsterer* reported that several piano makers had recently ordered marquetry *à l'Art Nouveau* for case decoration.

American versus French

Whether carved or inlaid, American pieces were generally heavier than the French prototypes. They often differed from the French in the choice of materials, colorings, finishes, fabrics, and craftsmanship. Whereas American manufacturers needed to control costs to keep prices competitive with other makers of high-grade furniture, designers of the best French pieces supervised every aspect of their designs, cutting no corners. Their creations were expensive handmade works of art, each unique. Most American Art Nouveau furniture, in contrast, was designed for limited mass production. The extensive hand carving on many of the pieces made them expensive, but the fact that relatively few examples seem to have been produced reflects a shortage of buyers rather than problems in manufacture. The limited American market for Art Nouveau furniture, along with cost and labor considerations of the mass manufacturers, clearly affected the American designs.

A major tenet of the French school was beauty and suitability of materials. The French artists stressed unusual natural materials in their work. Pieces on display at Bing's shop were constructed of walnut, ash, sycamore, lemonwood, orange, boxwood, maple, cherry, and oak as well as mahogany. Inlays were of rare woods in exquisite natural colors.

American manufacturers selected more prosaic woods. Although trade papers exclaimed over the beauty of the French woods with their matte finishes, the choice of materials used for American furniture remained limited. Mahogany was preferred for high-grade furniture in this country, and the

expensive carved pieces advertised were almost exclusively of this wood. Less expensive pieces were made of cheaper mahogany, finished hardwoods, and occasionally of oak.

While the French usually relied on natural wood tones to provide color contrast, American manufacturers sometimes used stains to provide variation. Stains were justified on the grounds that nature was prodigal in the use of color; therefore, adding color to complete the harmony of the work was permissible. Painted and pyrographed (wood-burned) floral designs, as well as decals, were also applied to American Art Nouveau furniture.

American manufacturers followed the French lead in abandoning high-gloss polishes on much of their furniture. The use of low-gloss wax finishes on all types of furniture became widespread during the first decade of this century. Numerous advertisements refer to the wax finish or satinlike surface of the Art Nouveau pieces.

Gilt and fabric

Americans also copied the French use of gilt. A boudoir suite exhibited by de Feure at the Paris Exposition was beautifully covered with gold leaf. This suite was illustrated in American publications, and gilding was endorsed as an important part of the Art Nouveau style here. Karpen Bros. offered its 1901 parlor suite in a choice of solid mahogany ($450) or genuine gold leaf ($620). Its relatively high cost may have kept gilding from widespread popularity.

Many American Art Nouveau pieces were upholstered, and fabrics played an important role in furniture design. European fabrics were imported in quantity and copied by American textile manufacturers so that many appropriate designs were available. The wilder, undulating designs were not popular, however. Favored fabrics often had strict symmetry and tightly controlled curves. Leather embossed in Art Nouveau patterns was also used as a chair covering. But American furniture manufacturers did not attempt to control other elements of the interior en-

Genuine Gold Leaf, covered in Grade Nos.

	150	200	250
Sofa	$310.00	$335.00	$360.00
Arm chair	250.00	265.00	280.00
Side chair	190.00	200.00	210.00
Total	$750.00	$800.00	$850.00

vironment—carpeting, draperies, wall coverings, metalwork, architecture—which contributed so much to the effect of French designs at the Paris Exposition.

American design: Strait-laced or sensual?

American Art Nouveau furniture made for mass manufacture cannot be compared to the Art Nouveau furniture of France, which was handcrafted and often one-of-a-kind. America's best-known designers of the time did not produce furniture in the French style. Frank Lloyd Wright and the Greene Brothers, for example, were architects and designers who addressed the total environment. But these men, like most Americans designing handcrafted furniture at the turn of the century, did not work in the French idiom. They rejected the ornate organic French styles in favor of the simpler forms that were more acceptable in this country. Louis Comfort Tiffany, the greatest American Art Nouveau designer, concentrated on the manufacture of glass. His interior design in the 1890s was of Moorish rather than French inspiration.

Turn-of-the-century America experienced a national wave of nostalgia for her pioneer past. The opulent French designs, however new and modern, recalled a history of decadent kings and courtiers. This country was searching for a native style to embody *American* history and myths. Extravagant French designs ultimately were rejected by middle-class Americans, who favored a new, moral style stressing straightforward craftsmanship. Ads for mission furniture used words like *clean, healthy, sturdy, simple,* and *honest.* Art Nouveau, with its aura of decadent sensuality, could scarcely compete. It enjoyed a brief vogue but quickly faded in popularity in the face of mission's rapid advance. In 1903 the *Upholstery Dealer and Decorative Furnisher* reported: "The Mission style has taken this country by storm, and seems to have filled the place in America that is occupied by l'art nouveau in France and the Arts and Crafts in England." ■

Charles F.A.Voysey

Voysey's simple furniture was a precursor to the American mission style. Its graceful, angular lines embodied the ideals of the British Arts and Crafts movement.

BY MARIAN PAGE

Charles Voysey sometimes has been cast as an Art Nouveau designer, sometimes as an Arts and Crafts designer, sometimes as a forerunner of the modern movement. But the difficulty in finding a proper niche for him lies in the indisputable fact that Voysey was preeminently himself. He didn't like Art Nouveau, which he called "a distinctly healthy development, but at the same time the manifestation of it is distinctly unhealthy and revolting." And he was strong in his denunciation of the modern movement. His furniture no less than his architecture is a highly personal interpretation, notwithstanding its decidedly English flavor.

If anything, Voysey's furniture has something of the spare beauty of Shaker furniture. It is characterized by the same kind of sobriety—simple in form, beautifully proportioned, and carefully made. There is, moreover, an uncommon harmony between Voysey architecture and furniture that is akin to the harmony of Shaker architecture and artifacts. This is not altogether surprising when one realizes that spiritual values run through all Voysey's work just as they do through Shaker designs.

In fact, the 82-year-old Voysey remarked to Nikolaus Pevsner in 1939 that "this new architecture cannot last. The architects have no religion. They have nothing exalted which they could try to approach; they are like designers who draw flowers and trees without remembering and honouring Him who created them."

Moreover, while Voysey appreciated William Morris's craftsmanship, he considered the man "too much of an atheist." Voysey respected plainness and soundness as the Shakers did. It isn't important that the Shakers were antiesthetic in their attitude toward art and Voysey was not. To Voysey esthetic and moral values were inseparable. Both the English architect and the American Shakers apparently came

Around 1907, The Essex and Suffolk Equitable Insurance Company commissioned Voysey to do their interiors and furniture, including the oak chair on the page opposite, which bears the company's initials. The Victoria and Albert Museum, London. Inset: Dining chair (1902–1905) with characteristic legs chamfered from a square top to octagonal feet. A recurrent motif is the pierced heart in the back splat. Royal Pavilion, Art Gallery and Museums, Brighton, England. *Moorcrag*, Gilhead on Lake Windermere, England, designed by Voysey. Photographs by Duncan McNeil, Sussex.

Despite his ardent individuality, Voysey worked within the general context of the Arts and Crafts Movement, utilizing simple shapes and forms and sharing the movement's respect for good craftsmanship. He himself was not a craftsman, but a designer. Above: Voysey designed this clock for himself in 1895, oil-painting its stylized landscape. Courtesy John Jesse Esq., London. The desk, below, is gracefully ornamented with functional brass strap hinges pierced with a pastoral scene. The Victoria and Albert Museum.

close to discovering what Voysey called "the true laws which govern fitness and beauty," even if it was a conscious search on Voysey's part and unconscious for the Shakers. In any case a belief in spiritual things seems to have wrought similar results.

It is also worth remembering, as Janet Malcolm explains it in the catalogue of the Shaker exhibition held at the Renwick Gallery in 1973–74, that when the Shakers spoke of "separation from 'the world,'" they meant the world of the cultivated tradition—of Victorian ornament, academic painting, and aristocratic manners." Voysey meant something similar when he wrote in *The Craftsman* in 1912: "A nation produces the architecture it deserves, and if in the main it is materialistic and sordid, we shall find all material qualities considered first and the moral and spiritual ones scarcely at all. Greed will crush out generosity and shams will smother poetry and sentiment." We should not labor the comparison too far, however, but be reminded of what Voysey once told an audience in Manchester: "Theories are so satisfying and yet so unsatisfactory in practice. I am more and more impressed by the difficulty, nay sin, of trying to dogmatize about matters of art."

True originality

Voysey came by his spiritualism and his individualism naturally. His father was a parson who was excommunicated from the Church of England for refusing to believe in the doctrine of everlasting Hell, and his beliefs had an important influence on the young Voysey. Of course the Shakers were also rebels against established faiths, and their individuality had its base in that rebellion just as Voysey's did. But Voysey would not have used the word *rebellion*. He described "true originality" as "having been for all time, the spiritual something given to the development of traditional forms by the individual artist." If the Shakers thought about such things at all, they surely would have agreed. "His work is *true*," as Voysey's contemporary M. H. Baillie-Scott put it. "One may imagine that he has re-

solved that it shall at least be that, leaving the rest on the knees of the gods. To such resolves the gods are gracious, for the best qualities of a building are those which are unconsciously obtained."

Voysey was born in 1857 in Yorkshire and, since he did not show any scholarly leanings, he was apprenticed to the architect J. P. Seddon, who was a friend of Morris and his group. He later joined the architect George Devey and around 1882 set up his own practice. Architectural commissions didn't come in immediately, so he designed some wallpapers and fabrics that proved highly successful both in England and on the Continent. Around 1888 he began to receive architectural commissions, mostly from middle-class people of simple but artistic taste and consciously "progressive" inclinations who wanted a house in the country. Some of his early clients, in fact, were Quakers who, he said, encouraged his pursuit of simplicity.

Voysey's influence quickly gained momentum, especially among the avant-garde, and by 1896 *The Studio* pointed out that a "Voysey wallpaper" sounded almost as familiar as a "Morris chintz" or a "Liberty silk." But the writer adds: "Mr. Voysey is an architect first and foremost. Like a few of the younger members of his profession, he is not only attracted by the possibilities of beauty in furniture and other complete, independent objects, but he is peculiarly fecund in the invention of patterns." As for his furniture, the writer thought it deserved

elaborate and patient study, for its one aim is "proportion, proportion, proportion," and that is a quality most elusive and difficult even to appreciate, much less to achieve. Even the most sanguine believer in the advance of taste must recognize that the classic restraint which marks Mr. Voysey's furniture could not hope at present to find a fit environment in every house awaiting its reception. But with its plain surfaces of wood, often enough stained green—with oil colour rubbed well in—its simple mouldings and its decoration (if any) confined to certain structural features—these show elements of a new style, which may possibly be the germ of the coming Revival of Classic Art which those who study the evolution of taste most deeply agree is not far off.

Admired on both sides of the Atlantic

Voysey's work was understood and appreciated by many of the art-minded in his own country. And in spite of, or perhaps because of, its distinct Englishness when it began to appear in the widely read *Studio*, it was quickly admired by designers on both sides of the Atlantic. It not only impressed such architects as Charles Rennie Mackintosh and the Glasgow group in Scotland, but it also seems to have been noticed by Frank Lloyd Wright and the prairie school architects in America. Moreover, it probably was largely Voysey's work that inspired the German government to attach the writer Hermann Muthesius to the German embassy in London in 1896 to study and report on the new domestic design in England. That study resulted in the three-volume book, *Das Englische Haus*, in which Voysey's work was prominently illustrated. In fact, so extensive was Voysey's influence that Walter Crane wondered in the *Journal of Decorative Art* in 1901 if there might not be danger of oak or green-stained furniture and white-washed walls becoming the outward sign of an inward spiritual grace "when perhaps they are only a fashion."

Voysey designed much of his best furniture between 1895 and 1910, when his influence was at its height. While it may not have been influential among the rank and file who were intent upon furnishing their houses with all the extracurricular clutter of the typical Victorian drawing room, what Voysey called "the tawdry pretentiousness of the bulk of modern furniture," it was clearly admired by the avant-garde.

In his autobiography, *Doubles Lives* (1943), William Plomer recalls two houses he visited as a child built by "that remarkable architect Voysey" which, he felt, combined more than a suggestion of the Pre-Raphaelite tradition of the style moderne or Art Nouveau, "with even more advanced and enlightened ideas both in their construction and decoration."

One of these houses, although not identified by name, was undoubtedly Garden Corner on the Chelsea Embankment in London, designed for E. J. Horniman in 1906–07 with "features

In 1905 and 1906 Voysey was both architect and interior designer of C.T. Burke's home, "Hollymount," near Beaconsfield, England. The whitewashed walls, plain rug, and general simplicity of the living room, below, suit Voysey's familiar oak chairs and tables. Architectural Drawing Collection, Art Museum, University of California, Santa Barbara.

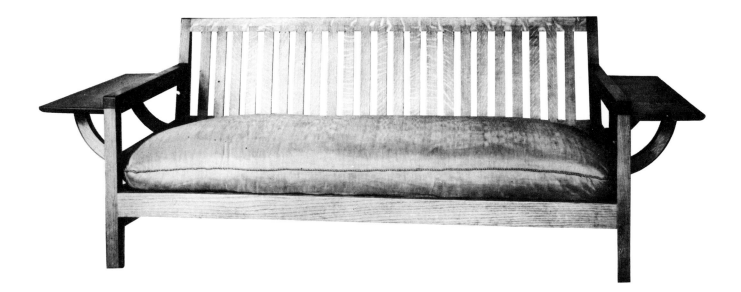

which would have impressed even an unobservant child (which I was not)." Those features included bathrooms lined with blue-green tiles, unstained oak paneling with "synchronized electric clocks let into it here and there," and lofty fireplaces, one of them ornamented with a wide expanse of plain gold mosaic.

The second house was Lowicks, built by Voysey in 1894 in Surrey, also for E. J. Horniman, and described by Plomer as

> equally beguiling and even more idiosyncratic, partly because everything was very high or very low. The roof, for instance, came down steeply almost to the ground; the casement windows were wide and low, and the window seats very low; but the latches on the doors were very high, and to open them one had to make a gesture like that of proposing a toast; straight and very high were the backs of the chairs which, like those in Chelsea, were pierced with heart-shaped openings. . . . It was still, this house, the last word, or at any rate the last but one, in modern taste and comfort.

Architectural historian David Gebhard has singled out the interior of Lowicks as a place where one can "sense Voysey's meticulous and loving care, ranging from built-in cabinets and storage areas to venting grills with their patterns of cutout birds and trees."

Unlike the Morris group and others of Arts and Crafts persuasion, Voysey designed furniture, but did not make it.

He recognized that "the human quality in familiar objects has in many cases been driven out by the machine. Nevertheless the machine has come to liberate man's mind for more intellectual work . . . ," he wrote in *Ideas and Things* (1909). Voysey supplied manufacturers with his designs whether they were to be carried out by hand or machine. He did this, moreover, before Frank Lloyd Wright delivered his famous 1901 speech "The Art and Craft of the Machine." And here again Voysey can be compared to the Shakers, who, it has truthfully been said, certainly would have used today's power tools if they had been available, and the results probably would have been even more craftsmanly.

Voysey seems to have been one of the first to show that the machine and ugliness need not be synonymous. "Ugliness," he believed, "was to be avoided as a form of sin."

The heart motif

Voysey was also unlike most Arts and Crafts designers, as Gebhard has noted, in that "his forms tend to be more traditional (vernacular); the individual components are much more delicate and refined. . . . He lightened his furniture by cutouts—usually of course using the motif of the heart—by elongating the vertical pieces, by narrowing the upright members at top and bottom, and by using hardware with cutout designs

as a surface pattern to enrich the object." That the heart was a particularly favored Voysey motif can't be missed by anyone who knows his work. Voysey, like his father, followed Emerson's doctrine that the goodness of God is visible in all things, and that concept, according to Alan Johnson in his review of the 1978 Voysey exhibition at the Royal Pavilion in Brighton (*Architectural Review*, July 1978), did much to explain his use of the heart motif in his designs, "for he regarded it as a means of transmitting virtue."

In a perceptive essay in the catalogue of the Brighton exhibition, Duncan Simpson points to other idiosyncrasies of Voysey's furniture, including his emphasis on supports. Corner supports or legs, as he says, invariably are carried above their necessary height, emphasizing their function. They are further emphasized by wooden capping pieces or finial-like elements that do not interfere with function. One can see in this, explains Simpson, "a working-out of Voysey's design ideal." Voysey spoke of the importance of "horizontalism" as suggestive of and creating a sense of repose, and for this reason, Simpson believes Voysey made his rooms broad and low. Any form of angularity, Simpson theorizes, suggests "opposite qualities of vigour or movement; so in his furniture designs Voysey played with these qualities, accentuating height by extending and attenuat-

Voysey's credo, "To be simple is the end, not the beginning of design," is exemplified in the 1906 oak settee, opposite page. The architect used it in several houses, including *Garden Court*, illustrated below. Strikingly clean lines distinguish the staircase hall in this Chelsea, London, home. Both Architectural Drawing Collection, Art Museum, University of California, Santa Barbara. Voysey's architecture harmonizes well with the simplicity of his furniture designs. The two chairs with the pierced heart in the back splat are identical to the one illustrated at the beginning of this article. Above: A Voysey oak dresser with typical strap hinges, ca 1898-1900. Royal Pavilion, Art Gallery and Museums, Brighton, England.

ing vertical members and breadth by such recurrent devices as the long strap hinge or moulded cornices."

But, Simpson concludes, "the effect, when one looks at the actual pieces of furniture, is really one created, not by Voysey's notions of design but by his sense, a very acute sense, of form and proportion." That, too, explains why he saw furniture less as individual pieces than as an integral part of his architecture.

Voysey's own ideas about furniture as set forth in the *Journal of the Royal Institute of British Architects* (1894) tend to support Simpson's theory that it was really his acute sense of form and proportion rather than his "notions of design" that was responsible for his furniture:

> Let every man judge furniture from the point of view of reason. Let us ask, Is it fit and thoroughly suited to the purpose for which it is intended? . . . And from the point of view of conscience ask, Is it true—is it all it pretends to be? Does it express qualities and feeling consistent with its owner and its surroundings? Is it faithful work? And for love's sake ask, Is it proportioned, coloured, and disposed as the natural beauties in creation? Are its lines and masses graceful and pleasing? Do any of its parts quarrel? Does it express sobriety, restraint, and purity? From the emotional point of view there are countless questions to ask: What are the associations which attract or repel me from this thing? Surely association is often the strongest force in governing taste, because reason and conscience are not cultivated and equally applied.

Keynote: simplicity

In the final analysis simplicity is the keynote of Voysey's furniture and everything he designed, and simplicity, as he himself said in his Manchester lecture in the 1890s, "requires perfection in all its details, while elaboration is easy in comparison with it." That too is what the Shakers discovered whether consciously or not. Simplicity was also the keynote of the man. Writing about his work in *The Studio* in 1897, the author thought it "only bare justice to record the fact that Mr. Voysey's simplicity of manner, his aim to use honest materials in a straightforward way, his occasional touches of humour, such as appear even in his most important

works—all these are the open expression of the man as well as of the architect."

Many were impressed by the simplicity and individuality of his clothes. Even his coat was "made without a lapel because it is a needless appendage," in the words of John Betjeman. "Everything he wore, owned or used, seemed to have been made to his own design by a craftsman," is the way he is recalled in *The Simpsons of Kendal, Craftsmen in Wood*, a recent monograph by Eleanor Davidson about the woodcarver and furniture maker A. W. Simpson, for whom Voysey designed a house in 1909. Voysey's individuality also was recognized in *The Craftsman*, August 1911, where the author states that, unlike other architects who express the tastes and ideas of the owners in the furniture and interiors they design, "Mr. Voysey is more apt to express his own highly cultured and original ideas, both as artist and artisan." The writer goes on to say that "although Mr. Voysey's style is essentially personal, recognizably so, it is also preeminently modern in spirit, so that his furnishings achieve complete harmony in the new English country house for which they are designed." Voysey's ideals, he adds, "are for rich and substantial interiors, but closely related to the modern idea of the people for whom he builds and designs. He plans his rooms for sitting rooms instead of great halls, for libraries where the young folks gather instead of a vast dais for haughty royalty, and the result is intimate rather than pompous."

Perhaps the intimacy and unpretentiousness his work invokes—combined with its fine proportions—makes Voysey's furniture, like Shaker furniture, still so pertinent today. The simple almost self-effacing grace of a Voysey chair is as appropriate as a Shaker chair in today's interiors—whereas a Frank Lloyd Wright chair may seem aggressive or cumbersome, even dated. It would be too easy to conclude that spiritual beliefs can be a significant component of furniture design, as well as of the other arts, but the work of Voysey and the Shakers does give us reason to speculate. ∎

Chicago Furniture

C*hicago furniture designs ranged from Renaissance Revival to modern Gothic to Prairie School, paralleling the city's most famous architecture. From 1870 to 1890 more furniture was made there than anywhere else in America.*

BY DAVID HANKS

After the Civil War, the furniture industry of the Midwest finally began to compete with the older, more established East. Philadelphia, Boston, and New York—leading 18th-century furniture centers—continued to be the most important for most of the 19th century. But Grand Rapids, Cincinnati, and then Chicago became serious rivals.

Chicago's skyline was changing in the late 19th century. And so was the look of the Chicago suburbs. With the new domestic architecture of Oak Park and other bedroom communities came

furniture to complement it. Old furniture styles were no longer suitable. The city's thriving furniture industry provided the technological and manufacturing skills necessary to support changing tastes.

Between 1870 and 1890, Chicago jumped from sixth to first place in total net furniture production. Although the great fire of 1871 destroyed many manufacturing companies, economic revival in the following decade revitalized the furniture industry. According to A. T. Andreas in *History of Chicago* (1866), this city led the world in the production of parlor furniture. Annual sales of upholstered goods and frames equaled New York, Boston, and Cincinnati's combined.

Furniture was Chicago's fourth largest industry, exceeded only by meat packing, clothing manufacturing, and iron and steel forging. The furniture business grew because of the city's excellent railroad facilities, rapidly growing population, low-cost labor supply,

and nearby lumber. Wisconsin and Michigan had extensive timber regions where quantities of white pine grew, and the Illinois bottomlands provided black walnut and other woods. Chicago's central geographic position permitted convenient distribution of goods all over the country.

"Modern Gothic" furniture

Chicago furniture of the 1870s was characterized by a variety of eclectic revival styles. Progressive designs of this period were designated "modern Gothic." The design reform movement began in England with the work of Augustus Welby Northmore Pugin, John Ruskin, and others. Christopher Dresser's work was also an important source for modern Gothic. Dresser, one of the most original and influential English designers of the late 19th century, visited Philadelphia in 1876 on the occasion of the Centennial Exhibition. His book *Principles of Decorative Design* set forth rules of constructing furniture copied by Philadelphia and Chicago craftsmen of the 1870s. According to Dresser, wood was to be used in a natural manner, worked with the grain to achieve the greatest strength. Furniture should have "simplicity of structure and truthfulness of construction." These principles characterized Chicago reform furniture.

Modern Gothic furniture borrowed elements from the architectural idiom of the Middle Ages, though it was not a literal revival of medieval furniture styles. A typical modern Gothic piece was rectilinear—in keeping with design reform precepts that furniture should eschew curves. Curves, said the reformers, were constructively weak and contrary to the "nature" of wood. A modern Gothic rectangular bookcase would be decorated with architectural elements such as turned columns or colonnettes, chamfered corners, rounded or pointed arches, tracery, crenellated moldings, and so on. The furniture also might have large strap hinges, incised with decorative designs, that functioned as an integral part of the ornament. Tiles painted with medieval themes were often set into modern Gothic pieces as an added decorative element. Light-colored woods or those with a decorative grain—ash, bird's-eye maple, birch, walnut, or pine—were preferred for modern Gothic, although some pieces were ebonized and decorated with incised foliate or geometric motifs.

A number of other interesting links between England, Philadelphia, and Chicago existed at this time. New ideas advocated by English reform designers and popularized by English architect, interior designer, and writer Charles Locke Eastlake are evident in the furniture designed by Philadelphia architect Frank Furness. Furness in turn influenced architect Louis Henri Sullivan. Sullivan, who had worked for Furness in Philadelphia, moved to Chicago. One root of Sullivan's beautiful, efflorescent architectural motifs is traced to the conventionalized ornament inspired by Furness. (Though Sullivan did not design furniture, he exerted a strong influence on American architectural ornament.) However, much of the furniture of the period adopted form and decoration from the architectural vernacular of the day.

Conventionalized ornament on modern Gothic furniture particularly characterized the style made in Philadephia during this period and has been associated with the shop of Daniel Pabst, a well-known designer and cabinetmaker there. Pabst made a three-piece bedroom suite in this style for his daughter

Late 19th-century furniture designers worked in a variety of styles, reflecting changing popular tastes. Opposite: Oak side chair, ca 1909, George Elmslie. The Art Institute of Chicago. Below, left to right: Wicker rocker, Heywood and Morrill, ca 1885; courtesy Pamela McGinley Scurry. "Modern Gothic" walnut side chair, 1875, by Frank Furness of Philadelphia; Philadelphia Museum of Art. Renaissance revival side chair, Wirts and Scholle, ca 1880; Smithsonian Institution.

Emma in 1878.

A Furness desk made for the Philadelphian's brother Horace Howard Furness in 1875 also typifies this style. The desk for Horace Furness's New York City home may have been made in Philadelphia cabinetmaker Daniel Pabst's shop since Furness's name appeared on his customer list. If this connection proves to be true, the association is key to the evolution of late 19th century furniture design in this country.

Isaac Scott was Furness and Pabst's counterpart in Chicago. Scott also worked in the modern Gothic style. His furniture helps to document the transfer of modern Gothic's reform precepts from England to Chicago via Philadelphia. Born in Manayunk, near Philadelphia, Scott was probably apprenticed in a shop like Pabst's, where he learned designer and expert craftsman's skills. In the Philadelphia city directories of 1867 and 1869, Scott was listed as a carver, an avocation in which he had a lifelong interest.

Scott moved to Chicago around 1873, as he is first listed that year in the Chicago directory as a designer. It is not known why Scott moved from Philadelphia, though Chicago's growing metropolis attracted many Easterners with its promise of jobs and opportunity. There Scott had the good fortune to find a kind, enlightened, and wealthy patron in John J. Glessner. According to Mrs. Glessner's journal, the family first met Isaac Scott in 1875. He made a large bookcase for them that year. This walnut bookcase is a masterpiece of Chicago furniture and is of comparable quality to the best modern Gothic furniture produced in the East. Its rectilinear form is inspired by Gothic furniture, and the inlaid cornice panel of birds, leaves, flowers, and a butterfly reflect Scott's fondness for nature. Although designed for their house at 261 West Washington Boulevard, the bookcase eventually was moved, along with other Scott-designed furniture, to the Glessner's famous house at 1800 South Prairie Avenue, designed by Henry Hobson Richardson and completed in 1887. By then, however, Scott had already left Chicago. He remained

Isaac Scott crafted the walnut bookcase on opposite page, top, for Chicago's Glessner family in 1875. Chicago Architecture Foundation; gift of Mrs. Charles F. Batchelder. Opposite, below: Oak table, 1902, designed by Frank Lloyd Wright for the William G. Fricke house, Oak Park, Illinois. Private collection. This page, top: Chairs made ca 1885 by the Tobey Furniture Company. Cherry. The Metropolitan Museum of Art; gift of Mrs. McCabe, 1968. Above: Card table, a rare example of Art Nouveau furniture designed by the Tobey firm. The Chrysler Museum, Norfolk, Virginia.

a lifelong friend, continuing to visit the Glessners in the summer in their New Hampshire house. There he taught woodcarving to the Glessner children.

Renaissance revival

Scott's furniture was exceptional in terms of its design and fine craftsmanship. But the prevailing style in America in the 1870s was not the modern Gothic, it was the Renaissance revival.

Renaissance revival furniture, typically architectonic and heavy, was often made of walnut, burled walnut, or darkly stained cherry woods. Case pieces were bilaterally symmetrical, with a raised crest often topped with a central medallion. Decorative medallions, cartouches, and classicals heads were frequently separately carved by mechanical means and applied (with glue) to appropriate parts of the furniture. Chairs in the Renaissance revival mode usually had trumpet legs and a central back splat topped by a cresting medallion ornament. Incised arabesques are found on many Renaissance revival pieces. In general, this furniture presents a formal appearance, in contrast to the sturdy but relatively informal "look" of many modern Gothic pieces.

More characteristic of Chicago's fine furniture than Scott's pieces were the tables, chairs, and settees made by Wirts and Scholle. The company manufactured all its parlor furniture, but its specialty was the Williams patent folding bed. Wirts and Scholle also sold a combination desk and washstand, made for it in Indianapolis. A side chair, part of a set of 15 dining chairs (now in the Smithsonian Institution's collection), was made between 1879 and 1885, when Wirts and Scholle were listed in partnership in Chicago directories. The chairs were originally in Chicago mayor Julian S. Rumsey's home (which was destroyed by the Great Chicago Fire and was rebuilt in 1874).

Chicagoans found that furniture produced by their own leading firms was compatible with the best from Europe and New York. In *Recollections of a Pioneer's Daughter*, Eliza Voluntine Rumsey, Mayor Rumsey's wife, wrote: "Some of the furniture for the house was made in New York by Herter and Company. . . . The dining room furniture was made by Wirtz and Sholle [*sic*] in Chicago." The Rumsey family was not alone in supporting New York's leading decorating firm, Herter Brothers and Company. The firm was well known to Chicago's rich and prominent citizens in the 1880s, including Marshall Field, John Glessner, and Potter Palmer.

Some of the most beautiful and innovative furniture produced in the 19th century was in rattan and wicker, and after the Civil War this intricately designed rattan furniture became increasingly popular. Renaissance revival works translated better into lighter rattan than into ponderous wood. Chicago's most famous rattan furniture manufacturer was Heywood & Morrill, begun in 1883. One Heywood & Morrill side chair was crafted in the Renaissance revival style. Two rival Eastern firms, Heywood Brothers & Company and the Wakefield Rattan Company, joined forces that year to establish a joint manufacturing enterprise. Henry Heywood and Amos Morrill of Heywood Brothers & Company found a suitable plant, which was to be the Chicago factory and warehouse until 1930. Heywood and Morrill were listed in the Chicago directories, in partnership, between 1888 and 1896.

Tobey Furniture Company: manufacturer of revival and reform styles

The Tobey Furniture Company, Chicago's most famous, also lasted the longest—99 years. Tobey produced furniture in revival and reform styles. Charles Tobey, the firm's president, was born in Dennis, Cape Cod, Massachusetts, in 1831. He came to Chicago in 1855 and opened a modest retail store that year. The following year he joined forces with his brother, Frank, and began to enlarge the business. In 1870, Frank Tobey and F. Porter Thayer organized the Thayer & Tobey Furniture Company; in 1873 they moved to a new building at State and Adams. In 1875 the brothers bought out Thayer's interest and reorganized as the Tobey Furniture Company.

The Tobey firm began in 1888 to specialize in a line of expensive, high-quality furniture which could be made to an architect's specification. One of the most impressive special-order examples attributed to the Tobey Company is a cherry dining table and chairs made about 1890 for Henry Lee Borden's house. Borden had purchased the house that year. The furniture and house are thought to have been designed by the same architect, because both dining room table and chairs carry out the same motifs. Unfortunately, since this set is not labeled nor is there a bill of sale, the attribution to Tobey rests on family tradition. In any case, the set is unlike documented Tobey furniture. In its architectonic form and integral use of naturalistic ornament, the Tobey dining table is an important example of Chicago furniture. Its proportions and solid rectilinear form anticipate the early furniture of Frank Lloyd Wright, as seen in the table designed for the William G. Fricke house (1902) in Oak Park, Illinois.

American Art Nouveau furniture was relatively rare, and the exuberant style that found such popularity in France at the turn of the century met with limited acceptance in this country. However, the label of the Tobey firm appears on an extraordinary Art Nouveau card table. Three almost identical ones also are known.

More acceptable to progressive Americans at the turn of the century was the Craftsman-style furniture, which Tobey also made. Its simple rectilinear forms and sympathetic use of natural materials were in keeping with reform precepts. Tobey was among many American firms producing craftsman-styled furniture in the early 20th century. The style was frequently advertised in catalogues and periodicals.

The prairie school

Architects in the so-called prairie school, named for the northern Midwestern landscape in which they worked, were responsible for designing the Windy City's most important contributions to the history of American furniture. George Washington Maher was among them. According to his con-

cept, furnishings should be designed as part of the total architectural scheme. Born in Mill Creek, West Virginia, Maher was first apprenticed at 13 to the Chicago firm of Bauer and Hill. He later joined J. L. Silsbee (along with Frank Lloyd Wright and George Grant Elmslie) before starting his own architectural practice in 1888. In 1891 Maher spent approximately three months traveling in Europe, an experience that was to strongly influence his work. Maher's design for the interior of John Farson's house (1897) in Oak Park reflects what he saw abroad. A carved lion-head motif—popular in Europe—was used throughout the house as an architectural design as well as on the dining-room chairs and other furniture.

In spite of strong European influence, Maher espoused an indigenous American architecture and described the Farson house as a "colonial" residence. An article in *Architectural Record* for June 1907 raised the issue: "Should he [the American architect] consciously seek to make his buildings a translation more or less adapted to American conditions of the traditional European technical methods and architectural forms? Or should he consciously seek to break away from the traditional forms and design buildings which are, as Mr. Maher puts it, 'indigenous'—the product of the American social and intellectual point of view and of the American physical facts?" In its strongly rectilinear form and discreet use of integral ornament, the Farson-house armchair was in keeping with reform precepts.

Maher's most intriguing and ambitious house was designed for James A. Patten in 1901. While the Farson house still stands, the Patten house in Evanston was unfortunately demolished in 1958. When completed, the Patten house received international attention. Stories about it appeared in periodicals such as *Studio* and *Western Architect*.

Louis J. Millet, who also executed some of the interiors for Adler and Sullivan, was the interior designer in charge of the execution of the Patten interiors, and it is likely he also contributed to the design. In explaining his choice of the thistle as the unifying decorative motif in the house, Maher said,

"... it has refinement of outline and a strong organic growth which could be most readily accommodated to the various materials that are employed in the construction of the building." The thistle—an especially appropriate motif in light of Patten's Scottish ancestry—adorns the home's reception room. Thistle was used throughout the house: it was painted on the walls, woven into the design of the rug, embroidered on draperies, portieres, and upholstery, and carved in relief on the furniture. The present location of most of the Patten furnishings is not known. A portiere incorporating the thistle is in the collection of the Art Institute of Chicago, and andirons were acquired by the Chicago Historical Society. Maher's Patten house best illustrates his motive-rhythm theory: "... each detail is designed to harmonize with the guiding motif which in turn was inspired by the necessity of the situation and local color and conditions." The chairs and table in the reception room also follow reform precepts: simplicity, predominantly rectilinear lines, and discreet integral ornament are qualities of both the modern Gothic furniture of the 1870s and of the prairie school furniture.

Under the influence of Wright, Maher was to substitute architectural motifs for thematic ones in the house in Hyde Park he designed for Ernest J. Magerstadt in 1908. Fortunately, this house, its beautiful art-glass windows, and some of its original furniture survive. A chair designed for the house with severely rectilinear lines and the absence of any ornament is reminiscent of some of Wright's furniture designs. It is also similar to a chair designed by Will H. Bradley in 1901 for the *Ladies' Home Journal* (February 1902).

George Grant Elmslie was a draftsman for J. L. Silsbee at the same time Maher apprenticed there. Sub-

sequently, Elmslie became chief draftsman for Adler and Sullivan and is usually credited with contributing to the designs of Sullivan's ornament. Whereas Sullivan apparently had little interest in designing furniture, Elmslie, like Wright, Maher, and others, attempted to create a total and harmonious scheme of interior and exterior architecture. In 1912, when Elmslie was in partnership with William Purcell, his firm was commissioned to design eight pieces of furniture for the Henry Babson House in Riverside, Illinois, which was designed by Louis Sullivan in 1907. Elmslie, who had worked for Sullivan from 1889 to 1909, designed a large part of the original interior. The face of a Babson clock—one of the eight Elmslie-Purcell pieces—was modeled by Kristian Schneider, probably in clay or wax for casting into bronze. (Schneider, who also had worked for Sullivan, would have developed his model from Elmslie's pencil drawing.) The clock hands, reproduced in recent years from an original photograph of the clock, were made to Elmslie's designs by Robert Jarvie of Chicago, and the works and chimes were imported from Germany.

The development of an indigenous furniture in Chicago paralleled that city's famous architecture. Its roots were in the English reform movement and the "modern Gothic" style of the 1870s which was transferred to Chicago via Philadelphia—and directly from England in succeeding decades. Chicago's furniture is especially significant to the evolution of furniture design in America because it included some of the most progressive modern designs in this country. The Chicago Historical Society is planning an exhibition on this subject late in 1980. The exhibit should be of great interest to those studying the history of American furniture. ∎

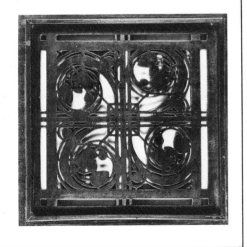

Opposite page, top: Dining room armchair, mahogany, designed by George Washington Maher for the John Farson house at Oak Park, Illinois, 1897. The lion's head motif ornamenting this chair (see detail) was used throughout the Farson house; it reflects a European influence on Maher's work. Both, The Art Institute of Chicago; lent by the Park District of Oak Park. Opposite, bottom: Side chair by George Maher, 1908, reflects the simple architectural lines of the Ernest J. Magerstadt house for which it was designed. Mr. & Mrs. Henry Field. Left: Tall mahogany clock with brass inlay (detail below) designed by George Elmslie for the Henry Babson house, 1912. The Art Institute of Chicago; gift of Mrs. Theodore Tieken.

Gustav Stickley

His popular Craftsman fur-
*niture of durable, utili-
tarian oak was emulated by
many other producers of the so-
called Mission style.*

BY BARRY SANDERS

Gustav Stickley, once an unknown cabinetmaker, revolutionized furniture design in America shortly after the turn of
the century, and very quickly became
the principal force behind the Arts and
Crafts movement in America. Stickley's
aesthetic and political inspiration was
the English designer William Morris,
who revolted against Victorian excess
in household and decorative arts and
the deplorable working conditions under which such art was produced.
When Stickley visited England in 1898,
he was overwhelmed by Morris's ac-

complishments: "[Morris] changed the
look of half the houses in London, and
substituted beauty for ugliness all over
the kingdom." On his return Stickley
formed the Gustave Stickley Company,
in Eastwood, New York, a suburb of
Syracuse, to manufacture what he
called Craftsman furniture, popularly
called "Mission." These new furniture
designs signaled Stickley's own revolt
against America's shoddy, hastily produced European imitations.

When Stickley first showed his furniture designs at the Furniture Exposition of 1900 in Grand Rapids, Michigan, he was 43 years old. By the next
year he had patented three designs: a
chair, a library table, and a round table.
That year he displayed several rooms of
furniture in a cooperative exhibition
with the Grueby Faience Company, at
the Pan American International Expo-

sition in Buffalo, New York.

In 1901 Stickley changed the name
of his company to the United Crafts, a
profit-sharing cooperative of cabinetmakers and metal- and leather-
workers modeled after the medieval
guild system. In England William Morris had attempted to revive the medieval guild with his own business, Morris
and Company. The United Crafts was
to be Stickley's attempt. With Morris's
inspiration the United Crafts would en-
deavor "to substitute the luxury of taste
for the luxury of costliness; to teach
that beauty does not imply elaboration
or ornament; to employ only those
forms and materials which make for
simplicity, individuality, and dignity of
effect." In addition, Stickley promised
his workmen conditions that would
make them neither "over-wearisome,
nor over-anxious."

Inspired by the work of design reformer William Morris and the English Arts and Crafts movement, Gustav Stickley used the functional parts of his furniture—especially the hardware—as integral ornament. Opposite page: Sideboard, ca 1905. Oak with decorative iron strap hinges. Courtesy Jordan-Volpe Gallery, New York. This page, left: Oak bureau, ca 1910, with hammered copper pulls. Courtesy Jordan-Volpe Gallery. Top, above: Gustav Stickley oak desk, notable for the small drawers with copper pulls mounted atop the writing surface. This desk was designed for comfort: the crossbar at the kneehole is located sufficiently far back to accommodate the sitter's knees. Collection of Barrie and Dee Dee Wigmore; photo, Mysak/Studio Nine. Immediately above: Sideboard of oak. Note the U-shaped iron pulls, usually found on examples of his earlier furniture. Collection of Barrie and Dee Dee Wigmore; photo, Mysak/Studio Nine.

In addition to larger pieces of furniture, Gustav Stickley's Craftsman Workshops turned out smaller decorative accessories such as the oak wastebasket at left. Collection of Barrie and Dee Dee Wigmore. Below: Unusual three-drawer library table crafted of oak. The dusky glazes of Rookwood pottery complement the warm oak tones of mission furniture: on the desk are (left) an early vase by Sara Alice Tooley, and (right) a larger vase by Lenore Asbury, who worked at Rookwood from 1899 to 1931. All, collection of Barrie and Dee Dee Wigmore; photo, Mysak/Studio Nine.

What makes it a Gustav Stickley piece?

"I tried to make furniture," said Stickley, "which would be simple, durable, comfortable, and fitted for the place it was to occupy and the work it had to do." Although people have argued over the origin of the name "Mission," there is general agreement over its description: Craftsman Mission furniture is straight-lined, hand-finished, well-made furniture, "constructed on primitive lines," as Stickley said, "planned for comfort, durability, and beauty, and expressing the true spirit of democracy." His furniture was unusually and intentionally heavy, since it was supposed to be set in place and left there.

Aside from a few pieces of inlaid furniture, Craftsman furniture was free of any decoration. Describing one of his designs, Stickley noted, "The piece is . . . first, last, and all the time a *chair*, and not an imitation of a throne, not an exhibit of snakes and dragons in a wild riot of misapplied wood-carving." Because Stickley insisted that any ornamentation be functional, he proudly ex-

posed mortise and tenon joints, not only to break up the straight lines and hard edges of the furniture but to create absolutely solid pieces. In larger pieces, such as bookcases or large trestle tables, these mortise and tenon joints were sometimes keyed for extra strength. Whenever possible Stickley used wooden dowels instead of nails; these too added strength and provided some accent and variety. Handles and pulls, made of either iron or copper, were given the same meticulous care as the cabinet itself. They were hand-wrought in Stickley's workshops, and finished in a dark color. Iron was treated to achieve a patina Stickley called "armor bright," while copper was darkened by "an old process of firing which gives a surface that mellows with age and exposure."

Although Stickley used mahogany and other woods, his first choice was native American white oak. This was quartersawn to add strength and to exploit the wood's medullary rays (the glasslike fibers that run across the grain, binding the perpendicular fibers together). Because he believed that a

piece of furniture's basic beauty was finally revealed through its color, Stickley refused to use commercially prepared stains, which gave the wood a painted appearance. Instead, he adopted a process called "fuming": Ammonia fumes reacting with the tannic acid in the oak produced what Stickley described as "a rich nut-brown color." Finally, a finish of one-third white shellac and two-thirds German lacquer was applied. Stickley also manufactured his own paste wax.

Stickley's motto, *Als ik kan*—"As I can"—adapted from the painter Jan van Eyck, was a version of William Morris's *Si je puis*. Provided the piece has not been stripped, it is not difficult to identify Stickley furniture, for each piece bears his Flemish motto in red within joiner's compasses. Stickley also signed his name across the bottom of the compasses. Later he used decals, and for a time he burned his logo into the wood. Some pieces carry a paper label pasted on the bottoms of chair seats, the undersides of tables, the backs of bookcases, and so on. Look for his red trademark in the drawers of desks and tables, on the rear stretchers of chair legs, on the backs of bookcases, the bottoms of umbrella stands, and the undersides of tables. Stickley registered all of these trademarks with the United States Patent Office. Through his elaborate use of trademarks, Stickley hoped to clearly distinguish his work from that of other Mission furniture manufacturers.

Dating Stickley pieces is more difficult than identifying them. The early *Als ik kan* signatures are framed within a small rectangle on chairs; early desks and cabinets have very large red joiner's compasses. If a paper label reading "The United Crafts" remains, the piece is early. Both early and late pieces are found with the logo burned into the wood. Though some collectors insist that the early Gustav Stickley pieces carry only the iron metalwork, there are early pieces with copper as well as iron metalwork. The surest way to date a piece is to become familiar with the catalogues (there are copies in scattered libraries, and they can sometimes be found in used bookstores), and match up the pieces with a catalogue picture. (But even the avid collector can be surprised: A filing cabinet that appears in no catalogue has come to light. Stickley apparently made some custom pieces, especially for businesses.) Browse through the pages of *The Craftsman;* a good many of Stickley' pieces are reproduced in the monthly magazine he edited and published from 1901. Check especially the earlier issues.

Stickley certainly was imitated. During the Arts and Crafts period Stickley's furniture was copied by firms like Sears Roebuck, Come-Packt, Macey, Gunn, Limberts Arts and Crafts, Retting, Hawthorne, Life Time, and others. Even Stickley's five younger brothers, who for a while were all in business with him, manufactured their own copies of Mission furniture. Charles Stickley had his own company. George and Albert manufactured under the names "Stickley Brothers" and "Quaint Furniture." Two other brothers, Leopold and Julius George (L. and J. G.), were Gustav Stickley's most successful imitators. (Many collectors feel that, after Gustav's furniture, L. and J. G. is the

Top: Clothes press, made of oak, copper and glass ca 1906. Note the highly decorative strap hinges of hammered copper. The Metropolitan Museum of Art, Gift of Cyril Farny in memory of Phyllis Holt Farny, 1976. Left: Fall front desk, oak with copper fittings. This is thought to be an early example of Stickley's work. The Brooklyn Museum; H. Randolph Lever Fund. Above: Hexagonal library table, ca 1906. The leather top of this strongly grained oak table is secured by copper nail heads. The stretchers are artfully tenoned through the legs. The Metropolitan Museum of Art, Gift of Cyril Farny in memory of Phyllis.

most collectible: Sometimes Gustav's pieces are difficult to tell from L. and J. G. Stickley's.) The novice may even become confused by the L. and J. G. trademark: a wood clamp (sometimes in red) over the Stickley name.

But close handling reveals differences between Gustav Stickley and even his best imitators—L. and J. G. Stickley. Where Gustav used solid boards, others were satisfied with veneers or laminations; where Gustav used quartersawn oak, others settled for straight-cut. His imitators replaced dowels with screws and even nails. Hardware was cast, drawers were not dovetailed. On the cheaper Mission pieces mortise and tenon joints were glued. A real mortise and tenon joint will not wiggle; glued ones will. These imitations were of inferior quality, but they were cheaper and therefore sold well. But Gustav Stickley's Craftsman furniture sold better.

By 1904 he dropped the idea of the profit-sharing United Crafts, expanded, and changed the name of his operations to the Craftsman Workshops. (He also changed the spelling of Gustave to Gustav.) In 1905 he moved the executive and editorial offices from Eastwood to his first Craftsman building in New York City. By 1913 he had rented a 12-story building in the city for his editorial and retail sales offices. *The Craftsman* contributed to his phenomenal success. It quickly became the vehicle for the dissemination of Arts and Crafts philosophy in America.

The Craftsman

Throughout *The Craftsman's* 16-year history (31 volumes were printed), Stickley and various staff and guest writers presented articles on art, architecture, poetry, drama, politics, economics, history, gardening, city planning, and education. But *The Craftsman* emphasized the household and decorative arts through long and short articles on furniture design, metalwork, jewelry, leatherwork, glass, pottery, textiles, and bookbinding. *The Craftsman* also included "how to" information on weaving, hammering copper, curing and finishing wood, building furniture, binding books, and tooling leather. (It is still a useful magazine for those who wish to build their own Craftsman furniture.) Over the years Stickley supplied his readers with 221 working plans for his Craftsman home designs.

As a forum for the Arts and Crafts movement *The Craftsman* became an essential source of information on the Arts and Crafts in America and abroad. It was in the pages of his own magazine that Stickley first reproduced pictures of his Craftsmen furniture, elaborating on its philosophical and aesthetic virtues.

On Wednesday, March 24, 1915, 15 years after he showed his first pieces, a petition of bankruptcy was filed against Craftsman, Incorporated. *The Craftsman* ceased publication with the December 1916 issue. The Arts and Crafts movement was to all intents finished. And with it vanished Stickley's most important contribution to the decorative and household arts: quality. For a short time after his bankruptcy Stickley experimented with a paint called Kem-Tone, but, according to one of his daughters, he never received any royalties. He died on April 12, 1942.

Today's market

Today Gustav Stickley's furniture still turns up in the occasional junk store or at the Salvation Army, but more and more often it is found in fancy antique shops, galleries, and auction houses at rapidly rising prices. More people are now aware of Craftsman furniture: The exhibition "The Arts and Crafts Movement in America," shown at the Princeton Museum of Art, helped; articles in magazines have also spread the word; and The Metropolitan Museum of Art in New York will soon have on display some of Stickley's furniture. The prices of Stickley furniture have been rising. At New York galleries single-door bookcases sell for around $1,000; big morris chairs sell for as high as $2,200.

Ladder-back chairs now sell in the posh galleries for $450 each, dining-room tables for around $1,500. But the furniture can still be found at inexpensive prices at less fancy stores and, at times, in used furniture and thrift shops. Identifying Craftsman furniture, however, is not always easy, especially if the signature has been obliterated or if the piece has been painted. But after handling a few pieces of Stickley's furniture, you'll soon discover the unusual heft, the careful selection and matching of woods, and the solid construction that separate his furniture from cheaper imitations. For instance, once the collector becomes familiar with a Gustav drawer, he won't confuse it with any other. Sides and bottom are oak, dovetailed front and back, and the drawer is unusually deep. The color of Stickley's furniture is also different from the rest, provided it hasn't been refinished; it has a deep, rich glow, a patina that distinguishes it from most other Mission furniture.

If you're buying for investment, you should probably buy only signed pieces. You'll of course pay more for early or rare pieces, and should expect to pay more for pieces that are in mint condition. Most pieces you find will probably be made of oak, the rest of mahogany. Mainly, you will see chairs, rockers, and more chairs. Sideboards, bookcases, and china cabinets surface

with some frequency. Liquor cabinets, three-door bookcases, and bedroom furniture appear less frequently. Occasionally, one of Stickley's table lamps or floor lamps will come up for sale. His copper accessories—ashtrays, wall plaques, chafing dishes, coal scuttles, chandeliers—appear now and then. They are usually stamped with the Craftsman trademark on the bottom of trays, on the sides of lamps. Inlaid pieces, which Stickley produced for one year, are most rare. Very few pieces need no refinishing, and every piece needs reupholstering. The most satisfying and reliable buying guide: Buy furniture you like; you'll never get cheated.

Gustav Stickley's furniture

Gustav Stickley manufactured furniture for virtually every room in the house. The amount of furniture he produced is staggering: The average number of designs for each of his catalogues is about 150 for the 16 years he was in business, and the workshop operated six days a week. Though it is impractical to describe all of his designs, it is possible to describe the six or seven most basic, important pieces of furniture that a person would be most apt to buy in 1909—the heyday of the Arts and Crafts movement. These are also typical pieces that today's collector is most likely to find. To furnish a Craftsman

Stickley, like his English counterparts, stressed the functional aspects of furniture. Despite his rather austere interpretation of functionalism, he designed chairs of surprising variety. Opposite page, left to right: Eastwood chair, ca 1901, quarter-sawn white oak with leather seat. Center: Spindle armchair with rush seat, quarter-sawn white oak, ca 1902. Right: Quarter-sawn oak with rush seat, ca 1902. This page, left to right: White oak armchair made between 1901 and 1904 with leather seat and brass studs; quarter-sawn white oak with original rush seat, ca 1903. All five courtesy, Jordan Volpe Gallery. Right: Oak side chair, 1901, marked with Stickley's red decal. Courtesy Robert Edwards Arts and Crafts Furnishings, Rosemont, Pennsylvania.

bungalow in 1909, you might have bought a morris chair, a rocker, a bookcase, a library table, a dining-room table and chairs, a china cabinet, and a sideboard. (Stickley also made bedroom furniture, now hard to find.)

The Craftsman living room

The morris chair was the center of any Craftsman living room. Big, roomy, and incredibly comfortable, it was a chair in which a person could spend an evening reading, smoking, listening to the windup record player or the radio, or simply dreaming the time away. (The chairs were named after William Morris, who had revived and made popular the Essex style chair, similar to this one.) Morris chairs had wide arms to accommodate ashtrays, pipes, or books, and a reclining back—on the principle of modern beach lounge chairs. The arms were either straight, slanted, or curved. The sides were open or slatted. Stickley's bigger morris chairs had mortise and tenon joints; both big and small had doweled joints. One could order cushions covered in sheepskin, cotton velvet, or "Craftsman canvas." The price for the largest style in 1909 was $41.50. Five dollars more would purchase a leather-covered footstool to place in front of the morris chair. For a bit more you could further enhance your living room with a handsome smoker's cabinet or a sheet-music cabinet.

The living room might have a rocker or two—the *sine qua non* of Mission furniture. Stickley's 1909 catalogue listed 18 different kinds of rockers, including a child's model. In fact, Stickley made a rocking version of almost every straightlegged chair he produced. He made rockers with and without arms; large, oversize rockers for easy contemplation; and low-seated, armless rockers for sewing, knitting, or slipping on shoes. Some had hard leather seats, some spring seats, and some slip rush seats.

Bookcases were also popular. Stickley made them in varying sizes—with one, two, or three doors—some with mortise and tenon joints, some with keyed joints, and others with doweled joints. Shelves were usually stationary and on line with the door mullions. Door pulls were of hammered iron or copper. The living-room library table might have one or two drawers, again with hammered iron or copper pulls. Most of these library tables could be ordered with wooden or leather-covered

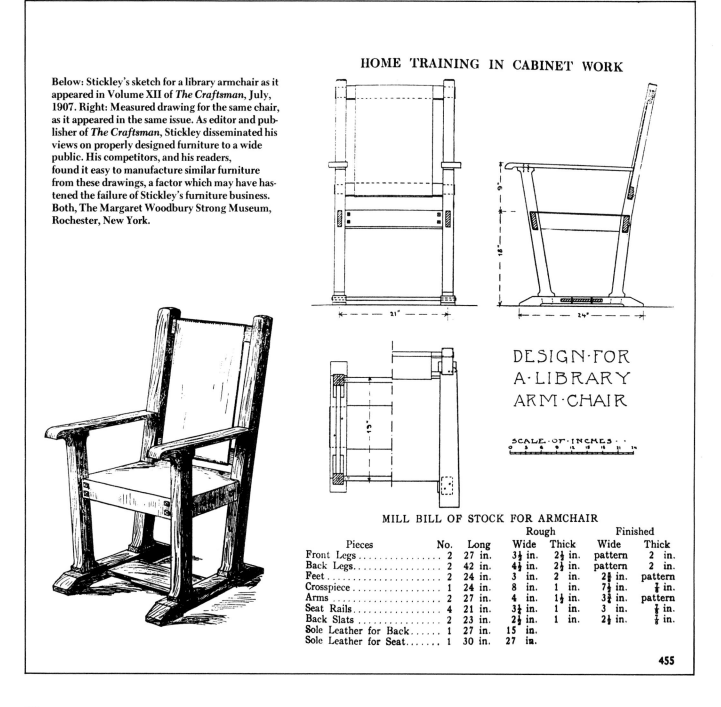

HOME TRAINING IN CABINET WORK

Below: Stickley's sketch for a library armchair as it appeared in Volume XII of *The Craftsman*, July, 1907. Right: Measured drawing for the same chair, as it appeared in the same issue. As editor and publisher of *The Craftsman*, Stickley disseminated his views on properly designed furniture to a wide public. His competitors, and his readers, found it easy to manufacture similar furniture from these drawings, a factor which may have hastened the failure of Stickley's furniture business. Both, The Margaret Woodbury Strong Museum, Rochester, New York.

DESIGN·FOR A·LIBRARY ARM·CHAIR

SCALE·OF·INCHES

MILL BILL OF STOCK FOR ARMCHAIR

Pieces	No.	Long	Rough Wide	Rough Thick	Finished Wide	Finished Thick
Front Legs	2	27 in.	3½ in.	2½ in.	pattern	2 in.
Back Legs	2	42 in.	4½ in.	2½ in.	pattern	2 in.
Feet	2	24 in.	3 in.	2 in.	2¼ in.	pattern
Crosspiece	1	24 in.	8 in.	1 in.	7½ in.	⅞ in.
Arms	2	27 in.	4 in.	1½ in.	3¾ in.	pattern
Seat Rails	4	21 in.	3½ in.	1 in.	3 in.	⅞ in.
Back Slats	2	23 in.	2½ in.	1 in.	2¼ in.	⅞ in.
Sole Leather for Back	1	27 in.	15 in.			
Sole Leather for Seat	1	30 in.	27 in.			

455

tops decorated around the edges with large iron or copper brads.

The dining room

The 1909 Craftsman catalogue featured dining tables in four different styles: a huge rectangular table that measured eight feet by four feet, and three round tables—one with a pedestal base, one with five legs, and a heavier model with four legs connected by stretchers to a center post. Most of Gustav Stickley's tabletops were quartersawn for appearance. They could be extended with leaves. He made a variety of dining chairs, with ladders, vertical-slat, or wide-splat backs. Some had straight tops, others were concave or convex. The ladder-back, the most popular in 1909, is the most sought after today. Though there are slight variations, ladder-backs have three slats, doweled at each end of the slat and at each point in the chair where a stretcher joins another structural member. The typical ladder-back came with a hard leather seat and was decorated at the corners with six of Stickley's characteristic square iron or copper nails for a finished, medieval look. (He also used these nails on some of his footstools.) In the corner of the dining room might sit one of Stickley's one- or two-door china cabinets. Some had a gentle architectural curve that swept across the base of the cabinet from leg to leg, others were straight. Some had mullions on the doors, some did not. Some had slab legs, some had individual square legs. China cabinets usually had doweled joints and door pulls of hammered iron or copper.

Stickley made two types of sideboard: delicate, small ones and larger, more primitive-looking ones, with hammered iron or copper straps running along the front of the side-compartment doors. These side compartments were used for storing tablecloths, napkins, and other table linen. Sideboards were fitted with a combination of wide and narrow drawers—some lined with a soft, nappy leather that Stickley called "ooze," for storing silverware. Doors and drawers had hammered pulls. ∎

Top, left: Detail of Stickley's distinctive red stamp as applied to furniture manufactured between 1901 and 1904. Within the joiner's compasses is the phrase, "Als ik kan," meaning "As I can." Stickley adopted this credo from the Flemish painter Jan van Eyck; it is a close approximation to design reformer William Morris's slogan "Si je puis"—"as I am able."
Top, right: Detail of a hand-hammered copper pull, about 2″ high. Both this pull and the one at top, left are found on pieces of furniture dating from about 1909. The functional hardware on many of Stickley's pieces doubles as ornamentation, in keeping with the Arts and Crafts notion that decoration should be integral to a piece, rather than fuperfluous. Stickley particularly favored the use of handcrafted hardware—hammered rather than cast iron and copper. This distinguishes many of his pieces from those of his competitors, who tended to use cheaper, mass-manufactured hardware. The smoky patina on genuine Gustav Stickley pulls, hinges, and handles was achieved by special processes. Photographs, courtesy Jordan-Volpe Gallery.

The Roycrofters

BY ROBERT EDWARDS

Roycroft furniture was simple, honest, and utilitarian, reflecting the ideals of the Arts and Crafts movement itself.

The Roycroft community, founded by Elbert Hubbard at East Aurora, New York, in 1893, produced Arts and Crafts furniture, books, metalwares, and lamps until 1938. Yet the products of the community are less well known than Hubbard's writings, particularly a small essay entitled "A Message to Garcia." More than forty million copies of this paean to blind obedience were printed by businesses and the military for distribution to employees and recruits. This and other examples of the

gospel according to "Fra Elbertus," as Hubbard called himself in a nod to the medieval associations of the Arts and Crafts movement, have tended to divert attention away from the physical products of the Roycroft community. The lore of East Aurora, spiced with Hubbard homilies, has proved irresistible to writers who have preferred to focus on the personal and philosophical idiosyncracies of Hubbard and his followers, rather than on the crafts produced at Roycroft.

It is time for a reassessment of the aesthetic merits of those crafts, but it is not easy to isolate the Roycrofter production from its philosophical context. Some collectors today, for example, regard all examples of Roycroft work as if they were pieces of the true cross; oth-

ers consider certain Roycroft objects to be high-quality works of art, but they dismiss Hubbard himself as an irrelevant huckster. These contradictory attitudes may stem from a paradox basic to the Roycroft movement: while the Roycrofters were in the business of making and selling crafts, Hubbard's real product was an ideal. This particular ideal, derived as it was from the Arts and Crafts philosophy of the Englishman William Morris, glorified hand craftsmanship, gave recognition to honest labor, and in its fullest expression, came to represent a sentimentalized, pastoral way of life that by the turn of the century had all but disappeared from an industrialized America. "To love one's friends, to bathe in the sunshine of life, to preserve a right mental attitude—the receptive attitude, the attitude of gratitude, and to do one's work—these make the sum of an ideal life," wrote Hubbard.

Hubbard was inspired to pursue his ideal after meeting William Morris, but it is well to remember that neither Morris nor Hubbard was financially dependent upon the success of his social experiments. Although it gave lip service to the Arts and Crafts philosophy of honoring the workman, the Roycroft community at East Aurora was emphatically not a socialist utopia. It was first and foremost a profitable business venture with Elbert Hubbard as its sole owner, director, and mastermind. There was no profit sharing as there was at the competing Craftsman workshops of Gustav Stickley. The Roycrofters divided their time between farming and craft work, for which they were paid a salary. "The Roycrofters are just plain folks," advertised Hubbard, "farmers with an artistic bias. The best work can be done only under certain conditions and in a certain environment. An artist must have what you call 'atmosphere'—the Roycrofters have supplied that opportunity."

The general work force at Roycroft was comprised of people with no particular art skills as well as those who were already master craftsmen. Many of the Roycroft products required little craftsmanship to execute and workers often moved from one shop to the next as needed. Still, out of about four hundred members of the community, the few genuine artists were recognized and, in some cases, given their own studios. Several artists who began as Roycrofters later achieved considerable fame on their own. Unlike designers at the Stickley or Limbert factories, who remain anonymous, many Roycroft artists are easily identified by their monograms, which are often concealed in the corners of their designs. For example, William Denslow, who already had a significant reputation when he began doing cartoons for Hubbard's periodicals in 1896, hid his logo, a sea horse or hippocampus, in the decorated initials of the books he designed.

Certain of Hubbard's pronouncements—"The world of commerce is just as honorable as the world of Art, and a trifle more necessary" or "Art: the vengeance of the ideal on the real"—suggested that art was an uninvited guest at the Roycroft philosophical feast. All of the community's products were well crafted, but they embodied a distressingly wide spectrum of taste: some aesthetically pleasing, some bad. Hubbard's own art lay in his ability to sell the whole range of these objects. It was no more difficult for him to sell the crudest objects—such as his "whole-skin pillow," merely two hides coarsely stitched together with the legs intact, or his "Ali Baba Bench," a parody of rustic furniture consisting of a split log retaining its bark and propped upon legs—as it was for him to sell a finely tooled leather waste basket by Frederick Kranz or an elaborate electric lamp by Dard Hunter. "The Business Man is a Salesman," Hubbard proudly pronounced, "and no matter how great your invention, how sweet your song, how sublime your picture, how perfect your card system, until you are able to convince the world that it needs the thing you have to offer, and you get the money for it, you are not a Business Man." To assure his status as a "Business Man," he saw to it that all of the results of his craftsmen's labor—books, furniture, and copperware—were self-perpetuating advertisements for the Roycroft ideal. Each edition of Walt Whitman poetry, each tall-backed chair, each hammered copper nut dish sold was boldly emblazoned with the Roycroft mark. In the purchaser's home it continued to sell the ideal.

Books, Roycroft's earliest product, were to be a mainstay of the business

White quarter-sawn oak bookcase, left, was made in the Roycroft shops between 1905 and 1910. Not pictured in any catalogue, it may be a unique piece, made to special order. The faceted beveling on the mullions is unusual, providing a decorative touch to an otherwise simple facade. The hardware is original, and like that of many other Roycroft pieces, is black-painted copper. The Roycroft mark is prominently emblazoned on the front of the bookcase. Courtesy Robert Edwards Arts & Crafts Furnishings, Rosemont, Pennsylvania. Opposite page: One of Dard Hunter's most elegant designs is that for the title page of *Justinian and Theodora*, written by Elbert and Alice Hubbard and published by the Roycroft Press in 1906. This striking black and orange graphic image is a clear departure from the meandering Kelmscott style previously used in the print shop. Photo, Rick Echelmeyer; courtesy Robert Edwards Arts & Crafts Furnishings, Rosemont, Pennsylvania.

until the shops closed. The first book, *Song of Songs*, was designed by Hubbard in 1896 in the style of his mentor, William Morris of the Kelmscott Press. It embodied the principles of the Arts and Crafts movement in which process and artistic thought were of utmost importance, and the sincere if unskilled efforts of the dilletante were considered as worthy as the refined results achieved by technically proficient artists. Crudely printed on handmade paper, hand illuminated, and printed "just as well as we could," *Song of Songs* was

tangible testament to Hubbard's homily that "As the quest is more than the achievement, so is the making of the thing more than owning it." However, if the book is judged by an aesthetic independent of the Arts and Crafts credo, the most that can be said for it is that it established a basic format upon which more talented Roycroft artists would later elaborate.

One of the best known of Roycroft's book designers, William Denslow, appeared on the Roycroft campus in 1896. Among his handsome creations

were editions of *Ye Ancient Mariner* and *Deserted Village*. Denslow's logo became so closely associated with Roycroft that it can be found elegantly entwined with the Roycroft trademark in the paper watermark used in books produced by the community both during and after Denslow's tenure at East Aurora. When—inevitably—Denslow's other illustration assignments took precedence over his Roycroft work, he left the community in 1900.

Another graphic designer, Samuel Warner, was a Fellow of the Royal

Society of Artists. Many of the books he designed for the Roycroft press owe a clear debt to his British training. No matter how derivative they might be, Warner's borders for the 1900 edition of Browning's *The Last Ride*, published by the Roycrofters, must be considered his most beautiful designs. They consisted of delicate Pre-Raphealite drawings, printed then painted with watercolors. Roycroft books decorated in this manner were designated "hand illuminated" in Hubbard's advertising and catalogues. This is somewhat misleading, because only a very few book decorations, including those on a copy of the Roycroft edition of *Deserted Village* presently displayed at the Elbert Hubbard Library-Museum in East Aurora, were completely executed by hand. Another Roycroft volume—Grey's *Elegy*, published in 1903—used the same border as *The Last Ride*. These Samuel Warner designs represent the last link to the 19th-century "medi-

eval" look; soon, a new Roycroft artist, Dard Hunter, would turn the direction of the Roycroft aesthetic away from Morris's precepts and toward a new, spare and elegant angularity.

Dard Hunter was the scion of a fairly prosperous family that ran the Lonhuda Art Pottery as well as a substantial printing establishment, so he was not dependent upon Hubbard's meager wages. He used the Roycroft shops as a starting point for his career in book and paper making. From 1903 to 1909, Roycroft provided a laboratory for Hunter's experiments not only in printing books but in designing stained glass. Even before he went to Vienna to study in 1908, Hunter was aware of the work of the Vienna Secession, a group of Austrian artists who eschewed the slavish imitation of historical styles in favor of the clean geometric stylization typified by Charles Rennie Mackintosh's Glasgow School design.

The windows he designed for the li-

brary of the Roycroft Inn are ample evidence of Hunter's development in this style. They are conservatively concieved in clear glass, leaded with a stylized rose motif which is only vaguely suggestive of Mackintosh influence; later windows and lighting fixtures make a strong geometric statement in glass of the mauve and yellow-green colors favored by the Glasgow School. The leading in these fixtures reiterates the gridwork theme so often used by Vienna Secessionist Josef Hoffman. Such advanced design seems out of place at the sturdily Victorian inn. A person familiar with the Inn only through Hunter's idealized illustrations in such Roycroft periodicals as *The Fra*, *The Roycrofter*, and *The Philistine* would be quite surprised when he arrived in East Aurora and found dark vaulted interiors rather than the light, bright, intimate spaces depicted by the artist. Although Hunter's magnificent leaded glass lighting fixtures replaced the dreary iron chandeliers that had been previously installed at the Inn (he also designed a china pattern to harmonize with these lights), he never effected a complete transformation to the more modern "Vienna" style, as period photographs of the Inn's interiors show.

Electric table lamps probably presented something of a challenge to Dard Hunter. Electricity had just come into general use, replacing lamp oil, and as late as 1910, a Roycroft catalogue offers to adapt their fixtures for electricity, gas, or oil. A stocky wood-framed electric lamp designed by

Hunter in the Mission style retains a form required for fuel-fired lighting. The broad rectilinear column of the base allows for a fuel font, and the truncated pyramid shape of the shade leaves an opening at the center for ventilation of the flame. Only the "modern art glass" panels, as they were described in a 1910 Roycroft catalogue, reflect the sophisticated ideas of the designer. A similar but clumsy version of this lamp appears in *Mission Furniture, How to Make It*, published by *Popular Mechanics* in 1910. Hunter's later lamp designs take advantage of the slender stem allowed by an electric cord and

enclosed dome shades.

The geometric motifs found in Hunter's three-dimensional designs were repeated in his two-dimensional graphics. His square rose motif became as closely associated with the Roycroft image as Denslow's sea horse had been a few years earlier. The rose, sometimes hiding Hunter's initials at its center, appeared on the cover of *The Fra*. It was tooled into leather, hammered out of silver, and leaded into luminous lamp shades. *Justinian and Theodora*, a play by Elbert and Alice Hubbard, was the finest book design produced by the Roycroft press. Dard Hunter's dramatic title page, printed in black and orange, was a striking departure from the meandering Kelmscott style previously used at the print shop. Decorations from this book were used again in *The Doctors*, another play by Hubbard.

The quarter-sawn oak dropfront desk at left was made in the Roycroft furniture shop around 1910. It is pleasingly embellished with copper strap hinges and hardware. While several of the Roycroft cabinetmakers have been identified, there is little documentation for the design origins of specific pieces of furniture, which were generally inspired by their English Arts and Crafts prototypes. Opposite page: Two examples of Roycroft china, designed by Dard Hunter for use at the Roycroft Inn. Their red and green motifs were intended to coordinate with the angular lighting fixtures Hunter also designed for the Inn. The plate on the left was made prior to 1910; the plate on the right, designed after 1910, clearly reflects the influence of the Vienna Secession on Hunter's work. Both pieces were fabricated at the Buffalo Pottery, which was run by a relative of Hubbard's. Photo, Rich Echelmeyer; courtesy Robert Edwards Arts & Crafts Furnishings, Rosemont, Pennsylvania.

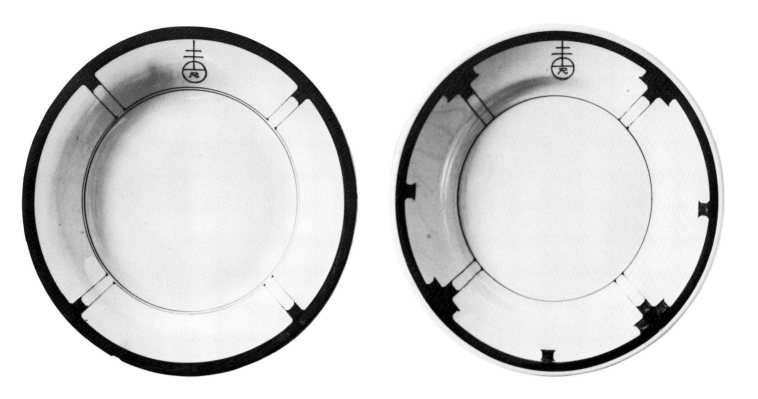

No other object better exemplifies the Roycroft style. Hubbard's disconcerting use of humor to mask serious thought is manifest not only in the text, which is a comedy dealing with the care of the insane, but also in the materials used to make the book—extraordinarily coarse handmade papers, rough sheep hide and burlap ties, intended to parody the Arts and Crafts book. Hubbard's advertisement for the book read:

> A silly play, eliminated for relief of the author, and now published for the first time. In the cast are doctors with whiskers, doctors clean-shaven, wise old doctors, fresh and forward internes, smart young surgeons, puffy family physicians, and a specialist who has traveled far and acknowledges that he knows nothing. Of course there are nurses and pretty patients, also a preacher and an obese limb of the law. Cupid enters, for you can't even keep the rogue out of a hospital, and all ends happily as a play should. Painfully illustrated on butcher's paper and illumined with cantharides. Bound in human hide, limp, lined with iodoform gauze, sewed with catgut and flavored with formaldehyde. Price, Two Dollars. P.S. Not being able to get enough human hide we are using suede sheep, instead.

Today, the humor of such copy palls, but the Hunter design stands as a beautiful distillation of American Arts and Crafts book design.

Although such "outside" periodicals as *Studio* and *Decorative Kunst* were in the Roycroft library, Dard Hunter probably had a hand in bringing modern European design to the metal shop through his friends Peter Robarge and Karl Kipp, a former banker who founded the Roycroft copper shop in 1908. Most of the metal work produced by the Roycroft shops had the look of die-cut mass production. Generally, the hand hammering was done to produce a planished surface texture rather than to expand the copper to form a unique vessel. The mechanical, geometric style of the Secessionists was particularly suited to Roycroft production methods. Those designs which most clearly derive from the Viennese school are the most successful, but the tapering vases decorated with gridwork cutouts, jade insets, or German silver appliqués were ahead of their time in this country and were therefore not widely popular. A lingering fondness for Victorian clutter was satisfied by the hundreds of desk sets, ashtrays and bud vases that formed the major part of the Roycroft metal inventory. Self-taught artisan Karl Kipp left the Roycrofters to start his own studio in East Aurora, the Tookay Shops. The cojoined Ks that were stamped on his work at this time are often the only distinguishing factors that can be determined between Roycroft and Kipp designs.

Roycroft furniture

From all accounts, the Roycroft cabinetmaking shops came into being in 1896 as a means of furnishing the inn Hubbard established to house his rich and famous admirers—the Fords, the Rockefellers, and actress Ellen Terry among others—who came to watch and occasionally participate in the daily regimen of the community. These visitors wanted to buy the chairs and tables built for the inn. Seeing a potential market for this furniture, Hubbard offered it in a catalogue. Since most work was done to order, the quantity produced was never as great as that turned out by the various Stickley factories. Unfortunately, no inspired furniture designer happened into Hubbard's web. Some of his cabinetmakers are known—Victor Toothaker, Albert Danner, and Herbert Buffum—but it is not known who was responsible for the ubiquitous Roycroft tapering leg which

While the Roycrofters were in the business of making and selling crafts, Hubbard's real product was an ideal.

terminated in a bulbous foot, or the ponderous proportions characteristic of much of the furniture. Its design appears to be a pastiche of English Arts and Crafts prototypes. For example, the leg shape was taken from a design by Arthur Heygate Mackmurdo and some of the copper hardware finds antecedent in hardware on a table by Herbert MacNair. Guidelines set by Hubbard to "Build your art horse-high, pig-tight and bull-strong," seem to be the only cohesive element in the highly varied offering. Bookcases, Morris chairs, china cabinets and dining tables, built with superb joinery from the best grades of wood, incorporate more handwork than the furniture made at other American factories of the period. However limited the aesthetic success of these designs, they were a successful representation of the Roycroft ideal. A piece of furniture had the potential to dominate the domestic environment. Books might be stored away on a shelf, the tiny stamp on a piece of copper might be overlooked, but the Roycroft insignia carved several inches high on the face of a cabinet or on the crest of a chair was a constant reminder of its origins. In Roycroft furniture, there was an implied message as well. Weight has traditionally been considered evidence of high quality and Roycroft designs had a reassuringly heavy appearance. Mahogany and bird's eye maple were sometimes used, but the predominant wood was oak, finished with a dark red-black stain. The wood grain was filled and polished to a high luster. Most pieces still in daily use retain this durable somber finish. Hubbard called his

Opposite page: White oak magazine rack, 37″ high, made at Roycroft between 1908 and 1910. The Roycroft stamp is prominently placed on this piece, as on most: Hubbard readily appreciated the publicity value of the mark. Courtesy Jordan-Volpe Gallery, New York. This page, left: Leather-seated white oak dining chair has stamped inventory numbers showing it was once in use at the Roycroft Inn. The distinctive foot on this chair, also seen in profile, was common to much Roycroft furniture. Photo, Rick Echelmeyer; courtesy Robert Edwards Arts & Crafts Furnishings, Rosemont, Pennsylvania. The 15″ lamp, above, combines amber-colored mica inserts with hand-hammered copper for an effect of grace and warmth. Jordan-Volpe Gallery, New York.

furniture "Aurora Colonial." Since there is no reference to 18th-century American furniture styles in his designs, it seems probable that Hubbard intended the wood stain to be associated with antique, aristocratic mahogany. It would therefore be compatible with Colonial Revival furnishings, the prevailing mode of interior decoration at the turn of the century.

Like Marshall McLuhan, Elbert Hubbard believed that "the medium is the message." That message, the Roycroft ideal, was never defined in its entirety in words, not even in those inspirational words printed at Roycroft and preciously bound in soft chamois, or "limp ooze" leather. The medium, however—the books, the copperware, the furniture—was fraught with meaning, which often promoted the noble tenets of the Arts and Crafts movement, and which nearly always propelled profit into Hubbard's pocket. One of his advertisements reads, "The Roycroft Inn was built, furnished, and is run by the Roycrofters—an Art Colony. Whether the Roycrofters have improved on the work of William Morris and John Ruskin is not the question. In any event, this institution has grown, slowly but surely." Hubbard never does tell us what the question is, let alone answer it. Very possibly, he did not, nor did he intend to, improve on the work of Morris and Ruskin. They gave him an idea for a business. This business, in turn, gave artists such as Dard Hunter, Karl Kipp, and William Denslow the opportunity to produce some of the best American work in the Arts and Crafts style. ■

Innovative
Furniture

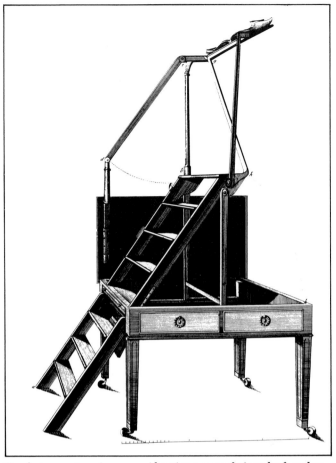

Comfort was not a primary consideration among chair and sofa makers until the High Victorian period, when overstuffed, upholstered seating became popular. Opposite: Both the cast iron spring and the bentwood back and arms of this rocker, patented by Heywood Brothers & Co., Gardner, Massachusetts, in 1873, were "innovative" applications of materials and technology. Private collection. Making furniture serve more than one purpose was the aim of many designers. Opposite, inset:

This windsor comb-back, common in the late 18th and early 19th centuries, cleverly combined a desk with a chair. Cooper-Hewitt Museum, New York. Windsors were among the first types of seating furniture made with "bent" wooden components. Above, left: Library steps, designed by Thomas Sheraton in 1793, fold down into the table. Photo courtesy David Hanks. Above, right: An example of Sheraton's concept, "in the wood." Courtesy Cooper-Hewitt Museum.

Design innovations have provided greater comfort, flexibility, portability, efficiency, and diversity in furniture. Utilizing new technology, materials, and above all ingenuity, many 19th century manufacturers worked to improve furniture design.

BY PAGE TALBOTT

Furniture, as we know it, is a relatively recent addition to man's world, following the more necessary inventions of tools, weapons, and agricultural implements. Among the earliest man-made seats and tables are those found in Egyptian records, and even these pieces are limited in form and material to low stools, chairs, and boxes constructed of wood, apparently made for members of the ruling class.

Remarkably, the use of furniture—particularly that which was heavily ornamented—continued to be limited to only the wealthiest members of the most civilized cultures until the Renaissance, when gradually the ownership of furniture became more widespread. Well into the 18th century, however, many homes were furnished only with stump chairs, log tables, and straw-mattress beds.

Throughout its history, furniture essentially has been limited to three basic forms—the table, the stool, and the box—from which all more advanced forms have evolved. Variations of these forms help to define innovation in furniture. Since "necessity is the mother of invention," most developments in furniture forms and functions have resulted from changing life-styles and residential patterns, as well as from shifts in the accessibility of materials.

Defining innovation

Furniture may be considered innovative if it offers a solution to man's need for portability, is made of new materials, uses a familiar material in a new way, combines the function of several pieces of furniture in one form to save space, or offers a unique solution to man's desire for seating and sleeping comfort. Furniture also may be considered innovative in terms of cost, efficiency, or advanced technology.

In certain cases the invention of one person or group may be said to be truly innovative, a key development in the progress of furniture design. More frequently, however, the development of those pieces of furniture that today are viewed as pivotal depended on a whole series of inventions that preceded them. A case in point is Michael Thonet. His ubiquitous bentwood furniture drew on the experiments of several earlier generations of craftsmen, including Windsor chairmakers, who bent hickory wood for use on hoopback chairs.

The problem of portability

A particularly fascinating furniture form that has withstood the test of time (it was invented as early as the 15th century B.C.) is the folding stool or chair. From our myopic vantage point, it is hard to believe that this clever invention could be 3,500 years old, but surviving Egyptian examples—as well as pictorial records of folding chairs used in Greece and Rome—attest to the popularity of this form in early cultures.

After Rome, however, the folding chair seems to have lost ground in favor of other, heavier forms of seating. It was rediscovered in the 19th century, when hundreds of patents were taken out for folding chairs. To the inventors and consumers of that century, folding chairs were truly innovative, embodying a wealth of technical and design changes, each an "improvement" on the one before.

Among the best known of the 19th-century folding-chair makers was George J. Hunzinger of New York City. Hunzinger registered many patents, including one in 1866 for a "reclining chair," with a back that tilted for comfort and legs that folded for portability. While Hunzinger's chair was meant for household use, much of the folding furniture of the period was "camp furniture" appropriate for picnics, traveling, or battlefield use.

Nineteenth-century inventors found many solutions to the problem of portability. The X-shaped leg configuration was the most common. Cued by their ancient predecessors, many designers connected either both sets of side legs, or front legs and back legs, with a collapsible metal brace, which when unlocked allowed the fabric seat to fold and the two sides or back and front to fold against each other. Among the most successful of the chairs using this "X" end formation was the one known today as a "director's chair," made in this country as early as the 1860s and manufactured by many firms including Gold Medal, Inc., of Racine, Wisconsin, in the latter part of the century. Such chairs featured front legs which folded up under the seat, while the seat itself folded against the back. Modern outdoor lounge chairs use this system, as did the A. F. Marks folding "invalid chair," patented in 1876. The lightest and most portable of the mass-produced 19th-century folding chairs were probably sling chairs made of canvas with metal or wooden frames, in production in the United States by 1895. Their prototype was patented in England in 1877.

Innovative materials

Furniture has been made of various materials from glass to paper, from plastic to steel. Almost as soon as a material has been invented, furniture designers have tried to put it to use. Charles Eames and Eero Saarinen, for example, capitalized on the technology developed during World War II in their experiments with molded plastic furniture. But most 19th- and 20th-century designers—including the inventors of portable furniture—who sought innovative materials found that most possibilities had been tested in earlier times. Frank O. Gehry, a Santa Monica designer, for example, experimented in the early 1970s with corrugated cardboard as a suitable material for low cost, lightweight furniture. But the use of paper in furniture construction did not originate in this century. Paper furniture was known as early as the second century A.D., when the Chinese used papier-mâché to make decorative and utilitarian objects. And papier-mâché was widely used in England in the mid-19th century for chairs and tables in the rococo-revival style.

The Chinese also can be credited with the invention of cast iron, originally used for small domestic objects but adapted for furniture making by the early 19th century. While such pieces are now considered appropriate primarily for outdoor use, cast-iron benches, tables, and chairs commonly were found in the best-appointed parlors of the mid-Victorian period. They were more sturdy and less expensive than pieces crafted of wrought iron, reflecting an ongoing search for better and cheaper materials for furniture making.

In addition to cast and wrought iron, 19th-century furniture makers used steel wire strips, rods, mesh, and tubes, followed in the 20th century by such modern materials as chromium and nickel, and various kinds of plastics including acrylics, polystyrenes, nylon, fiberglass, and melamines. Rubber and other petroleum-based products are also being used experimentally, particularly by today's European designers.

Of course, wood continues to be the most popular material for furniture—pulled, stretched, and bent to its limits. Wood-bending under steam pressure was a technique developed in ancient times. But it was not applied to furniture until the 18th century with the development of the Windsor chair. Beginning in the 1840s bentwood began

Above, left: Cast iron garden chair, patented in 1866 by Lalance & Grosjean of New York. Private collection; photo courtesy Smithsonian Institution. Above, right: Although Michael Thonet is credited with inventing bentwood furniture, other designers preceded him. Bostonian Samuel Gragg's 1808 "elastic chair" was perhaps the first American example. Smithsonian Institution; gift of Dr. Richard H. Howland. Above: New Yorker C.B. Sheldon's popular 1876 reclining chair, which could be folded up for easy moving. Private collection; photo Studio Nine. Left: The Paine Furniture Co. of Boston introduced this amusing piano hide-a-bed in the 1880s. Photo courtesy Smithsonian Institution.

to be used for other chair forms, as attested by the number of wood-bending patents on record at the United States Patent Office. Laminated wood—many layers glued together and worked as one unit—or plywood had an 18th-century counterpart. Thomas Chippendale made dining-room chairs for Osterley Park circa 1773 with back splats of "three-ply" mahogany. Michael Thonet, best known for his experimental use of bentwood toward the middle of the 19th century, also made chair parts from narrow strips of veneer, bent in molds under heat and then glued. The earliest American patents for plywood were issued in 1865 and 1868, starting a furniture-making revolution in this country. Foremost among American furniture makers using laminated woods was John Henry Belter, whose work is so well known to the 20th-century student and collector that his name has become the generic designation for all laminated rococo-revival furniture. Another well-known 19th-century firm, Gardner and Company, had salesrooms in New York City and developed award-winning three-ply veneer chairs that were shown in an impressive booth in the 1876 Philadelphia Centennial Exhibition.

In this century Gilbert Rohde and Charles Eames continued to design bent and laminated wood furniture. Rohde's chair, manufactured around 1930 by Heywood-Wakefield Company, consists of a seat and back of one piece of wood, with separate bent and laminated wood supports. Eames's chair was put into production in 1946 by Herman Miller. This design was particularly innovative because the molded panels of the back and seat were bent in three directions to fit the human body. Today's furniture industry continues to experiment with new materials. Although the past two centuries have witnessed extraordinary experimentation, the possibilities seem in no sense exhausted for new ways to work with basic materials.

Multipurpose furniture

In every era, furniture makers have attempted to attain maximum utility in minimum space for each piece of furniture. Limited only by imagination, some furniture makers pushed their designs to the point of absurdity: Bruschke Ericke of Chicago, Illinois, advertised a combination of bathtub and sofa in the December 1883 issue of *Decorator and Furnisher.* It was described as the "common sense invention of the age" because it placed "a household necessity within reach of all." Among the more plausible dual-purpose furniture forms were combination table and dictionary stands, library stairs that converted to chairs, and bookcases that unfolded to reveal beds.

Because of their bulk, beds were the items most commonly concealed in other, less space-consuming forms. Beginning in the 17th century and possibly before, beds were hidden in trunks, disguised as cupboards, or conjured from chairs and lounges. By the 19th century, beds were masked as pianos, bureaus, writing desks, and wardrobes, among other pieces. In some cases the forms that hid the beds were functional, but in other instances they were merely false fronts, allowing the bed to be placed undetected in a parlor or library.

The most common furniture combination in the last as well as the current century has been the sofa bed. By the late 1800s the desire to combine the

Opposite page: Gilbert Rohde's fascination with industrial materials helped create a modern American esthetic. Using a plastic called bakelite for the top and tubular steel for the legs, Rohde designed this striking desk for the Troy Sunshade Company of Ohio, ca 1934. Private collection; photo courtesy Smithsonian Institution. Right: The Chinese made papier mâché furniture as early as the 2nd century. Frank O. Gehry, an American, revived the tradition in 1970 with this corrugated cardboard lounge chair. He called his low-cost, light-weight cardboard furniture "Easy Edges." Private collection; photo courtesy David Hanks.

function of seating and sleeping furniture reached epidemic proportions: hundreds of patents were registered for a seemingly inexhaustible number of combinations, alterations, and improvements. Typical solutions to the problem of combining the two forms involved sofa backs that unhinged to fall backward, supported by hidden legs; seats consisting of double mattresses which folded out on springs; and the 20th-century "convertible" version, which has collapsible metal springs and a frame that supports a folding mattress.

Innovating for comfort

While certain earlier forms, notably the wing chair of the 17th century and the French bergère of the 18th century made concessions to comfort in seating, it was not until the High Victorian period that most sofas and chairs were purposely designed to be comfortable. The increased prominence of the upholstering trade, the plethora of patents for supporting springs and frames, and the new esthetic appeal of "stuffed" furniture all contributed to the popularity of upholstery during the Victorian era.

Overstuffed furniture epitomized this new desire for comfortable seating, but other chair forms reflected the same concerns. The reclining chair in its many variations was also largely a 19th-century phenomenon, although it too had precedents in earlier times. Some recliners used ratchets to raise and lower the backs, while others depended on concealed legs to support the back in its inclined position.

The most popular reclining chair was based on a prototype designed in England by William Watt and executed by Morris and Company, beginning in 1883. Known today as the Morris chair, this form was produced widely in the United States by such makers as Allan and Brothers of Philadelphia, who in 1894 patented their own version, incorporating further mechanical innovations. Today upholstered recliners are standard in most American homes, continuing a tradition of comfort established by our forebears of the past century.

The invention of spiral springs—iron wire coiled into two inverted cones—was one of the most significant innovations in furniture making. While

springs were widely used in the pre-Revolutionary period, mostly to ease the ride of wagon and carriage passengers, they generally were not applied in household furniture until the Victorian era. One of the best-known pieces of early spiral-spring furniture, the "revolving armchair" designed by Thomas E. Warren, of Troy, New York, was shown at London's Crystal Palace Exhibition of 1851. This "very handsome" chair was described in the *Illustrated Exhibitor* (London, 1851) as "made wholly of cast iron, the base consisting of four ornamental bracket feet mounted on casters and secured to a center piece, to which eight elliptical springs were attached." The Warren chair was the first of many chairs—in particular, office chairs that provided maximum flexibility in a small space—to use springs in this fashion.

Research into patent records, trade journals, and catalogues of 19th-century furniture firms has only touched the surface of the innovations in design, technology, materials, spatial economy, and comfort. Current interest in this period will no doubt lead to further discoveries. ■

Thonet and Bentwood

Using innovative technology, German-born Thonet developed distinctive laminated and bentwood chairs between 1830 and 1857. They were mass-manufactured by his descendants well into the 20th century.

BY CHRISTOPHER WILK

In the history of furniture design, few events have been more significant—or more taken for granted—than Michael Thonet's development of bentwood furniture from 1830 to 1857. During these years, the German-born Thonet brought furniture-making from the realm of handicraft into the industrial age. In the following half-century, he and his successors built the largest furniture company the world had ever known, while creating a most enduring and successful type of furniture.

It all began in 1830, at Thonet's birthplace, Boppard-on-Rhine, in a one-man cabinetmaking shop he'd owned for 11 years. Thonet fabricated his first bent furniture parts from pieces of laminated veneer. He continued to experiment and by 1836 constructed his first bentwood chairs.

Only a few of these first chairs survive. Except for the seat, they were made by a new process: thin, narrow pieces of veneer were stacked and tied together, then soaked in boiling glue. Thonet bent these pliable parts into wooden molds, allowed them to dry,

and assembled them. He applied an additional surface layer of veneer to unify the design.

Between 1840 and 1842 he made a second group of similarly constructed chairs with fewer parts. This desire to simplify construction, to reduce the number of parts and the amount of labor necessary to produce a chair, remained a constant in Thonet's career as a craftsman and manufacturer. Thonet's chairs were considerably lighter in weight than carved chairs of similar design, and they were lower in cost.

Thonet and his Central European contemporaries regarded the process for making furniture from bent pieces of laminated veneers as an "invention." They were apparently unaware of earlier chairs of partial bentwood construction, such as English and American bow-back Windsor chairs, the patent chairs made by Samuel Gragg in Boston between 1808 and 1815, and certain French chairs of the first decade of the 19th century. Thonet surely must have found inspiration for his bending technique in the traditional bending methods of craftsmen such as barrel makers, wheelwrights, shipbuilders, and carriage makers. His particular innovation was to develop a bending process specifically geared to large-scale production of chairs and other furniture.

Although technically innovative, Thonet's chairs were stylistically very much a part of the contemporary Biedermeier style of furniture design that dominated Central Europe between

1815 and 1848. Derived from French Directoire and Empire furniture, Biedermeier was a restrained, unornamented style that relied primarily on a richly grained surface veneer for decoration. Thonet's chairs were quite similar to carved Biedermeier chairs. The use of elaborately curved chair parts, which appeared to be of bent construction, was quite common in Biedermeier furniture.

Early in Thonet's career, his work appeared at exhibition in Koblenz, where it attracted the attention of the celebrated Prince Klemens von Metternich, chancellor and foreign minister of the Austro-Hungarian Empire. Metternich was much impressed with Thonet's bentwood furniture. After giving him a private audience at his castle on the Rhine, he urged Thonet to move to the capital city of the Empire, Vienna, where his work would find a more appreciative audience. In 1842 Thonet, his wife, and five sons moved to Vienna.

The renovation of the palace of the Liechtenstein family provided the Thonets with their first commission; they made elaborately bent pieces for parquet floors and manufactured a large number of chairs in three designs.

Remarkably restrained and delicate

A Thonet advertisement, ca 1873, illustrates the wide variety of furniture forms they manufactured from bentwood. Note pictures of Thonet factories, together with addresses of the firm's branch offices at the top of the document. All photographs, courtesy Thonet Archives.

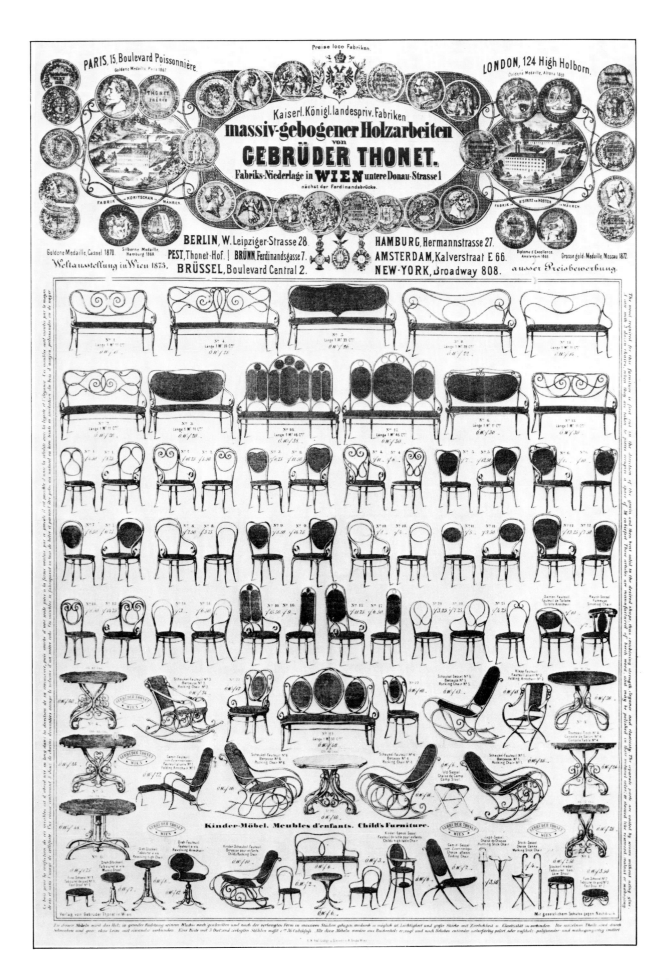

Above, left: Bentwood chair. Thonet Brothers, late 19th century. The unusual configuration of the back and legs approximates the appearance of rustic furniture. Philadelphia Museum of Arts, Marie Josephine Rozet Fund. The music stand at left, ca 1890, is a virtuoso example of the art of steam bending. Courtesy Thonet Archives.

in design, the Liechtenstein chairs were completely unrelated to any contemporary European counterparts. They demonstrated the originality of Thonet furniture and were proof of his belief in bentwood construction as the ideal method for chair making.

Although these startlingly original chairs appeared to have been made from solid bentwood, they actually were made from long pieces of laminated veneers rasped to a less rectilinear (in some cases almost round) profile. These chairs showed that although Thonet was already thinking in terms of solid—as opposed to layered—bentwood chairs, he was unable to successfully produce furniture of solid wood. During the next several years Thonet devoted much energy to solving this technical problem.

After completing his work for the Liechtenstein Palace in 1849, Michael Thonet opened his own furniture workshop and in the same year received his first large independent commission:

chairs for the Café Daum in Vienna. Thonet eventually produced several hundred of these chairs in laminated construction. The Daum chair was later added to the Thonet catalogues as model No. 4. During the 1850s, Thonet made a large number of new chair designs for specific commissions, including Vienna's Schwarzenberg Palace, while continuing to work on the problem of how to manufacture furniture of solid bentwood.

In 1851 Thonet sent some furniture for display at London's Great Exhibition, housed in Joseph Paxton's Crystal Palace. These examples of elaborately decorated fancy furniture (which the exhibition jury described as "curious"), brought the Thonets the first of many awards which they received at each subsequent exhibition they entered. Their success continued practically unabated until the First World War.

On November 1, 1853, the Gebrüder Thonet, or Thonet Brothers of Vienna,

was formed, named for Michael Thonet's five sons. That year they received an imperial monopoly patent "for the production of chairs and table legs made of bentwood," which expired in 1869. International exhibitions in Munich (1854) and Paris (1855) created a large international market for bentwood furniture. By 1855 orders were received from as far away as South America. Precisely at this time the final obstacles to the mass production of solid bentwood furniture were overcome. Copper beech trees grew abundantly in Central Europe, and their wood was ideally suited to bending. Long rods of beechwood were steamed until malleable and then bent into iron molds. After the pieces were allowed to dry in the molds, they were sanded, machined, stained, caned, and finally packed for shipping.

By 1856 the small Thonet factory of 70 workers in Vienna was unable to keep up with the ever-increasing number of orders. Michael Thonet moved to the beech forests of Moravia (present-day Czechoslovakia) to supervise the construction of the first of seven large factories. The Thonets designed and built most of their own machinery and tools. At this time they stopped using skilled cabinetmakers and joiners. Henceforth they relied exclusively on unskilled labor. Each worker learned only one of the steps involved in the carefully regimented process of factory production. During its first year, 1857, Thonet's new factory produced 10,000 pieces of furniture, mostly chairs; in the following year the total rose to 16,000; and by 1860 the factory produced the extraordinary number of 50,000 pieces of furniture.

The new solid beechwood chairs, sold almost exclusively for commercial use in cafés, restaurants, and hotels, were immediately successful for several reasons. A simple bentwood side chair was made from six or eight pieces of bent beechwood screwed—not glued—together. The result was a chair without joints, remarkably durable and strong. The chairs were extremely lightweight, ideally suited for situations where furniture was moved a

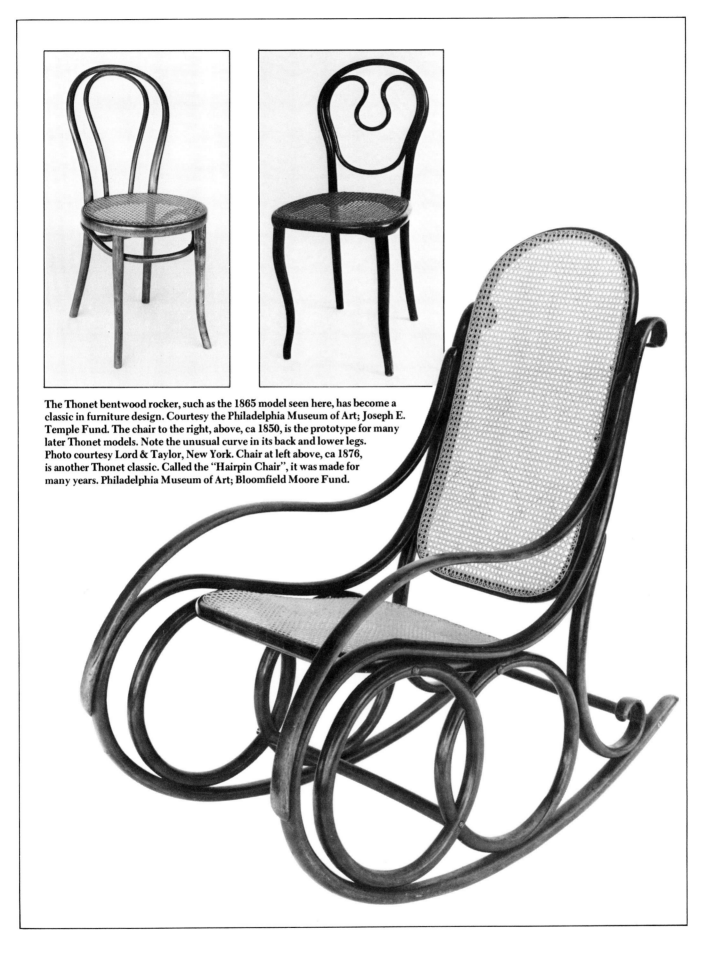

The Thonet bentwood rocker, such as the 1865 model seen here, has become a classic in furniture design. Courtesy the Philadelphia Museum of Art; Joseph E. Temple Fund. The chair to the right, above, ca 1850, is the prototype for many later Thonet models. Note the unusual curve in its back and lower legs. Photo courtesy Lord & Taylor, New York. Chair at left above, ca 1876, is another Thonet classic. Called the "Hairpin Chair", it was made for many years. Philadelphia Museum of Art; Bloomfield Moore Fund.

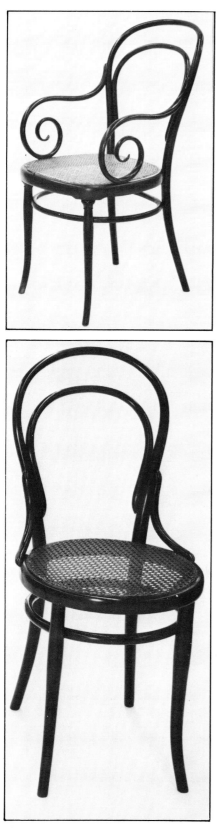

The Thonet firm was best known for its simply constructed, inexpensive chairs. This page, top: Thonet armchair, ca 1859, is a variation of the "Vienna Café Chair" beneath it. This staple item, #14 in the catalogue, was the first widely affordable Thonet design. All photos, courtesy Thonet Archives.

great deal. The chairs were shipped unassembled in large crates (or, as the bentwood industry referred to it around the turn of the century, "knocked-down"), thereby greatly reducing shipping costs.

The design of the chairs, which may have influenced their initial success less than their price or weight, was totally novel. An English writer looking back on twenty-five years of Thonet furniture documented the public's reaction: "Slowly these goods were received, at first with some disfavor, having a decidedly foreign look about them, but they have surely steadily increased in popularity."

The ever-growing demand for Thonet bentwood furniture is one of the most remarkable stories of the Industrial Revolution. Many countries, especially England, exported large amounts of furniture in the 19th century, but no company approached the volume of export sales achieved by Thonet. The explosion of sales was matched by an enormous increase in the number of models available. In 1859 Thonet published a catalogue containing 26 items. Seven years later, Thonet had branch offices in Budapest, Paris, London, Berlin, Hamburg, Rotterdam, and Brno, and offered 70 items; in 1888 the figure was 348; in 1895 the total rose to 848; and by the turn of the century Thonet offered its customers over 1,000 designs of furniture.

The largest-selling item—several million were sold during the 19th century—was model No. 14, one of the simplest, most understated chairs ever designed.

In 1860 the Thonets introduced their first rocking chair. Influenced by the steel and brass rockers exhibited at London's Crystal Palace, bentwood rockers were one of the few Thonet models made for domestic use. During the 1860s Thonet also introduced swivel office chairs, folding chairs, and children's furniture. Although the side chair remained the core of the Thonet line, almost all of the side-chair designs began to be offered with accompanying armchairs and settees.

Michael Thonet died in 1871, but during the 1870s and 1880s his sons ex-

panded the repertoire of bentwood furniture to include virtually every major form. Stools, chaises longues, rocking couches, theater seating, beds, walking sticks, cribs, garden furniture, plant stands, towel and coat racks, dressing tables, screens, easels, music stands, invalid furniture, and every possible type of table were offered at this time.

When Thonet's imperial patent expired in 1869, other bentwood companies began competing for a share of the large market he had developed. The largest and most successful of these, the firm of Jacob and Josef Kohn, began building factories in the same towns or villages where the Thonet factories were located. Like those of other competitors, Kohn's catalogues featured exact copies of Thonet models, even using the same model numbers for identification. By 1894 at least 52 companies producing bentwood furniture were located in a number of European countries, including Russia, Germany, France, Italy, Belgium, and Romania.

Bentwood furniture was exported to the United States in small quantities from the 1860s, but popularity greatly increased after Thonet opened a New York branch store around 1873. Thonet and Kohn displays at the 1876 Philadelphia Centennial Exhibition aroused further interest. Among the many bentwood companies having agents or sales offices in the United States—mostly in New York—were Fischel, Mundus, Hoffmann, and the Austrian Bentwood Furniture Company. Although no competitor offered as many models as Thonet, virtually all of them sold standard models that were often indistinguishable from the original Thonet versions. Around the turn of the century, competition between the various companies became particularly intense, and price wars were common.

In the period between 1899 and World War I, both Thonet and J. & J. Kohn produced the designs of leading Viennese architects and designers, including Adolf Loos, Josef Hoffmann, Otto Wagner, Koloman Moser, Gustav Siegel, Marcel Kammerer, Josef Urban, and Leopold Bauer. Kohn's and Thonet's sale of furniture by "name" designers marked the first instances of fur-

The spiralling curves of bentwood furniture influenced the Art Nouveau style. Chaise longue, beechwood and cane, made by Thonet Brothers ca 1870. The Brooklyn Museum; The Woodward Memorial Fund.

niture manufacturers marketing ready-made, mass-produced, reasonably priced architect-designed furniture. Despite the significance of this event, contemporary writers made little note of it, and the "name" designers received no credit in the Thonet or Kohn catalogues.

Such architect-designed pieces showed a predilection for geometrical forms, generally rectilinear. Although *The Studio* magazine commented that "the process by which any curve can be given to wood is particularly applicable to the modern taste for "line," these designers eschewed the sinewy curves of the art/nouveau style to which the writer was referring. The spiraling curves of Thonet bentwood furniture were always recognized as an "Austrian specialty" (as described in the same article), but it was primarily

in Belgium and France that traditional Thonet bentwood furniture had its influence on the new, modern style called art nouveau.

At its peak Thonet had more than 30 international branches and employed more than 6,000 workers, who produced almost 2,000,000 pieces of furniture per year. But World War I brought an abrupt halt to the bentwood industry. Recovery from the war was not achieved until the 1920s, when Thonet merged with a recently formed furniture conglomerate composed of the old Kohn and Mundus companies. Under the Thonet name, this new firm continued the production of traditional bentwood furniture but also added a large number of new architect-designed bentwood and tubular-steel models.

During the late 1920s and early

1930s, when it manufactured the designs of architects like Marcel Breuer, Miës van der Rohe, and Le Corbusier and his associates, Thonet again reached preeminence in the field of furniture design.

In 1939, on the eve of World War II, the company moved its headquarters to the United States, where it remains today. Other individual Thonet companies, originally part of the large conglomerate, now exist in Germany, France, and Austria.

Michael Thonet revolutionized furniture design, production, and marketing. At the basis of all of his work was the process itself, the steam-bending of beechwood, which was brilliantly and artistically reflected in his furniture. His bentwood furniture and that of his successors and rivals remains an important contribution to design history. ∎

George Hunzinger

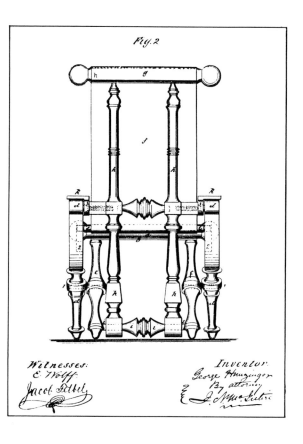

Best remembered for his patent furniture, including ingenious collapsible chairs, Hunzinger worked in a distinctive variant of the Renaissance Revival style.

BY RICHARD W. FLINT

George Hunzinger was a German immigrant chairmaker whose eclectic, patented works adorned Victorian parlors. Hunzinger's work first received attention from scholars and collectors in The Metropolitan Museum of Art's 1970 exhibition "Nineteenth Century America." Marilynn Johnson described it in the exhibition catalogue as "turned wooden parts that look like the components of an engine, or, in the base, cast-iron piping. . . . Gazing at these chairs, one can only feel that turning a knob might set all the wheels and cogs into motion."

The best-known chairs Hunzinger made are an 1866 patented folding chair and one designed with a diagonal side brace patented in 1869. Also important was an 1876 patent for attaching metallic strips as seating and one in 1882 for a platform rocker. Such occasional chairs, "fancier" or different in design from other furniture, were used by Victorian Americans to provide diversity and accent in a parlor.

American decorative taste changed frequently in the 19th century. There were many styles of furniture, and while Hunzinger's creations might be said to fit within certain genres, he was hardly a conformist. His whimsical work appeals to collectors and historians alike, and the prosperous condition of his business indicates that his work appealed to Victorians too.

The early years

George Jakob Hunzinger was born in

Tuttlingen, a German city near the Swiss border, on September 12, 1835, the oldest of four children. His family had been settled in Tuttlingen for many generations, working as cabinetmakers since 1612. Today Hunzingers in Tuttlingen still produce interior cabinetwork as well as reproductions of cabinets and restorations of antique furniture. Some of the many styles and designs produced by Hunzinger in America were manufactured in Germany from about 1850 until World War I.

Hunzinger's birthplace is in the province of Württemberg, the same area where John Henry Belter was born in 1804. Unlike Belter's unsigned American rococo furniture, most all of Hunzinger's work bears a clear label indicating where it was manufactured. This identification is often a boldly incised stamp on the back of a leg or brace marked with the date of patent.

While post-Civil War designers revived traditional styles, innovators such as Hunzinger created new forms for patent furniture. Opposite: Illustration for a Hunzinger reclining chair from patent papers issued in 1866. Top left: Ambrotype of Hunzinger, ca 1860. Above: Walnut folding chair, patented 1866, with upholstery added later. Inset, right: Detail of Hunzinger's stamped inscription. All courtesy The Margaret Woodbury Strong Museum, Rochester, New York.

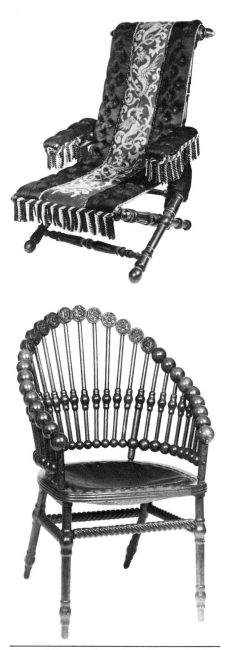

Top: Folding armchair, 1866. Ebonized walnut and gilt; original horsehair and needlepoint upholstery with fringe. Courtesy the High Museum of Art, the Crawford Decorative Arts Collection. Above: Oak side chair, patented 1877, shows Hunzinger's light touch. Courtesy The Strong Museum.

On his patent rocker, the label is paper.

George Hunzinger's mother died when he was 11, and his father remarried three years later. Young George did not get along well with his stepmother and, following his apprenticeship, he spent much of his time as a journeyman in Geneva, Switzerland. The young cabinetmaker was part of a large wave of German immigrants when he came to America and settled in Brooklyn during the 1850s. The impact of German culture on America was strong, and within the furniture business the national origin of cabinetmakers and upholsterers was heavily Germanic. Of the 5,071 men and women working in New York City in 1870, the census reported that 3,103 were German. In Brooklyn Hunzinger met a woman who also came from Tuttlingen, Marie Susanne Grieb, and they were married on Christmas Day, 1859 in the German Evangelical Church on Schermerhorn Street, Brooklyn.

Hunzinger's first patents

In 1861 Hunzinger obtained the first of many patents he would receive. It was for an improved reclining chair with a footboard designed to serve as a table; the whole unit could also be folded for transport. Two years later Hunzinger improved the folding arm, patented the invention, and assigned its use to C. Henry Glinsman, a New York City furniture manufacturer and, possibly, Hunzinger's employer.

In 1865 Hunzinger received his United States citizenship and in the following year he obtained another patent for a folding reclining chair. Furniture that moved, folded, or converted into other uses fascinated the American public as much as did the variety of elaborately embellished Victorian styles. Platform rockers, folding chairs, and hideaway beds were only a few of the many pieces that were invented and patented by their designers.

There are different kinds of patents: trademark, design, and invention. By 1875 Hunzinger discovered that there were other patentable parts to his 1866 chair and he was reissued a patent protecting those inventions. Such *camp chairs* or *stools*, as Hunzinger called them, were not new. What he claimed for his patent was not a design but an invention for a stronger structural system.

George Hunzinger prospered from his patents. In 1866 he went into business for himself in New York at 192 Laurens Street. Within two years he built up a stock worth $10,000 and regularly employed four or five men. In 1869 he received his fourth patent for a diagonal brace on a chair that connected, on the sides, the front feet of the chair with the upper back. The brace strengthened the chair's support, for, as Hunzinger himself explained in his patent application: "The back legs of chairs are very liable to become loosened at the point of connection with the seat. . . . This looseness arises from pressure against the back of the chair, and from tipping the chair backward upon the hind legs." Such tipping of the chair was a very American habit and the immigrant chairmaker was attempting to design a durable seat for his new countrymen.

Prosperity on Seventh Avenue

Hunzinger sold $50,000 worth of goods in 1869 when he received the patent for the chair most frequently encountered by today's collectors—the "diagonal-brace" chair. In 1870, with his business growing and prospering, he leased new quarters at 402 Bleecker Street. Hunzinger was regarded by his contemporaries as "industrious & hardworking" and with a reputation for "fair dealing & promptitude" in business affairs. Between 1871 and 1873 his capital worth grew from $25,000 to $60,000. The rapid growth of his business probably contributed to his breaking the five-year lease on Bleecker Street in 1873 to move to Seventh Avenue.

In his earliest years, Hunzinger described himself as a "manufacturer of patent Folding, Reclining and Extension Chairs," other times as a cabinetmaker, or, most often, simply as a chairmaker. The description he chose in the 1880s—maker of "fancy chairs" and "ornamental furniture"—seems best to us today. His creations represent a merriment of design unlike anyone else's. The angular arms and braces utilizing wheel-and-cog-like elements disrupt expectations of traditional design. While Hunzinger's firm primarily produced chairs, especially in its early years, it also made sofas. A spectacular parlor suite comprising sofa, gentleman's chair, and two lady's side chairs—now at the Margaret Woodbury Strong Museum in Rochester, New York—bears the 1869 patent date. The furniture feet represent cloven hooves, and the pieces are embellished with carving. As the firm prospered in the 1870s and later, its designs became more conventional, but George Hunzinger continued to be fascinated with new ideas.

In 1876 Hunzinger received a patent for a springlike woven-wire chair seat and back. The patent was for a series of peripheral grooves and pins that held the wire band to the chair frame. It also protected the wire bands, which were described as "finely tempered flat steel ribbons or springs . . . covered with a durable web of silk or worsted, not sewed, but woven around the steel." In 1878, the U.S. Patent Office assigned him the use of Chester D. Flynt's patent for a spring seat of arched steel bands. Three years later, Hunzinger himself received another patent for woven-wire seat coverings similar to his 1876 invention. His fascination for spring seats reflected ideas that went back at least as far as a 1793 design by Thomas Sheraton. Spiral springs for use as chair cushions were patented in England in 1826, and woven-wire mattresses were invented about 1870.

Disaster by fire

Hunzinger's growing prosperity in the 1870s was interrupted by the kind of calamity that occasionally brought havoc to 19th-century businesses. On October 17, 1877, Hunzinger's factory, along with several other structures, was

Top: Unusual folding rocker, painted black and partially covered with brass strips, without Hunzinger's usual knobs and turnings. Courtesy Charles and Helen Sporn Collection; photo Mysak/Studio Nine. Right: Two walnut side chairs, both examples of Hunzinger's 1869 patent diagonally-braced chair. Courtesy The Strong Museum.

Above: Side chair, 1869, black lacquer with gold striping. The 1869 patent diagonally-braced chair is frequently encountered by today's collectors. Courtesy the Sporn Collection; photo Mysak/Studio Nine. Top: Detail of Hunzinger's business letterhead. Courtesy The Strong Museum. Inset: Stereoview, ca 1875, showing a Hunzinger side chair. Courtesy The Strong Museum.

"Tipping chairs backward was a very American habit, and Hunzinger was attempting to design a durable seat for his new countrymen."

destroyed by fire. Hunzinger's loss was $50,000, but the total estimated loss for the entire conflagration was $238,000. The other principal losers were also furniture factories: Pierre J. Hardy lost $80,000 and the prestigious firm of Roux & Co. lost $55,000.

The three furniture factories of Hunzinger, Hardy, and Roux, each 50 by 100 feet and built of brick, formed a **T** shape. Roux's five-story factory faced 18th Street, back to back with Hardy's six-story structure on 19th Street. The rear of Hunzinger's five-story building on Seventh Avenue abutted the rear of the other two factories. Numerous other small houses filled the corner lots on Seventh Avenue between 18th and 19th streets. The three factories, each connected by iron bridges, shared a common steam engine that was thought to have ignited the lumber store in the yard.

Hunzinger's insurance amounted to only $20,000, less than half his loss. A series of three temporary locations housed his factory for the next two years as Hunzinger awaited completion of his new $26,000 building which still stands at 323-327 West 16th Street.

Hunzinger's rockers

The Hunzinger company continued to grow under conservative management in the 1880s. But his recovery from the fire and the firm's prosperous condition were due to George Hunzinger's most successful invention, a platform or spring rocking chair patented in 1882. In his patent application Hunzinger noted that such rockers had "long been regular articles of manufacture" but his was a simple device composed of two compound hinges each connected to the base and rocking chair and with contractile springs connecting the middle portion of each hinge.

The rocking chair was a particularly American phenomena and very popular with the middle classes. It was in the 1870s that the patent rocker became

Above: Walnut folding chair. In 1876 Hunzinger patented the webbed upholstery construction of steel ribbons covered with silk or worsted. Private collection.

prominent, and in his *Book of Designs* J. Wayland Kimball offers an explanation:

> Foreigners call the rocking chair a peculiarly American luxury, yet the necessary length of the rockers on the floor causes this favorite chair to be occasionally in the way, and not infrequently too noisy for comfort. These disadvantages have been very ingeniously overcome in the chairs of certain makers who, in different ways, build them so that there is no rocker on the floor and the movements are also noiseless.

Patents for platform rockers appeared from the late 1860s through the turn of the century. These rockers became a popular American form of seating. Hunzinger began producing experimental models before he patented his version in 1882, and many of his rockers also incorporated other Hunzinger patents. Each platform rocker bears a paper label on the underside of the stationary base identifying his duplex spring and reminding the owner that "one drop of Oil from your Sewing Machine can in every joint of hinge will prevent noise."

Hunzinger goes international

In the late 1880s George's two sons entered the business. George, Jr., was born in 1862 and Alfred in 1868. Alfred's congenial personality would serve him well as the firm's superb salesman. By the 20th century the sons' six sisters would share in the firm's ownership.

Hunzinger sought to establish a foreign market and, in 1889, traveled to London and Paris. In Paris he bought tapestry from Leon Chanee & Co. At Clair-Leproust he found embroidery for use on chair seats and backs. In addition, he shipped to New York several tables, chairs, and sofas from the same house. Elsewhere in Paris, Hunzinger bought several chairs, including some of bamboo. He wrote to his sons about the purchases: "... all this furniture was bought simply for samples to be copied, every one being different and mostly in common wood partly not finished and partly in frames without seating. ..." He closed by telling his children that "Mama is hardy and well and getting awful fat."

From Paris Hunzinger and his wife traveled to London. A London letter to his sons gives some insight into furniture operation in 1889:

> This morning I was to see Angus and found Cutler from Buffalo with him; they have been to Paris together and just returned. He sells Cutler's desks. I found mostly American goods in his place and he showed me all his house; he gets every thing shipped K[nocked] D[own] and has cabinetmakers to put it together and finishers to finish it. He does a large business and I seen thousand cases not unpacked yet. The stuff as he gets it is in a rude state and packed close as solid wood. He has immitated our rockers from those sent to him, improved the lines and is now making new patterns. He gets our spring cast in large quantities, has them gilded; they shine like gold. I don't know how it is made. He makes them in all sorts of plush and gets as he says 50 shillings for them and he says that they pay him the best profit of all things he deals in. I asked him what House he thought could

Above: Rocker, with woven wire seat and back first patented in 1876. Three decades of Hunzinger patents—for structural inventions rather than esthetic designs—guaranteed him a comfortable living. Courtesy D. Magner Antiques, Brooklyn Heights, New York.

handle our goods as they are now if we would give the sole agency for England. This was water on his mill and he thought to make a fine thing out of it and said he was the only man that could do this to advantage. In ten years he has build up with nothing an immense big business. [If] I should send the frames K[nocked] D[own] unfinished at a lower price then I calculate . . . he would garante [sic] a business of 40,000 a year of course all benefit for him and none for us. He is smarter than the best Yank you ever met. I am sorry my time here is so short but I will see what I can do to meet my ambition to establish our goods here.

Although Hunzinger investigated a few locations and agents, it is unknown if he established an English market. Family members, recalling legend, say large shipments were loaded on ships in New

York harbor.

Hunzinger obtained a total of 20 furniture patents. Examples have not been found for every one. But even as late as November, 1979, a rocker was discovered illustrating a "lost" chair patented 100 years earlier. The patent, for metal tubing on the frame of a chair, claimed the metal strengthened the chair, but it is one of the few cases where Hunzinger admitted that his invention essentially "becomes ornament to the wooden chair-frame."

The year 1883 saw Hunzinger patent a method for applying straw braid to furniture and cabinet ware, also for primarily ornamental reasons. No examples have been found. A folding bedstead came from the drawing boards in

1887 and, as Hunzinger wrote in a considerate tone, "The object of this invention is to furnish a sufficient space in the wardrobe-bedstead when folded for the pillows to lie flat in the ordinary position, so that they will not be crumpled. . . ." Thoughtful Germanic-Yankee genius.

In the 1890s Hunzinger was intrigued by tables. An 1892 patent improved an 1890 design for a combined table and chair. In 1894 a game table with a flip-top was patented, and in 1899 the executors of his estate patented his last invention, a chair with arms that could be raised to make a writing surface.

Following their father's unexpected death at age 63, the family continued to operate the business. Son George headed the firm, with Alfred as salesman; several of the daughters worked in the office. The style of furniture was more conventional than their father's early creations and included, according to the firm's letterhead, chairs and rockers, library suites, Morris chairs, card tables, three-position chairs, and sun-parlor furniture. Markets were found through the frequent Grand Rapids trade shows and Sloane's in New York. Large sales were made to resort hotels along the Jersey shore, including the Essex, Sussex, and Marlborough-Blenheim. The factory is said to have employed some 80 cabinetmakers, mostly of Swiss, German, and Irish background. In the 1920s unions tried to organize the factory workers. While the family could have made more money by selling the firm as a going business, they jointly decided to close it down. George Hunzinger & Son then became a real estate and stockholding company for the family. Wealthy and retired, the children made a vacation trip to Europe and, until their deaths, remained a close and insular family.

Hunzinger's productive life corresponded to the age of patent furniture in America. His creations—so many perhaps because of the innovative spirit of the age—added whimsy to Victorian parlors. Hunzinger customers rocked and tilted in chairs which, with their turnings and carvings, were as fun to look at as to use. ■

Top and above: Sofa, armchair, and ladies' chair. Patented 1869, walnut with incised, gilt line-decoration. Although chairs were Hunzinger's primary interest, he also produced sofas, bedsteads, tables, and cabinets. This suite does not have the airy quality of much of his other work, but it does feature his characteristic carved embellishments and bolt-like connections. Right: Walnut side chair, patented 1869. On this variant of the diagonally-braced chair, the C-shaped curve from the back to the underside of the front probably indicates 1870s construction. Courtesy Lyndhurst, Tarrytown, New York, Property of the National Trust for Historic Preservation.

Wicker

BY KATHERINE MENZ

R attan furniture was manu-factured for virtually every room in the house during the decades after 1850, in a variety of styles to suit every taste and pocketbook.

Wicker has never lost its place as an American home furnishing. At one time or another since the 17th century it has been used in every room in the house, from elegant town-house drawing rooms to country-cottage living rooms, and out of doors as well. Wicker has always been relatively easy and inexpensive to make, which partially explains

its long-lasting success. Because it can be crafted into a variety of pleasing shapes and designs in a rainbow of colors it can be adapted to suit the changing tastes and life-styles of people each decade and century. For the 19th-century craftsmen who were responsible for wicker's golden age, the pliability of the material allowed them to execute fantastic shapes. And finally 20th century furniture makers put their skills to the test by experimenting with new wicker materials.

The term *wicker* covers a variety of woven furniture materials from straw, willow, and rattan, to twine, prairie grass, sea grass, and fiber. An 18th-century dictionary defines wicker as "a

green twig of an osier . . . that will bend very easily." Another calls it anything "made of small sticks." The term itself probably comes from the German word *wickeln,* meaning "to roll over," because wicker is made by twining one twig over another. The earliest materials used were probably straw, willow, and reed.

A short history of early wicker

Although wicker is commonly associated with Victorian fashions, written references to wicker actually occur in Europe as early as the 14th century. There is also evidence that woven furnishings were no strangers to ancient Egyptian homes, as closely woven

This page, top right: Vanity side chair, ca 1890. This chair has an oak frame and is decorated with elaborate curlicues on back and legs. Top left: Highchair, ca 1890s. Spider cane back with oak frame. Above: Rocker, ca 1880s. Made by the Heywood Brothers, this rocker has an unusual front stretcher. Bottom right: Sewing basket, late 1890s. This simple, well-woven basket and stand is also from the Heywood Brothers. Opposite page: Shellback armchair, 1880s. Note the curlicues on the arms of this dramatic, bold piece. All of the above Mysak/Studio 9, courtesy Pamela McGinley Scoury, The Wicker Garden.

Top: Lamp, late 1890s. This unusual lamp, constructed by the Heywood Brothers and Wakefield Co., has a square shade with a cross-weave design. Bottom: Plant stand late 1890s. The original green stain decorating the stand can still be seen. All of the above Mysak/Studio 9, courtesy Pamela McGinley Scoury, The Wicker Garden.

high-backed wicker chairs appear in Egyptian, Greek, and Roman art.

In America the earliest known existing example of wicker furniture is a cradle dating back to the Plymouth Colony. Seventeenth- and 18th-century inventories frequently list such wicker ware as baskets, chairs, and cradles, and one 17th-century Rhode Island colonist owned a wicker chair that, oddly enough, was more expensive than a turned wood chair.

The style of 17th-century American wicker varied remarkably little from its ancient Egyptian, Greek, or Roman counterparts. The same tightly woven hooded chair with enclosed arms has remained popular for centuries. References to "basket chairs"—as they were often called—are found in 17th-century inventories, and such chairs are still made today. (In its contemporary form, the basket chair is suspended from the ceiling.) Wicker's association with the tradition of basket weaving may be a possible explanation for the slow evolution of style and weave: neither basket weaving nor wicker furniture has changed much over the centuries.

Early 19th-century basket weavers were the first known craftsmen to advertise wicker furniture. (It is possible that 17th- and 18th-century basket weavers might have done so as well but we have no record of such ads.) Peddlers who sold woodenware and baskets frequently also sold wicker chairs.

During the early 19th century, rattan replaced straw and willow, which was the major material used in wicker furniture-making in the 17th and 18th centuries. The word *rattan* comes from the Malaysian word *rotang*, which is a type of trailing palm native to Malaysia, India, Sri Lanka, and China. This plant grows several hundred feet long and

has a hard, thin bark jointed like bamboo. The outer bark was used for chair caning, while the inner reed was used to weave furniture. Rattan was imported by the East India Company in the early 17th century; however, it probably was not available in America until direct trade with China opened up after the American Revolution.

Though there are isolated early examples of American wicker on view at the Plymouth Plantation in Massachusetts (such as the Plymouth cradle previously mentioned), few pieces exist that were made prior to 1870. Consequently, little is known about 17th- and 18th-century wicker furniture. Illustrations from the mid-19th century picture wicker furniture with closely woven cane seats and looped reed backs and arms. The frame, made from hickory or oak, was steamed and bent into shape and then wrapped with split cane. It was not until this time that wicker furniture-making changed from a craft to an industry.

Mid-19th-century wicker

The woven chair was an ideal medium for experimentation by 19th-century furniture makers who also worked with a wide range of materials such as papier mâché, iron, and laminated wood. The woven chair—inexpensive (because materials were plentiful and sturdy) and relatively easy to make as well—drew more and more attention from innovative designers. In 1851, the author of *Rural Homes*, Gervase Wheeler, recommended wicker furniture for country houses because, "the principal excellencies of cane as a material for chairs, sofas, baskets, etc., are its durability, elasticity, and great facility of being turned and twisted into an almost endless variety of shapes . . ."

By the 1850s homeowners could buy rattan furniture for every room in the house. Settees, rocking chairs, ladies' workstands, ladies' sewing chairs, office chairs, children's chairs, waste baskets, and footstools were advertised. *The Housekeeper's Own Book,* written by Stephen Smith in 1856, recommended rattan furniture for "country houses, piazzas, front halls and upper rooms." In *Rural Homes,* Wheeler suggested specific styles for different settings; the rattan with arched and pointed backs for Gothic-style cottages and Chinese-style rattan sofas for "old-fashioned and quaint-looking sitting rooms."

Between 1860 and 1880, the popular cane on rattan chairs was called the "star back" pattern because of the design in which the cane was woven—many six-sided stars. Chairs with this cane set into a rectangular framework are among the earliest we know. Examples of these chairs are rare, but may still be found today. The star back pattern was made until about 1910.

The earliest examples of the closely woven, all-reed, crisscrossed-pattern chairs appear in magazine advertisements in the 1870s. (Reed consists of the pith of the rattan material.) After World War I, a wider weave, less expensive and easier to make, superseded the finer crisscross weave. Although the wider weave had been available as early as the 1880s, most of it was made in the 20th century.

In addition to the plain-weave styles, late-19th-century wicker manufacturers produced a large variety of elaborate and intricate designs intended for parlor furniture mainly for the middle class. Entire parlor suites were available, but most often this very ornate furniture was intended as an accent piece. The isolated ornamental

Left: Peregrine White cradle, ca. 1620. Peregrine White, an infant born aboard the Mayflower in 1620, used this cradle, the earliest known example of wicker in America. Courtesy the Pilgrim Society, Plymouth, Massachusetts. Above: Wicker divan and young boy, ca. 1900. The exoticism associated with wicker made it a popular photographic prop in portrait studios. Right: Egyptian-style armchair, 1898. Below: Rocker, ca. 1915. This chair was made of prairie grass, one of the many materials used in woven furniture. All three courtesy Katherine Menz.

This page, left: Rocker with bird design, ca. 1880. This page, right: Rocker, ca. 1880. Excellent example of the star back pattern, popular from 1860 to 1910. Opposite page, left: Armchair, ca. 1900. This closeweave wicker chair with cane seat is from the Wakefield Rattan Co. catalogue. Opposite page, right: Hooded wicker seaside chair, ca. 1890. This chair is actually part of a painted prop in a photography studio. People stuck their heads through holes to appear as part of the scene. All four courtesy Katherine Menz.

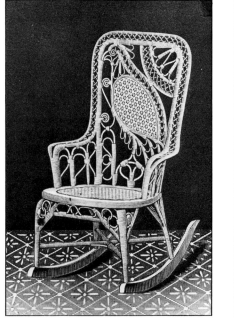 

chair, usually described in contemporary catalogues as "a fancy reception chair," was particularly popular. According to Ella Rodman Church, author of a household advice book published in 1881 called *How To Furnish A Home*, the "Sets ordered of an upholsterer . . . are seldom satisfactory to a person with an eye for simple beauty, and quite destroy the charm of interest and variety that is produced by having few things alike."

Wicker was made in a variety of styles and in a range of colors. An advertisement for the Wakefield Rattan Company in an 1883 issue of *Century Magazine* lists "Mahogany, Pompeian Red, Cherry, Ebony, etc. . . . and Copper, Silver or Gold Bronze." The ad continues:

"The new and original idea of color work is having great success, and meets the popular demand for novelty in fall furnishing." Articles about French rattan—which was particularly admired because it was lacquered in a variety of

colors—first appeared in the early 1890s. By the end of that decade, American manufacturers were also offering multicolored wicker in combinations of red, yellow, white, and green.

During this time wicker was available with upholstered backs and seats as well. The author of *Our Homes; How To Beautify Them* (New York, 1888) recommended bright plush with silk embroidered peacock feathers, although for most, cushions were the more popular alternative. A fad in the 1890s was to weave colored ribbons into the wicker and place fancy bows at the corners of chairs and stools. Wicker furniture fit many of the late 19th-century criteria for stylish home furnishings. One magazine article in 1885 noted: "Quite an acquisition is being made to art in the later and more elaborate production of rattan furniture. The material itself encourages freedom of design. . . . Admitting of being colored and combining delicate details with great strength, it presents many of the

effects of wood carving."

During the early 20th century, wicker meant for outdoor use was usually painted a solid color. If used indoors, wicker could be stained mahogany or oak. Some multicolored wicker from the twenties and thirties has survived with original paint. The most popular color combination for sofas and chairs was green with a red and black diamond-shaped design in the center back. The design was both woven and then painted on seat furniture for dramatic accent.

Wicker in its prime

Wicker furniture reached the height of its popularity between 1875 and 1910. By the turn of the century one wicker manufacturer claimed, "No up-to-date, well furnished house is complete without a few pieces of reed and rattan furniture."

The great popularity of wicker at this time coincided with several other trends led by a decorative arts reform

movement in England and America. The proponents of this movement were afraid that mass-produced furniture would destroy the care and individuality so cherished in handmade furniture. Charles Lock Eastlake's book, *Hints on Household Taste* (1868), was the first of many household advice books concerned with what was called "artistic" furnishings. He and his followers advocated a return to the handmade look. As a result of this reform movement homemakers became more aware of the need for "artistic" furnishings, a revived interest in Orientalism being one of the direct results of this need. The term *Orientalism* was used loosely in the late 19th century to refer to anything exotic and far away, including the Far East and Japan, as well as Moorish Spain and Byzantium. The opening of Japan to the West in 1859 and the International Exhibition in 1862—with its display of Japanese decorative arts—marked the beginning of this interest, a trend that became even

more widespread after the publication of the household advice books. (Oriental knick-knacks and *objets d'arts*, judiciously placed, were believed to enhance the home by creating the necessary artistic surroundings.)

The association of wicker with exotic foreign countries was probably the largest single factor behind wicker's popularity in the late 19th century. Since the rattan material itself came from the Far East, some wicker manufacturers could capitalize on the mystery of its foreign origin. In furniture catalogues, wicker was described as "East India Chairs" and "Chinese Hourglass Chairs." One Milwaukee manufacturer of reed and wicker furniture—A. Meinecke and Son—advertised furniture made with Chinese matting as "India Punjab Furniture: Artistic, Odd, and Inexpensive." Some rattan furniture was undoubtedly imported from the Orient, such as the well-known, fan-backed chair, but most was manufactured domestically.

Orientalism inspired many wicker designs. The asymmetry of Japanese art is the first most noticeable influence. Japanese fans used in wicker chair-backs, latticework, arabesques, strapwork (a kind of latticework), diaper patterns (crisscross diamond effect), arches and ogees (s-curves) taken from Moorish and Byzantine art and architecture are some examples. Harriet Spofford in her book *Art Decoration Applied to Furniture*, very popular in 1878 when it was written, recommended wicker in her chapter "Oriental Styles." She described a wicker armchair in terms suggestive of Moorish art by saying that the frame was "black lacquered and gilt in odd minglings of alphabetical characters and traceries."

Companion furnishings to wicker, according to contemporary household books, were Oriental accouterments, such as ebonized hanging cabinets with exotic curios, tiles, and scrolls. Japanese fans and parasols were suggested as

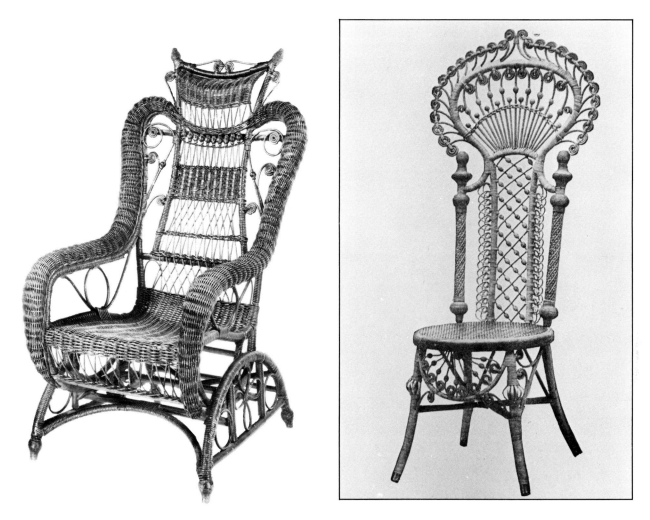

ceiling and wall decorations, and Oriental materials were often used to upholster wicker furniture. Virginia Shortridge, in an article appearing in the June 1893 issue of the widely read magazine, *Decorator and Furnisher*, wrote: "Many of the wicker chair seats are draped and cushioned with Oriental fabrics, thus producing novel and artistic effects."

The exoticism associated with wicker made it an often-used photographic prop in portrait studios. The setting for these pictures also often includes painted backdrops displaying a lavish scenery with waving palm trees. Old photographs show the variety of unusual wicker forms used in the studios. In fact, ornate wicker became so popular as a photographer's prop that the Heywood Brothers and Wakefield Company manufactured a wicker "posing" chair, illustrated in their 1898–99 catalogue. Designed for use exclusively as a prop, the seat is too narrow for normal sitting. When photography was

still new and mysterious, the excitement of a family visit to a photographer's studio must have been enhanced by these bizarre settings. Book illustrations, particularly 19th-century romantic novels and illustrations in advertisements, also often featured women reclining in wicker furniture.

Wicker's loose weave was considered particularly suitable for invalids, and children. It was also perfect for summer furniture. Its sturdy position in the American marketplace was further confirmed in the 19th century because it was associated with sanitation and health. In 1898 Carrie May Ashton wrote in the magazine *Decorator and Furnisher:* "Rattan and bamboo are used more and more every year for tables, cabinets, writing desks, bookcases, lounges and chairs. These are especially desirable from a sanitary standpoint."

Wicker was made into both reclining chairs and wheel chairs (called "rolling chairs") for the invalid. One wicker furniture company, The Paine Manufac-

turing Company (in 1891), advertised the healthful qualities of its furniture with the claim that invalids in the Azores were the first to discover the "wonderful pieces of reed furniture."

Rattan furniture for children also had its roots in the 19th-century concern for ventilation. As early as 1851, Gervase Wheeler wrote of a child's wicker bedstead: "The lightness, sweetness, and coolness of the article, particularly adapted as it is to ventilation must greatly recommend it."

Although the initial popularity of rattan baby carriages in the baby-carriage boom of the turn of the century may have been due to its sanitary appeal, the ensuing increase in popularity reflected a combination of factors. Perhaps the most important of these was the idealized image of childhood that took place late in the 19th century. Children were no longer treated as adults, as they had been, but were venerated for their childlikeness. This changing attitude was translated natu-

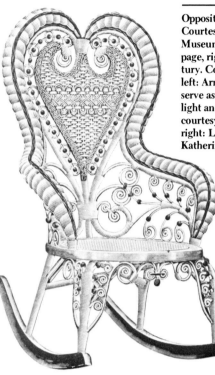

rally into rattan creations: the material was extemely adaptable for the fanciful baby carriage designs adults thought children would find fascinating, forms ranging from seashells to miniature cars equipped with glass and brass fittings.

Wicker was also considered an ideal furniture for the outdoor relaxation desired by the many wealthy 19th-century Americans who migrated each summer from cities to the seaside and mountains in search of fresh air. Vacation houses and resort hotels were constructed then with wide verandas and sleeping porches so that guests could get as much exposure to the country air as possible, and wicker was the fashionable furniture for this purpose.

Later wicker designs

After World War I taste for the elaborate curvilinear looped-reed design of wicker furniture of the 19th century was replaced by a preference for more angular shapes and solid patterns. Instead of inventing more fanciful designs, wicker manufacturers began to experiment with materials other than rattan—especially with prairie grass and fiber.

Prairie grass ("From the Prairies of America to the Homes of the World," as Ludwig Bauman & Co. advertised) was a wire grass from the prairie marshes of northwest America, converted into a pliable twine and woven into furniture. Manufacturers stressed its suitability for indoor, winter furniture because it had a natural greenish-brown color not intended to be painted. Sea grass was manufactured and woven in a similar way. Fiber—a twisted paper stiffened with glue sizing—was perhaps the least expensive of all woven materials. In 1917 a wicker-weaving machine utilizing fiber material was invented by Marshall B. Lloyd and was·called the Lloyd loom.

As the 20th century progressed, the skilled labor needed to weave wicker in the United States became scarce, and imports replaced domestic manufacture. The history of Schober and Company, which began making wicker in Philadelphia in 1892, illustrates this trend in the wicker industry. After World War I, Schober started to import wicker furniture from the Far East and by World War II it no longer made any here in the States. Interestingly enough Schober continues to import wicker furniture to this day.

The history of wicker furniture and its rise to popularity is particularly revealing of Victorian tastes and attitudes regarding the home. Wicker satisfied both the prerequisites of the 19th-century tastemakers, such as Charles Lock Eastlake, and the romantic fancies of homemakers of that time. As one of the most popular furniture forms of the last quarter of the 19th century, wicker furniture played an important role in the domestic life of American Victorians. And true to its history, wicker, old or new, still decorates a part of many American homes today. ■

Cast Iron

To furnish the romantic gardens of the 19th century, chairs, settees, vases and urns of decorative cast iron were mass manufactured throughout much of the 19th century.

BY ESTHER MIPAAS

After 100 years of invention and discovery, spanning the 18th and 19th centuries, scientists achieved a malleable iron that could withstand the stress and vibrations of railroads, mills, bridges, and steamboats.

Iron became the innovative material of the age. Mass production along with mass marketing was thriving by 1851, the year of the Crystal Palace Exhibition in London. (The Crystal Palace itself was an architectural *tour de force* of cast iron and glass.) In England the Coalbrookdale Company, largely involved in engineering iron long-span bridges, regularly manufactured parlor stoves and grates, but it also made garden vases, flowerpot stands, settees, and railings. Its products and those of other English and French foundries were sold in America; they also provided patterns that U.S. firms bought and variously copied.

The widespread mass manufacture of cast-iron furniture and decorative items coincided with a period of renewed interest—in both England and

"A truly precious metal," said a Scottish chemist in reference to iron in the 19th century, ". . . capable of being cast in molds of any form . . . drawn into wires of any desired strength or fineness . . . of being sharpened, hardened, and softened at pleasure." Opposite page: Bench, Snug Harbor Cultural Center, Staten Island, New York.

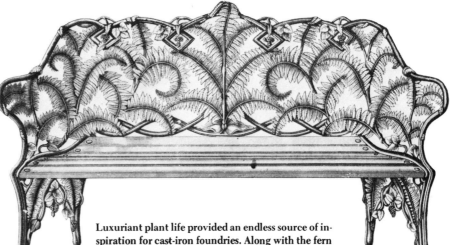

Luxuriant plant life provided an endless source of inspiration for cast-iron foundries. Along with the fern motifs shown here, they also frequently produced designs based on vines, morning glories, and oak trees. The catalogue bench illustrated above utilizes the fern frond as a design motif. Left: Detail from cast-iron bench, Woodlawn Cemetery, Bronx, New York. Both The Friends of Cast-Iron. Top: Settee by John McClean, Evergreen Cemetery, Brooklyn, New York, ca 1890. Photo by Esther Mipaas.

America—in landscape and garden architecture.

Landscape and residential architect Andrew Jackson Downing, an important tastemaker in mid-19th-century America, adapted the romantic "natural" English garden to what he called the economical taste of his countrymen. A picturesque—or romantic—English garden of the late 18th or early 19th century might include serpentine streams and meandering paths that opened into surprise views. For contemplating such surprises, architects of this type of garden might well provide a seat or settee for two at an appropriate spot. Large estates designed in the picturesque, or romantic, style might include covered sitting areas, pavilions, belvederes, lookouts, and bowerlike retreats. These devices—and the seats they contained—might be made of stone, wood, or cast iron. Thus a demand grew for suitable outdoor cast-iron furniture that conformed with the romantic idea.

For suburban living, Downing especially favored Italian-style villas. The balustraded porches and terraces of these houses cried out for decoration, and uncovered urns or vases filled with trailing plants were deemed suitable. Though Downing preferred terra-cotta or artificial stone (less expensive than actual cut stone) for such vases, they were also economically manufactured in the newly popular medium of cast iron.

Cast-iron vases decorated some fashionable buildings in such stylish resort areas as Saratoga Springs. (Even before *The Last of the Mohicans* described upstate New York as virgin wilderness, Saratoga Springs was acquiring the same elegant reputation as the continental spas. The springs were not a new discovery. Their medicinal properties were known to the native Indians, and the area had been the scene of major action during the French and Indian War. During the 19th century, Saratoga Springs was commercially developed as a fashionable resort.)

Dr. John Clarke, owner of the Congress Spring, bottled the spring waters for sale nationwide. By 1824 he built Saratoga's third hotel, the Congress Spring Hotel. In improving the grounds to attract guests, he placed among the plantings and furnishings a pair of iron amphorae. They were decorated with molded bas-reliefs reproducing Bertel Thorwaldsen's medallions showing "Morning" and "Night." The spun-sugar serenity of this influential sculptor's work was so attractive to the popular level of neoclassic taste that copies were used to decorate everything from porcelain and terra-cotta to cast iron. The style was in tune with white wood Doric columns and iron railings decorated with Greek frets or anthemia that characterized the Greek revival style in America.

Where the Saratoga vases were produced is not known. They may have been fabricated in one of the foundries operating in Troy or Albany, New York. (Several of these foundries were making ornamental heating stoves as well as plowshares and tools at that time.) It is possible that they were produced by the Royal Prussian Foundries in and around Berlin, Germany. (During the Napoleonic wars, precious metals were scarce in Germany. Cast iron was worked to a marvelous degree of virtuosity, producing a range of artwares from fine filigreed jewelry and medallions to larger-than-life-size statues.)

Subsequent visitors' guidebooks to Saratoga Springs, issued decade after decade, illustrated the Thorwaldsen vases flanking the pavilion of the Congress Spring as not-to-be-missed objects. Surviving a fire that ravaged the hotel in 1866, today they stand fresh and brightly planted in Congress Park, which is owned by New York State.

A leading cast-iron manufacturer

At the New York Exhibition of the Industries of All Nations in 1853-54, railings designed by John B. Wickersham and manufactured at his New York Wire Railing Works surrounded the exterior of the building and set off displays from one another inside. He used the newly improved malleable iron to crimp and weave thin rods and ribbons of iron into continuous lengths of fencing that were strung between cast-iron support posts. (The rods varied in diameter from ⅛ to ⅜ inches.) In the previous seven years Wickersham had designed ways of using his fencing for gardens, parks, cemeteries, gazebos, and verandas. Other uses included window grilles and cages for bank tellers. He also designed railings for hospitals that extended along tiers of balconies and stretched the lengths of two and three stories so that patients could enjoy the fresh air and sunshine. In style Wickersham's fencing was either an even lattice or was drawn into more ornamental bent-wire patterns reminiscent of calligraphy. At this time, objects were designed in the restrained

Opposite page, left: Vase, ca 1825. A pair of these iron amphora, decorated with bas-relief reproductions of Bertel Thorwaldsen's "Morning" on one side and "Night" (shown here) on the other, are located at Congress Park, Saratoga Springs, New York. Left: Detail of urn by J.W. Fiske Ironworks. Both photos by Esther Mipaas.

Below: Warwick vase as shown in J.L. Mott Iron Works catalogue. The original Warwick vase was excavated in 1771 from Hadrian's Villa in Rome and came to England as the property of the Duke of Warwick. It was widely reproduced in the 19th century. The Friends of Cast-Iron.

and airy Greek revival style. They were not made to show mass and shadow, as designs favored later in the 19th century did. Wickersham's railings were shipped over the nation's new canal networks to cities all along the coast and Gulf states—notably to New Orleans and Galveston. (The Wickersham sales catalogue of 1857 states emphatically that its workmen would go anywhere in the United States to install their product.)

While crimped and bent wire in combination with cast-iron posts—for making bank-teller cages and city-brownstone railings—were the central focus of the New York Wire Railing

Works, the company was also the sales agent for the products, including garden furniture, of other iron manufacturers. Receiving items in parts, the company assembled and displayed articles at its showroom at 312 Broadway in New York City. The illustrated New York Wire Railing catalogue shows the popular furnishings of the day. Although the catalogue was not large, it offered several items suitably ornamented for garden seating.

Typical motifs found on such garden furniture in the mid-19th century included naturalistically treated plant forms: clusters of grapes, vine leaves, rustic branches and twigs, and fern

fronds. A Gothic touch of pointed arches, scrolls, and strapwork was also evident.

Other manufacturers of cast-iron furniture

In addition to the New York Wire Railing Works, several other foundries operated at this time. They produced heating stoves—with cast-iron decoration—and, in the 1850s, components for cast-iron buildings. Several of these firms also manufactured garden furniture. George Cornell and George R. Jackson advertised iron bedsteads and iron tables and chairs, along with railings and verandas, in the 1840s and

While little is known about the designers of most cast iron furniture the bench shown immediately above provides a notable exception to this rule. Washington Irving sketched the design for the bench in a letter he wrote to George Harvey, dated November 15, 1836. Gouverneur Kemble later cast two benches according to Irving's design and gave them to Irving as a house-warming present Left: Bench, mid-19th century. Both Sleepy Hollow Restorations. Tarrytown, New York.

1850s. Boston, New York, Baltimore, and Philadelphia were the headquarters for many of the foundries. In Boston, Chase Brothers and Company sold settees in the Gothic style, one of which is held by The Metropolitan Museum of Art. In Baltimore, the Haywood and Bartlett Company produced ornamental architectural parts, as well as plumbing and heating appliances. In Detroit, the E.T. Barnum Wire and Tool Works made wire cloth and roof crestings. This firm also made a cast-iron chair with a naturalistic fern design, an example of which is on display in The Brooklyn Museum's decorative-arts hall.

Later in the century other firms included the North American Iron Works, which developed as a subsidiary of the J. L. Mott Iron Works, New York City had a cluster of companies with retail showrooms that flourished all through the later half of the 19th century. They issued illustrated catalogues, and sold their wares across the country.

Producing a full range of garden embellishments, including settees and planter vases, the J. L. Mott Iron Works (1828) and the Janes, Beebe and Company (1847—after 1857, the Janes, Kirtland and Company) started out as manufacturers of cast-iron stoves in lower Manhattan. The Mott works later moved north to a location on the Harlem River that since 1848 has been called Mott Haven.

The Janes company issued an illustrated catalogue along with a separate price list in 1859. The catalogue alludes to its great project then under construction—the Library of Congress's huge coffered ceiling. Janes, Kirtland and Company also moved uptown to more extensive grounds, about a mile east of Mott Haven, in the south Bronx. Neither of these companies participated in the Crystal Palace Exhibition in London in 1851, nor in the New York Exhibition in 1853-54. Evidently these were the years they metamorphosed into mass-production industries from family operations in which the owner was the master craftsman.

In 1858 Joseph Winn Fiske opened offices and a showroom at Park Place in New York. Later he moved to Barclay Street. He is known for the weathervanes he manufactured in great number and variety (although they actually are manufactured art, they are considered folk art today). The J. W. Fiske Company continued production of garden and park ornaments until well into the 20th century.

Unless the name of the foundry is cast into the frame of a garden chair or settee or a name tag is welded to the back, it is unrealistic to try to date or identify the manufacturer of such a cast-iron piece. Because these marks were not always applied, one can do no more than estimate that a piece was popular and in production after a particular decade and was made by one of several ironworks. (There were only about a dozen patterns made altogether.) The settees, chairs, and tables ceased being mass-produced when cast synthetic stone benches proved more economical.

Cast-iron vases

During the years when cast-iron seating was widely manufactured, similar cast-iron vases were made by all the cast-iron firms. Models for the vases, manufactured in a variety of materials, imitated classical designs, which were known and favored by almost everyone in the 19th century with taste and an art education. The Warwick vase is a case in point. It was illustrated in the *Official Catalogue of the New York Exhibition* in 1853 and exhibited in marble carved by Nicola Marchetti of Carrara, Italy. Contemporary critics said that if judged by the number of reproductions in bronze, terra-cotta, and artificial stone, this antique vase could be called a universal favorite. The original ancient vase, excavated in 1771 from Hadrian's Villa in Rome, came to England as the property of the Duke of

Left: Detail of chair by Robert Wood. Many pieces of cast-iron furniture carry a mark indicating the foundry where they were cast. Wood's mark is clearly visible in this detail. Courtesy Israel Sack, Inc., New York.

Above: Bench by Eugene T. Barum, Detroit, ca 1880. Clusters of grapes and grape leaves were the inspiration for the design of this popular bench. Note the legs fashioned from the leaves. Collection, Greenfield Village and Henry Ford Museum, Dearborn, Michigan.

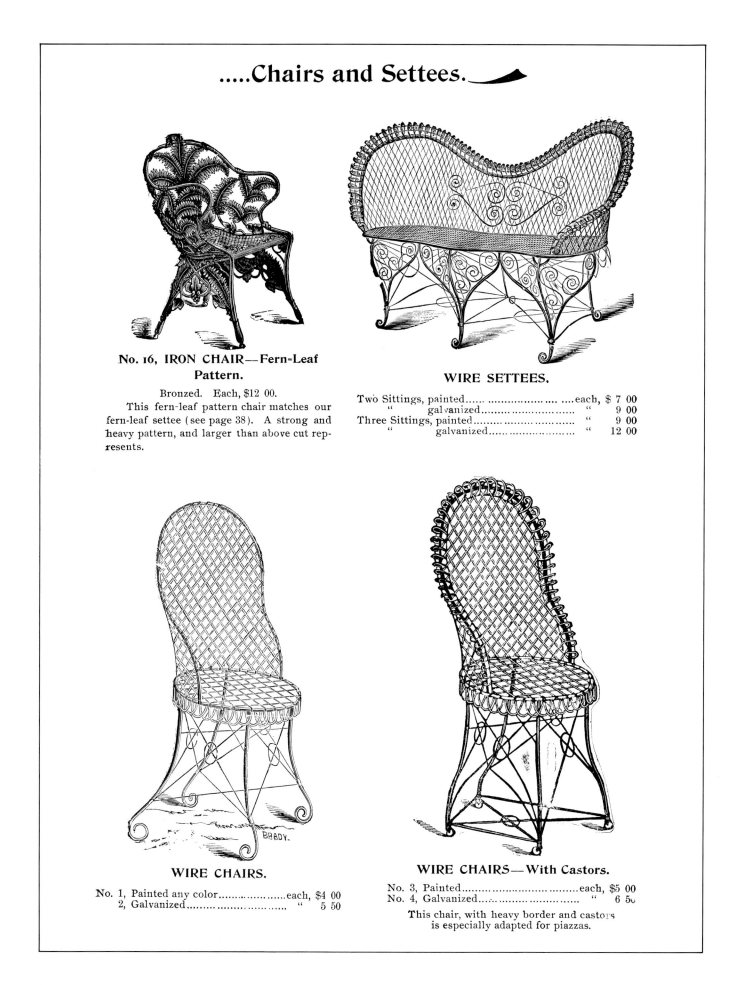

No. 16, IRON CHAIR—Fern-Leaf Pattern.

Bronzed. Each, $12 00.

This fern-leaf pattern chair matches our fern-leaf settee (see page 38). A strong and heavy pattern, and larger than above cut represents.

WIRE SETTEES.

Two Sittings, painted...... ....each, $ 7 00
" galvanized........................... " 9 00
Three Sittings, painted............. .... " 9 00
" galvanized....... .... " 12 00

WIRE CHAIRS.

No. 1, Painted any color......................each, $4 00
2, Galvanized......................... ..... " 5 50

WIRE CHAIRS—With Castors.

No. 3, Painted................. ....each, $5 00
No. 4, Galvanized.......... .... " 6 50

This chair, with heavy border and castors is especially adapted for piazzas.

Above, left: Urn as shown in James Kirtland & Co. catalogue, 1857. This cast-iron urn could be ordered in a variety of sizes. The one shown here was 6 feet 8 inches high. The Friends of Cast-Iron. Cast-iron furniture makers drew from all periods and styles for inspiration for their designs. Greek revival, rococo and gothic styles were favorites. Above, right: "Veranda Furniture," ca 1880. Culver Pictures.

Warwick. The decoration is a band of satyr heads with grapes and vine leaves in their hair entwined in bacchic revelry. Reproductions of the Warwick vase were illustrated in the Janes, Beebe catalogue and were available in sizes of 15 or 25 inches across the rim. The J. L. Mott Iron Works catalogue of 1875 also showed it.

Pedestals to hold the vases were sold separately. A customer could choose from several patterns which matched a vase or not. Pedestals most frequently used with the vases were designed as traditional plinths with square cross sections. Another favorite was the stand formed by three cranes standing back to back. This was a device copied from the ancient Etruscans by way of 18th-century archaeological finds. The style passed through various versions in the neoclassic mode. American post-Civil War cranes of iron were more naturalistic, recalling waterfowl at momentary rest. One crane pedestal, standing on a lawn in Snug Harbor, Staten Island, is seen supporting a vase with a modified geometric handle (a design treatment associated with the Eastlake influence).

Until late in the century, contours of vases, decorations on their surfaces, and the flare of their handles were similar to classic models. The elongated amphora shape reflected earlier neoclassic taste. The krater (a bucket with low handles) was no less classic and was cast by foundries throughout the century. Typical ornamentation might include handles resembling lions' heads or woodsy twigs. The body might be embellished with a medallion portrait of George Washington. Frequently a relief showed a procession of figures as described by John Keats in *Ode on a Grecian Urn*:

O Attic shape! Fair attitude with brede

Of marble men and maidens overwrought,

With forest branches and the trodden weed.

Footed, fluted basins with flaring rims were most popular. They came in many sizes, from 15 inches to as much as 3 feet across, and looked like giant goblets spilling over with geraniums and ivy.

Before the rage for iron garden vases died down, some larger and more elaborate ones were made. The balanced proportions of the classic models were redrawn into more exuberant shapes. Swags of conventionalized palmettes and lotus, vines, and bandings of egg-and-dart molding embossed the surfaces. Handles gave heightened relief. They were sculpted in serpen-

tine shapes, using swans, serpents, or strings of beads. Sometimes rams' heads and dragons' heads with twisting horns worked as handles. Judging by the dates of the houses in whose areaways the large cast-iron planters presently stand, it was in the 1880s and 1890s that spirited, abundant decoration became popular. And if any maker's name is cast into the bases of these ornate vases, the chances are that it will be J. W. Fiske.

The sculptors in all the ironworks were anonymous and highly skilled. They carved the wooden models or shaped plaster forms from which the sand molds for casting were impressed. The sculptural iron art of these unknown artisans gave a focal point to suburban lawns and city front yards, expressive of an opulent though short-lived era. A word of caution: some patterns are being cast today from worn-out molds that produce a blurred relief decoration; they are sold in shops that somehow have inexhaustible supplies of French bakers' racks and other reproductions now in vogue with decorators.

Example of 19th-century cast-iron furniture can be seen in the decorative-arts collections of museums and restoration foundations and in older gardens that for some special reason have not been destroyed for a modern design. ■

Adirondack Hickory

To furnish America's summer resorts and cottages, Indiana factories turned out vast quantities of simple, rustic furniture toward the end of the 19th century.

BY CRAIG GILBORN

There's more hickory in the Adirondacks than you can shake a stick at, yet few hickory trees grow in the woodlands of the Adirondack Park. Tucked away in dozens of Adirondack camps and hotels are hundreds of chairs and tables manufactured between 1898 and 1940 at several factories in Indiana, where hickory trees flourished. Intended for "porches, lawns, summer homes, country clubs, gardens, pavilions, parks, dens and sanatoriums," in the words of one maker, this hickory furniture was shipped to all parts of the United States. It met the demand for sturdy pieces to furnish countless summer resorts and cottages being constructed from Maine to California and Florida. Simple and functional, the furniture did not look as though it belonged in anything resembling a parlor, which suited the buyers just fine. They wanted woodsy living spaces that were not mirror images of their city and suburban homes.

The quantity of hickory furniture imported to the Adirondacks was staggering, and a visitor to summer places today will see enough to leave him wondering about all the pieces that were lost to fire and rot. Historic photographs and postcards of hotels and children's camps show dining rooms filled with hickory chairs and tables. Old timers in Old Forge, New York, which mediated between the outside world and resorts in the Adirondack interior, recall boxcars of hickory furniture ar-

riving by rail at nearby Thendara, bound for hotels and camps farther east. In 1922 the proprietor of the Higby Club purchased upwards of 150 chairs for his dining room, and three years later two orders were shipped by way of New York City and Old Forge to O. M. Edwards, a stockholder in three railroads, whose summer home was situated on one of the lakes in the

OLD HICKORY
PORCH *and* GARDEN
FURNITURE

THE SOLARIUM, CAMP NAWITA, SEVERANCE, N.Y.   574,

Simple, sturdy furniture was needed for the summer resorts that flourished in the Adirondacks in the first years of this century. Between 1898 and 1940 several factories in Indiana produced thousands of tables, settees, and chairs made from the region's plentiful hickory trees. Above: A catalogue cover from the Old Hickory Furniture Company, 1922. Left: A postcard showing the hickory-furnished solarium at Camp Nawita, Severence, New York, from about 1915. Both courtesy the Adirondack Museum. Opposite page, left: This hickory piece is listed in a 1911 catalogue of the "Rustic Hickory Furniture Company," La Porte, Indiana. Courtesy Robert Edwards Gallery, Rosemont, Pennsylvania.

149

Fulton Chain. Covewood Lodge, on Big Moose Lake, retains more than a hundred hickory chairs and tables dating from the twenties, and Kamp Kill Kare, perhaps the showiest and best-kept of the large, private camps in the Adirondacks, acquired its quota of hickory at about the same time.

The Old Hickory Chair Company

The person chiefly responsible for this influx of Hoosier rusticity into the Adirondacks was Edmund Llewellyn Brown, founder of the first and most important of the three or four Indiana factories that produced hickory furniture, the Old Hickory Chair Company. His daughter, Dr. Francis T. Brown, a lively lady perhaps in her seventies who is now a pediatrician in Indianapolis, supplied much of the information

about her father's venture. Mr. Brown was born in Memphis, Tennessee, in 1873, and lived as a boy in Little Rock, Arkansas. He attempted to start a hickory operation in New Decatur, Alabama, but eventually, about 1895, settled in Martinsville, a small town about 25 miles south of the Indiana capital. There were large natural stands of hickory trees in that region and they were often grown by farmers as a harvestable cash crop.

By 1898 Brown was in business, operating at first for two or three months and then for longer periods as orders came in from individuals, department stores, and furniture outlets. In 1901 he filed a patent for a bark-splitting machine; other patents probably were taken out, according to Dr. Brown, though these may have been in the name of the Shireman brothers, who were Edmund Brown's partners until,

in Dr. Brown's words, they "froze him out." Apparently, the Shiremans had the cash and Brown the ideas.

The company's name was borrowed from Andrew Jackson. The association of the resolute American general and President with the hickory furniture was pointed out in the company's advertising. A company catalogue for 1922 boasted, "The sturdiness of such able pioneers as Andrew Jackson, whose nickname 'Old Hickory' designates this distinctive furniture, is typified by its long-wearing qualities." To put the furniture in its proper setting, Mr. Brown built a two-story log house outside Martinsville, named "High Rock," which he opened as a showroom for customers vacationing in the country nearby.

To construct his furniture, Brown utilized immature hickory saplings, called *poles*, which were bent into

Above: After about 1940 the Old Hickory Company began substituting caning and nylon webbing for bark in the backs and bottoms of their chairs. This later chair also exhibits the more streamlined design of the later furniture. Courtesy Mr. and Mrs. Richard Cohen. Right: One of the Old Hickory Furniture Company's most popular pieces was the rocking chair with splint webbing on the seat and back. 1922. Adirondack Museum.

150

Because of its sturdy simplicity hickory furniture received the praise of the Arts and Crafts movement. One writer for *Craftsman* magazine liked its "personality and air of definite sincerity." Left: A Rustic Hickory Furniture Company table made before 1933. Courtesy Hemlock Hall Hotel, Blue Mountain Lake, New York. Below: Rocker, branded with Old Hickory Furniture Company, Martinsville, Indiana, ca 1910–1940. Private collection; photo Peter and Rosine Lemon.

AN INTERIOR AT CAMP PINE KNOT.

Period photographs and engravings—as well as contemporary ones—attest to hickory furniture's popularity in country homes and resorts in the late 19th and early 20th centuries, and today. Above, top: A living room of a camp at Blue Mountain Lake, New York, with hickory and rustic furniture dating from 1920-1940. Private collection; photo Peter & Rosine Lemon. Left: A hotel porch with hickory rockers, 1920-1940. Courtesy Hemlock Hall Hotel, Blue Mountain Lake; photo Peter & Rosine Lemon. Above: An engraving from a late 19th-century guide to the Adirondacks. 1887. Private collection.

shape on patented metal frames and fitted together, Tinkertoy fashion, into a remarkably wide variety of seats—armchairs, side chairs, rockers, settees, swings and the like. That work was done by men. The weaving of backs and bottoms was done by women and children, according to Mary Neal, who retired in 1977 from the Old Hickory Furniture Company, where she had been employed for 42 years as a bookkeeper. The inner bark of the hickory tree, cut in strips and soaked to make it pliable, provided the material for weaving. The firm offered a smaller selection of tables with tops of varnished oak in addition to such sundries as stools, coat stands and boxes, and baskets for flowers. Fences, rustic screens, swings, and summer houses were also available. These were assembled from young sassafras poles. Altogether, the 1922 catalogue listed nearly 120 different items for the discriminating buyer, ranging in price from $4.25 for a small dining chair to $300 for a summer house 12 feet in diameter with a floor and green-stained shingle roof.

All the company's products were marked, usually with a brand on a rear leg or under the tabletop. One such mark, intended to distinguish the product from imitations, is oval and reads OLD HICKORY/CHAIR CO/MARTINS-VILLE, IND. From 1898 to 1920 the Martinsville firm was called the Old Hickory Chair Company. In 1920, the word *Furniture* replaced *Chair*, and the company was chartered in Delaware. After about 1940 the company began substituting caning and nylon webbing for bark in the backs and bottoms, and as a further concession to the modern era, design became more streamlined. Legs, arms, and backs were formed by single, continuous members. Miss Neal said that the company ceased making hickory furniture about 1970, following a fire. By that time the hickory line was a shadow of what it had been. Its doom was sealed by dwindling supplies of hickory poles and splints and by a shortage of people who could do the weaving.

Other manufacturers

Old Hickory had its competitors. The

largest of these may well have been the Rustic Hickory Furniture Company, which began operations in a barn in La Porte, Indiana, in 1902. That was also the year that Edmund Brown sold his interest in the Martinsville firm. The new company, formed by E. H. Handley, turned out furniture similar to Old Hickory's. It employed a brand and two or three paper labels to identify its products. One chair, in Blue Mountain Lake, bears the impression RUSTIC HICKORY/FURNITURE CO./LA PORTE, IND. In 1933 the company was forced into receivership and may have gone out of business.

A third hickory company was started at an unknown date by a former employee of Old Hickory, Emerson Laughner. Edmund Brown also may have been involved with the Indiana Hickory Furniture Company, which ceased operating in the early years of the Depression. An armchair in Piseco, New York, in the southern Adirondacks, carries the brand INDIANA HICK-ORY/FURNITURE CO./CONFAX, IND. on a back leg.

Two children's seats, a chair and rocker, found recently at Covewood Lodge, carry paper labels on which only the words *Terre Haute, Ind.* are legible. Dr. Brown speculated that this unidentified factory specialized in juvenile furniture and that it was absorbed by the Indiana Hickory Furniture Company.

The sturdiness and functional merits of hickory were obvious. But a moral significance also was ascribed to hickory furniture. Magazine writers under the intellectual spell of the craftsman's movement—which originated in England and espoused handmade furnishings over those which were mindlessly stamped out by machines—proselytized in favor of traditional crafts and functional design. In *Craftsman* magazine an anonymous writer praised hickory furniture for its "personality and air of definite sincerity."

The Indiana makers were aware of fashionable trends, however. Three small spindles are sometimes found between two top rails in the backs of hickory chairs. The three-spindle motif is characteristic of much furniture associated with Charles Locke Eastlake, an Englishman who inveighed against Victorian fussiness and therefore helped to prepare the way for the craftsman's movement.

Hickory, however, was meant to be used, not admired. Hikers exploring unoccupied Adirondack camps may well find a jumble of legs and rockers in a corner of a porch, stacked there in haste by some long-ago vacationer whose family members were impatiently waiting in the car to return to home, business, or school. Hickory furniture is as immutable as any human object can be under an unwritten law which says that indifference is the bliss of the Adirondack summer camp, and neglect its usual consequence. ■

153

Selected Bibliography

Ames, Kenneth L. "Grand Rapids Furniture at the Time of the Centennial." *Winterthur Portfolio 10* (1975): 23–50.

Aslin, Elizabeth. *The Aesthetic Movement, Prelude to Art Nouveau.* New York: Frederick A. Praeger Publishers, 1969.

Battersby, Martin. *The World of Art Nouveau.* New York: Funk & Wagnalls, 1968.

Bishop, Robert. *Centuries and Styles of the American Chair, 1640–1970.* New York: E. P. Dutton, 1972.

———, and Coblentz, Patricia. *The World of Antiques, Art, and Architecture in Victorian America.* New York: E. P. Dutton, 1979.

Bridgeman, Harriet, and Drury, Elizabeth, eds. *The Encyclopedia of Victoriana.* New York: Macmillan, 1975.

Butler, Joseph T. *American Antiques, 1800–1900: A Collector's History and Guide.* New York: Odyssey Press, 1965.

Catalano, Kathleen M. "Cabinetmaking in Philadelphia, 1820–1840: Transition from Craft to Industry." *Winterthur Portfolio 13* (1979): 81–138.

Clark, Robert Judson, ed. *The Arts and Crafts Movement in America, 1876–1916.* Princeton: Princeton University Press, 1972.

Comstock, Helen. *American Furniture: Seventeenth, Eighteenth, and Nineteenth Century Styles.* New York: Viking Press, 1962.

———, ed. *The Concise Encyclopedia of American Antiques.* 2 vols. London: The Connoisseur, 1958.

Davidson, Marshall B. Vol. II: *The American Heritage History of American Antiques from the Revolution to the Civil War.* Vol. III: *The American Heritage History of Antiques from the Civil War to World War I.* Reprint (3 vols. in 1). New York: Bonanza Books, 1979.

Durant, Mary. *American Heritage Guide to Antiques.* New York: American Heritage Publishing Co., 1970.

Eastlake, Charles L. *Hints on Household Taste in Furniture, Upholstery, and Other Details.* London: Longmans, Green and Co., 1868. Reprint. New York: Dover Publications, 1969.

Fales, Dean A., Jr. *American Painted Furniture, 1660–1880.* New York: E. P. Dutton, 1972.

Fales, Martha Lou Gandy. *Regional Characteristics of Empire Furniture.* Wilmington: Winterthur Museum, 1954.

Garrett, Wendell D., and others. *The Arts in America: The Nineteenth Century.* New York: Charles Scribner's Sons, 1969.

Giedion, Sigfried. *Mechanization Takes Command: A Contribution to Anonymous History.* New York: Oxford University Press, 1948.

Grand Rapids Museum. *Renaissance Revival Furniture,* Grand Rapids: The Grand Rapids Museum, 1976.

Hanks, David A. *The Decorative Designs of Frank Lloyd Wright.* New York: E. P. Dutton, 1979.

Hope, Thomas. *Household Furniture and Interior Decoration*. London: Longman, Hurst, Rees & Orme, 1807. Reprint. New York: Dover Publications, 1971.

Howe, Katherine S., and Warren, David B. *The Gothic Revival Style in America, 1830–1870*. Houston: The Museum of Fine Arts, 1976.

Jervis, Simon. *Victorian Furniture*. London: Sydney Wardlock, 1968.

Kenney, John Tarrant. *The Hitchcock Chair: The Story of a Connecticut Yankee—L. Hitchcock of Hitchcocks-ville—and an Account of the Restoration of This 19th Century Manufactory*. New York: Clarkson N. Potter, 1971.

Madigan, Mary Jean Smith. *Eastlake-influenced American Furniture, 1870–1890*. Yonkers, New York: The Hudson River Museum, 1973.

———, "Charles Locke Eastlake and American Furniture Manufacture." *Winterthur Portfolio 10* (1975): 1-22.

Mayhew, Edgar deN., and Myers, Minor, Jr. *A Documentary History of American Interiors: From the Colonial Era to 1915*. New York: Charles Scribner's Sons. 1980.

Miller, V. Isabelle. *Furniture by New York Cabinetmakers, 1650 to 1860*. New York: Museum of the City of New York, 1956.

Naeve, Milo M. *The Classical Presence in American Art*. Chicago: The Art Institute of Chicago, 1978.

Otto, Celia Jackson. *American Furniture of the Nineteenth Century*. New York: Viking Press, 1965.

Philadelphia Museum of Art. *Philadelphia: Three Centuries of American Art*. Philadelphia: Philadelphia Museum of Art, 1976.

Quimby, Ian, and Earl, Polly Anne, eds. *Technological Innovation and the Decorative Arts*. Charlottesville: The University Press of Virginia, 1974.

Saunders, Richard. *Collecting and Restoring Wicker Furniture*. New York: Crown Publishers, 1976.

Schwartz, Marvin D. *American Interiors, 1675–1885: A Guide to the American Period Rooms in the Brooklyn Museum*. New York: The Brooklyn Museum, 1968.

———. *Victoriana: An Exhibition of the Arts of the Victorian Era in America*. New York: The Brooklyn Institute of Arts and Sciences, 1960.

———; Stanek, Edward J.; and True, Douglas K. *The Furniture of John Henry Belter and the Rococo Revival: An Inquiry into Nineteenth-Century Furniture Design Through a Study of the Gloria and Richard Manney Collection*. New York: E. P. Dutton, 1981.

Seale, William. *The Tasteful Interlude: American Interiors Through the Camera's Eye, 1860–1917*. New York: Praeger Publishers, 1975. 2nd rev. ed. Nashville: American Association for State and Local History, 1981.

Tracy, Berry B., and Gerdts, William H. *Classical America, 1815—1845*. Newark, New Jersey: The Newark Museum Association, 1963.

———; Johnson, Marilynn; and others. *19th-Century America: Furniture and Other Decorative Arts, An Exhibition in Celebration of the Hundredth Anniversary of The Metropolitan Museum of Art*. New York: The Metropolitan Museum of Art, 1970.

Van Why, Joseph S., and MacFarland, Anne S. *A Selection of 19th-Century American Chairs*. Hartford: The Stowe-Day Foundation, 1973.

Wilson, Richard Guy; Pilgrim, Dianne H.; and Murray, Richard N. *The American Renaissance, 1876-1917*. New York: The Brooklyn Museum, 1979.

Index

About the Authors

RUTH BERENSON, art critic for *National Review*, writes regularly for *The New York Times*.

CAROL L. BOHDAN, formerly publisher of *Nineteenth Century* magazine, is now an independent consultant in the arts.

KATHLEEN CATALANO is a curator with the National Park Service at the Longfellow House, Cambridge, Massachusetts.

ED POLK DOUGLAS is a consultant, author, and lecturer on 19th-century taste.

ROBERT EDWARDS is a Pennsylvania antiques dealer and scholar of the Arts and Crafts movement in America.

RICHARD W. FLINT, formerly assistant curator at the Strong Museum, is a consultant to the Smithsonian Institution's Division of Performing Arts.

CRAIG GILBORN is the director of the Adirondack Museum of Blue Mountain Lake, New York.

DAVID HANKS is a specialist in 19th-century furniture, coauthor of *Innovative Furniture in America* (Horizon Press, 1980) and a guest curator at the Smithsonian Institution.

KATHARINE MORRISON MCCLINTON is the author of many books on art and antiques.

KATHERINE MENZ, formerly curator with the National Park Service at Harper's Ferry Center, West Virginia, completed her master's thesis on American wicker furniture at the Henry Francis du Pont Winterthur Museum and the University of Delaware.

ESTHER MIPAAS is a New York-based writer and photographer of historical subjects.

MARIAN PAGE is a writer on design and architecture and the author of *Historic Houses Restored and Preserved* and *Furniture Designed by Architects* (both Whitney Library of Design, New York).

BARRY SANDERS is on the faculty of Pitzer College, Claremont, California.

PAGE TALBOTT, coauthor with David Hanks of *Innovative Furniture in America* (Horizon Press, 1980), is a Philadelphia-based consultant on the arts of the 19th century.

BETTY TELLER is exhibitions coordinator for the Smithsonian Institution Traveling Exhibition Service.

CHRISTOPHER WILK is a freelance writer and curator whose field is modern architecture and decorative arts.